McBRIDE - MAST

FAMILIES

By John McBride Eacott

ISBN 978-0-9878227-5-8

Published by John Eacott

Copyright 2018 by John Eacott,

Orders for copies of this book, or permission to quote or reproduce may be submitted to the publisher, John Eacott at eacott@execulink.com or to his current address.

My websites   www.eacott.info   or   eacott.weebly.com

This work is accumulated from different sources and it is believed that all material used is taken from the public domain.

Other works by John Eacott include "Of Other Times" 1980; "Becoming John"; "The Eacott History"; "Sunshine Sketches of Nizwa, Oman"; "Eacott Reynolds Families".
Most works are print available at www.lulu.com

version 2

McBride - Mast

There was a reunion in Boone NC in June 2001 of the McBride - Mast families. At that time, none of the cousins, even the first cousins, ever knew Thomas Clark McBride. Some never even knew his wife Mary Elizabeth Mast. This is the story of the families who share together their common roots with Thomas and Mary.

I hope this information adds to your understanding of your back ground. I have referenced from the book "Valle Crucis, a History of an Uncommon Place" by I. Harding Hughes Jr. 3rd printing 1999 by Bookcrafters Inc. distributed by Mast General Store, Valle Crucis NC 28691 and from a web site "Ancestrees.com" and a Mast web page which has detailed genealogy, with information about the Ohio Masts and others. I also referenced "Kinships Concealed" by Roth and Cranford and the detailed work of C.Z. Mast in 1911. There seems to be a lot on the Masts. They clearly are prolific pioneers, moving across America to North Carolina, Ohio, Texas, Missouri , Oregon and elsewhere as the frontiers opened.

When I started this project, I had just names. However my goal was to get an insight of the lives of our ancestors. Gradually I began to sense that what I was looking at was a great big slice across the history of America. We don't go back to the Mayflower but we were here for the Revolution and all the events since. The Mast, McBride and their related lines have been active participants in a growing nation. I only wish I knew more of their stories. These are our relatives. This is part of our story.

John Eacott
Curries Ontario
July 2018

THE STORY

I was a small boy when my grandmother Mary Elizabeth Mast McBride died. I knew her best when I was about five years old. She was very much of another time and place. Born of mountain stock from Watauga County NC she lived a simple life marked by her rural Appalachian ancestry. She lived at the time in a small Victorian ,white frame dwelling near Scottsville, Virginia. Behind the house was a well with a crank. An old bucket was lowered to haul out water. Off in the corner of the yard was an old log cabin used as a smoke house. It was dark and dank and cool and smelled of smoke. On the other side was another barn and a chicken shed. There were chickens around the yard. Some were to be eaten. On one occasion a man didn't bother to chop off their heads but was able to quickly snap their necks with his hands. There were also other fowl to play with including little ducklings who would follow me around. A cow with a bell was in the pasture behind the house. At night there were the fireflies to delight and collect in a bottle. As a boy I recall her hitching up an old horse or mule to a one furrow plough, the reins over her shoulder and her hands guiding the plough. This was for a garden across the road from her home. Beside the garden was a small old barn where the horse lived. Grain was also stored in this barn. I can still recall the smell of that old barn full of mice, corn and horse droppings.

I helped crank the glass jar with its wooden paddle to make butter. I also loved to crank another device of tins inserted inside each other with a packing of ice and salt between them. With this we made ice cream. I learned how to make a corn stalk fiddle and a corn stalk whistle. She made a shirt for me out of an old flour sack. As it was war time, the bags were printed with patterns as a war saving effort. On the porch was an old trunk which held an old, old flag of the United States. I do not know its significance. It did not have a lot of stars.

Grandma McBride always seemed patient, her temperament mild and her wisdom firm. She was obviously independent, said to be advanced in her thinking for the time. She was revered by her family and those who knew her. However, for me she was Grandma. As I grew up her picture taken sitting on a bench before her house in her simple dress and apron was a reminder of a special place and time. It was a time from the past which I saw briefly as a boy. It was a time that shaped me in many ways.

My mother was born Rhoda Mast McBride April 22, 1910 at Newmarket TN in the foothills of the Great Smoky Mountains.

THE SMITHS

Rhoda Smith, my mother's grandmother, was born March 22, 1839 and died May 13, 1910. Mary Elizabeth Mast named her youngest child Rhoda after her mother who died only three weeks after the birth. An earlier Rhoda Smith (Aug 27, 1799 - June 3, 1829) married Hiram Reese (Reece) (Mar 12, 1798 - July 9, 1872) of Watauga in 1816 and had two sons Johiel (Dec 20, 1818 - Nov 10, 1837) and Asa 1820. Perhaps this Rhoda was an aunt. She was buried at Old Cove Creek Church in Watauga. Rhoda shows up as a name in other Smith records. Abner Smith born May 1770 died Mar 3 1855 was married to Mehetabel, who bore an ancient biblical name. All of these Smiths are buried in the **Cove Creek Baptist Cemetery** as are Elizabeth Smith born Jan 10, 1801 died Feb ? and her husband Bennet Smith born 1802 - died Nov 18, 1841. There are some Masts in this cemetery and most of the McBride ancestors as well.

Rhoda Smith was the daughter of Elizabeth Lacey Dugger born about July 1806 died April 18 1893. and Jehiel Smith also born 1807 married 11 Sept 1833 and died 1885.

Her brothers and sisters were: Ebenezer Smith 1828; Bennet Smith 1835 married Jane Greene; Wiley 1836; Carolina 1838; Rhoda 1839; Henry 1841; William 1842; Mary 1845 married Tillet Combs; Martha 1847 married D.J. Lowrance; Jeheil 1849. So Wiley would have been Mary Elizabeth Mast's uncle and she named a child Wiley.

Elizabeth Dugger was descended, in order, from David, Benjamin, Daniel, John, and William Dugger. William came to USA before 1656 and was a member of the Virginia House of Burgesses. The Dugger family served in the revolutionary war, and fought at the battle of Lookout mountain. They also served under Andrew Jackson. Duggers were in the mine (iron) owning business and were quite prosperous. They were Daniel Boone settlers. These were people who had come with Boone as their guide through the mountains to find their new homes.

Elizabeth's father David Dugger 1777 -1850 married Margaret Ernest 1787 -1836 and their children were Henry; Polly; Elizabeth and William.

From J.P. Arthur "History of Watauga" 1915

Smith Family.-- George Smith was the first of this family to come to the mountains, arriving about 1780. According to his bible, he died April 30, 1838 aged ninety-one years and fifty days. Elizabeth, his wife died March

8, 1842, aged ninety-two years.

Their children were: Abner, died May 20, 1850, aged sixty-nine years. Mehetabel was the wife of Abner. She was born a Fairchild and died March 3, 1855, aged eighty-four years, nine months and sixteen days.

The daughters of the first Abner were: Rhoda, born August 27, 1799; Mary, born February 27, 1802; Elizabeth, who married Jacob Reese, March 17, 1825; Susannah, who married Jacob Moody April 28, 1831; Rebecca, who married Jacob Norris March 27, 1835; Mary, who married William Roland June 6, 1835. Son Jehiel was born September 16, 1806 and died January 10, 1885. He was twice married, his first wife having been Rachel Adams and his second wife Elizabeth Dugger whom he married September 15, 1835.

He had two sons, Bennett and Jehiel.

Bennett Smith married Elizabeth Moody December 23, 1824. Bennett died November 15, 1844, aged forty-two years, eight months and twenty-two days. Bennett Smith's children were: Abner, who married Chaney Green; Polly, who married George Hayes. Bennett's Abner children were: Bennett, who married a Kimes; Polly, who married James Rayfield; Elijah, who married Emma Austin; Elizabeth, not married; Sally, who married Pink Henson; George, who married, first, Emma Price, and second, Mary Bingham; Rebecca, who married Julius Isenhour.

Jehiel's children were: Ebenezer, born March 3, 1828; Bennett, Born January 29, 1835, and married Jane Green December 6, 1856; Wiley, born June 27, 1836, never married; Carolina, born January 5, 1838, never married; Rhoda, born march 22, 1839, married Finley P. Mast; Henry, born March 3, 1841, never married; William, born September 18, 1842; never married; Mary, born October 9, 1845, married Tillett Combs; Martha, born June 15, 1847 married D. J. Lowrance, and Jehiel, born October 27, 1849.

Bennet Smith married Jane Green December 6, 1856, and their children were: Carolina, born May, 1857 and died April 26, 1859; John C. Smith, born January 28, 1861, and married Sarah C. Mast January 2, 1881. Abner and Bennett Smith settled at Silverstone. Abner was elected to the legislature in 1821 and 1825, while his great-grandson, Abner W., was elected in 1914.

THE MASTS

Mary Elizabeth Mast was born December 19, 1868, the second child of Finley Patterson Mast and Rhoda Smith. Her older brother Charlie was born in 1867 and her sisters Mattie (1871) and Lillie(1882). Jack was her younger brother and Emma was the youngest. She was raised on her father's farm at Valle Crucis, North Carolina. It was said she became the first woman in Watauga County to go away to school, in this case a high school. The school was across the mountain in Globe N.C. When she was 18, she married Thomas Clark McBride of Sugar Grove. More of their life later.

Mary's father Finley Patterson Mast was descended from a German\Swiss family of Amish Mennonite faith. There appears to have been a Mast coat of Arms. Mary had a copy. " Argent (Silver) signifies sincerity and peace. Gules (red) signifies military fortitude and magnanimity. Cross signifies tribulation and affection, or a symbol of resolution. The cross signifies tribulation and affection or a symbol of resolution. The cross being in the center of the escutcheon signifies dominion or authority. Escallops were the ancient badges of pilgrims, those who were truly brave. The crescent signifies enlightenment and honored by the gracious aspect of his sovereign Also the symbol for the hope of greater glory. Stripes all red, outline of escutcheon is black with silver background." (as copied by Rhoda Mast McBride from a coat of arms at Mary Mast McBride's whose copy was obtained through her family).

John Mast (gen 1) (American generation one) was born in Switzerland in 1740 into a Mennonite family . The children reputedly had been orphaned and came to America with an uncle, Johannes Mast ostensibly to avoid religious persecution. John,10, his older brother Jacob, 12 and four sisters, Elizabeth 14,Anna 8, Magdalena 7, Sarah 6 sailed from Rotterdam on the ship "Brotherhood" with 324 other people and landed in Philadelphia Nov 3, 1750. At least 3 other Mast families were already in America. One source identifies John's ancestry as this: Hans (John) Mast was born abt 1570 in Guggisberg, Switzerland (south of Berne east of Friborg in a farming area). He married Elsa Alben. Peter was born to them about 1600. Peter married Anne Zwehlen July 6, 1629. Uli was their child born 1664 and he married Elsi Beyeler Jan 18 1660. Their son Hans married Anna Mischler and their children were: Johannes Mast born 1695 in Guggisberg died Berks Co. PA. Christian Mast 1697, Barbara Mast 1699, Jacob Mast born 1705 died 1772 in Berks Co. PA., Anna Mast 1704 and ? Mast born 1710. This unnamed Mast married and his children were: Anna born 1734, Magdalena 1735 born in Switzerland and died 1827 in Holmes co.

Ohio, Jacob born 1738 and John born 1740.

When the name Mast or Maust was first started is not known, but C. Z. Mast in his "Annals Of Conestoga Valley" states that in the vicinity of Brookhausen, in Westfalia, Germany, there is in the year 1429. A Dietrich Mast, named as a landowner. In Kurkfalz, Germany, in officers record of 1717 is the name of a tax recorder, Peter Jacob von der Mast.

The first Mast in America came in 1727, but he was not supposed to have been a Mennonite. Not until 1727 did more Amish appear. Three more families came in 1733, Johannes Lapp, Johannes Reichenbach and Johannes Slabach.

Then in 1736 on September 1, Jacob Hostedler, Johannes Lorentz, Peter Rupp, and Jacob Gochenauer landed. Melchoir Detwiler also came the same year. But the next year 9 families arrived October 8, 1737 on the ship "Charming Polly" from Rotterdam, Holland, controlled by Captain Charles Stedman. The landing is recorded in series 2, volume 17 of Pennsylvania Archives and there was listed 105 men, 107 women, 25 boys. C. Henry Smith in his "the Mennonite Immigration to Pennsylvania," states the 9 families (Amish) were Jacob Beiler, Hans Schantz, Hans Gerber, Jr., Christian Kurtz, Jacob Mueller, Hans Zimmerman, Christian Hertzberger, Jacob Mast and Christian Buerki. One woman named Barbara Mast may have been Jacob's wife. Jacob was on the sick list. Jacob located in Berks County, PA. Land was bought from the sons of William Penn as they inherited much of Pennsylvania. Some land was bought for as little as 16 cents an acre.

The ten year old John grew up in the Northkill Congregation of Amish Mennonites near the present town of Bernville PA. This was the oldest Amish congregation in America. The children lived with the Eli Hochstetler family. John was apparently married in 1756 at the age of 16 in Pennsylvania to (choose one!!) Catherine Barbara Harmon (born about 1833 in Germany) daughter of George or Jacob Harmon and Mary Wiley or Maria Pauschen.(a parentage problem exists!!) His first child was Nancy Mast born 1757 died 1859 in Montgomery Co. Ohio. She married James Curtis. When John was 20, in 1760 the community was attacked by Indians and they moved to the Conestoga Valley between the Schuykill River and Conestoga Creek in Berks Co. PA east of Morgantown. John's second child Elizabeth was born here in 1760.(died 1831) Here also, Jacob erected a log home and married Magdalena Holly (who had sailed over on the same boat) Jacob raised 12 children. The Conestoga Congregation, the third established, was to become the first permanent settlement of the Amish. Jacob was elected the second bishop of the church in 1788. Some of his descendants remained in Pennsylvania and some went to Holmes Co.

Millersburg, Ohio. Jacob died in 1808 and his wife in 1820. All this is documented in an 800 page book by C.Z. Mast "A Brief History of Jacob Mast and Other Mast Pioneers" published in 1911. The section on John Mast the brother is on pages 666 to 689.It also includes notes on the Ohio and Texas descendants up to 1900. There are still Amish Mast families.

John left his newly married brother and set off with his wife, Barbara (Harmon, Hermon or Lapp or Lopp or ?) and 4 children for North Carolina. (Nancy 1757-1859; Elizabeth 1760 -1831; David born 1761 in Lancaster Co PA died Aug 1836 in Montgomery Co. (Dayton) Ohio; John Jr. Born 1762 in Lancaster PA died Sept 12, 1832 Miami Co. Ohio (Also going to North Carolina with John were his sister Magdalena who married Michael Troyer and the Beiler and Fisher families. This move may have been precipitated by a falling out with his brother. (His other 3 sisters apparently never married.) On Feb. 17, 1763 he bought land in Rowan county North Carolina having largely walked all the way south with his family. (Note Rowan County then included Ashe and what is now Watauga county) Joseph was born March 25, 1764 in Randolph Co. NC and died 1835 in Watauga Co. NC. Hanna was born 1766; Catherine 1768 - died Nov 1809 in Miami Co OH. She married Andrew Sheets in 1788; Mary Mast born 1770 in Randolph died 1806 in Montgomery Co. OH; Jacob Mast born 1770 Randolph died 1809 in Ashe Co (Watauga) NC; Mary Magdalena Mollie Mast born March 20, 1772 in NC died Nov 27 1850 in Miami Co. OH. She married 1. Martin Davenport, March 1795, 2. John Waggoner 1801, 3. George Sinks after 1802; Susanna Mast born 1775 died July 30, 1830 in Miami Co. OH; and last was Stephen Mast born 1784 and died after 1833. John having settled in Randolf County NC (then a part of Guilford Co.) eventually had five sons and seven daughters. So while John went to North Carolina, several of his children went to Ohio where they may have reconnected with other Mast family coming from Pennsylvania.

During the revolutionary war it was thought that the Masts had participated in the siege of Charleston. However the record actually shows the name to be Mash. David Mast was born in 1761 and was styled Captain although it is not certain that he ever was a military leader. The primary reason for this is the fact that in 1779 John Mast and Andrew Fouts, Fred Waymire and Andrew Hoover all refused together to take the oath of allegiance presumably because they were pacifists or loyalists to the crown. While John Mast was not a Quaker, the others above were. The will of George Harmon who died in 1786 in Randolph Co. notes Cutliffe and other sons but makes no reference to a Barbara or other daughters. David Waggoner is noted as a son in law and John Maste and Adam Bowers as friends. Now this seems odd since if John Mast had married his daughter Barbara Harmon he would have been recognized as family not friend. Did John marry Stephen Fouts daughter Barbara or Jacob Harmon's daughter? Most of this group of friends relocated together to North Carolina one way or another. David Mast (1761 - 1836) married Nancy Ware (? - 1816) in 1778 in Watauga. John's second son, Joseph (born and died in Randolph Co. born 1764 died 1809) married Eve Bowers (born Dec. 30, 1758) daughter of George and Margaret Bowers. Eve had been born in South Carolina between the Saluda and French Broad Rivers May 30, 1783. Shortly afterwards Joseph and Eve moved to what became Valle Crucis. However he also bought 100 acres along the Uwharri River on Jan 5 1787.

Apart from Joseph who had relocated to Valle Crucis the rest of the family lived around Randolph NC. In 1798 Captain David Mast accompanied by his brother John Mast as well as David Hoover and others known to be Quakers went land hunting into Ohio. The reasons were perhaps related to the Quaker religion and a dislike of slavery. When they returned they organized themselves and on Christmas day 1800 the first group left Morgan Bryan's community at the Forks of the Yadkin R. in Western North Carolina for Ohio. This may have included John Mast (born1762 died 1832) who became the first settler in Miami Co. Ohio (just north of Dayton). John Jr. achieved the rank of private in the Revolutionary War and enlisted in North Carolina. He took part in the Siege of Charleston. He is listed as having children starting in 1775, but this seems too young to be probable In 1798, he, brother - David Hoover, Martin Davenport and Benjamin Iddings went on a land hunting expedition from North Carolina to evaluate Miami Valley in Ohio as a new territory for their families to live in. John Jr. remained in Miami Co. while the others returned to NC to bring their families. He was literally the first settler in what became known as West Branch, Miami Co., Ohio. His brothers Jacob and David, and all his seven sisters and their husbands proceeded to move to the Stillwater River Valley on adjoining properties in Miami and Montgomery counties in Ohio on their return trip in 1801. By 1801, John had built a flour mill (grist mill) that stood until a 1955 fire burned it down. The quality of the flour from his mill was listed as "superfine". He also ran a gunsmith shop. This John was taxed in Miami Co., Ohio in 1810 and 1816. He was in the deed records for Union Twp., Miami Co., Ohio in 1813, 1817, 1824, 1826, 1827,1828, 1830, 1831, and 1832. He is listed in the Census of 1827 for Union Twp., Miami Co., Ohio. He had his will probated in Miami Co., Ohio 1832. Henry Hoover, his wife's nephew, was one of his executors. Henry was the great, great uncle of President Herbert Hoover. John's wife was Susanah Hoover.

Nancy Mast(born 1762) and her husband James Curtis may have migrated at this time. Others may have waited a little longer before departing.

On the 10th of September 1801 David Mast (1761 - 1836) and his wife Nancy Ware (died 1816) began the migration to Ohio with brother Jacob (died 1809) married Nancy Sinks,(but had no kids) and his sister and their husbands, Elizabeth and Leonard Eller, Hanah and Daniel Hoover, Mary and David Hoover, Mary Magdalen (Mollie) and John Wagoner, Catherine and Andrew Sheets, Susannah and Henry Houts. David was known by the name of Captain Mast because he was one of the two leaders, the other being David Hoover. They brought 64 families from North Carolina to the Stillwater area of Ohio in 1801/2. David built five cabins in 1802 according to a website by Judith Baker. One of them was still lived in as of 1918 and in 2002 it still existed in Butler Twp., Miami Co., Ohio at 2151 Kershner Road. The logs were covered by clapboard by 1914.

David is the Capt. Mast listed as living in what is now the Poke Grove, Randolph Twp. area of Montgomery Co., Ohio in 1806. Originally the 64 families settled on lands on a 4 mile stretch along the Stillwater River. It encompassed lands in what was then Butler Twp., Clay Township and more in Union Twp., Miami Co., Ohio. However, boundary changes in 1825 placed David's land in Randolph Twp., Montgomery Co., Ohio instead. His cabin was the first to be notched in the Stillwater Woods with many others following for the large party of families they brought to Ohio. The beautiful large two story home he built afterwards has been restored by Cinda Lightner Kratzner and is located just outside of the town of Union in Randolph Co., OH on State Route 48. He was taxed in 1804, 1810 and 1816 in Montgomery Co., Ohio. He was in the deed records of West Milton, Miami Co., Ohio in 1836 dealing with Lot 50. Absalom, one of his son's, apparently used the same title as displayed in a letter quoted below.

W.H. Beers in "The History of Montgomery County, Book III," (1882) on pages 54-56, give a very interesting account of David Mast's migration to Ohio with his family. The account is quoted from a letter written by son, Capt. Absalom Mast. "*On the 10th day of Sept. (1802) ... my father, with four of his sisters and their husbands, bid adieu to old North Carolina, in company with one or two more families. They resided in Randolph County, (NC), of the Hewary River. They were all in low circumstances; had money enough to make their entries, and to buy some provisions during the winter. They halted for winter quarters at what is now called Ridgeville, eight miles north of Lebanon; rented a log cabin of Luther and Calvin Ball . . . Our*

Carolina tramps, or families, left Ridgeville vicinity (just north of Lebanon, OH) on the 4th day of March, 1802. They proceeded to the Stillwater woods, (arriving on 20 Mar.1802) where they had previously made their selections and on my father's purchase the first house or cabin was raised or notched." An interview with Mary Hoover of the same Montgomery Co., Randolph Twp. area, Ohio adds further interesting detail. *"They had to cut a road north, through the wilderness, as they moved on their entries of land, which were purchased in 1798. . . David Mast settled on the northwest quarter of section 3."* Nearby neighbors included Daniel Hoover, Daniel Hoover, Jr., and David Hoover. *"Indians were numerous then but never molested the settlers of this township, although as settlers arrived and rumors of Indian depredations were being committed, there were block-houses built and the neighbors were collected in them at night for mutual protection against the Indians, but every morning the settlers would disperse to their respective clearings."* Capt. Mast has several letters quoted on these pages of Beer's book.

Another accounting of this same story comes from his grandson, Wesley J. Mast, in a letter he wrote at age 85 on Sep. 3, 1910 to Mr. C. Z. Mast. *"David Mast, his two brothers, John and Jacob, seven sisters and their husbands came here in the early part of March 1802. They had left their homes in North Carolina in 1801 and had spent the winter in Ridgeville, Ohio north of Lebanon, Ohio. The sisters were Nancy, Elizabeth, Hannah, Mary Mollie, Catherine, Susannah. Their husbands were James Curtis who married Nancy, Daniel Hoover who married Hannah. John Waggoner who married Mollie. It was Henry Fouts who married their families."*

" all bid adieu to the Uwharrie River, family and friends and although in low circumstances they had enough money to make their entries and buy winter provisions. They wintered at Ridgeville north of Lebanon where they rented cabins. On Mar 4 1802 they arrived at Stillwater River where they had previously made their selection (in Montgomery and Miami Counties Ohio.)"

This account was written by Absalom Mast years later. This was a predominantly Quaker community although these Masts were never officially members of the church except by marriage to members and by participating in activities.

David Mast had the following children: Obedience, Rebecca, John 1791-

1863 who died in Butler OH, Nancy, Sarah, and Absalom. This branch of the Mast family later went to Indiana and Missouri. They appeared to be an industrious and progressive lot.

A fourth son, Stephen who never married went to Maryland and farmed on land that is now part of Baltimore. He visited his siblings in Miami and Montgomery Co., Ohio in 1833, but was never heard from again. In 1895 a Baltimore newspaper published an account of his land in an attempt to find his heirs. He had apparently leased it out.

There are records for the Jacob's descendants and the Ohio branch. This history has not researched them as it concentrates on Joseph Mast's descendants.

~~~~

Joseph Mast (gen 2) John's second son was born in Randolph Co. (March 25, 1764 - died 1835) and was the only child to remain in North Carolina. Joseph married **Eve Bowers** who was six years older than he (born Dec 30, 1758 in South Carolina between Saluda and French Broad Rivers.) They were married May 30,1783. Her parents were George and Margaret Bowers. She died 1830.

Sometime during the 1780's Joseph moved to Valle Crucis, Watauga Co. NC (although as late as 1787 he bought land in Randolph Co.) This was territory that the explorer/settler Daniel Boone helped populate between 1769 and 1790. Not many people had come to the Watauga area at that time, nor did many come until the 1840's.

Why would Joseph Mast take his family from the developed lands into a remote mountain area? This was a hard to access place in 1780 and apart from river bottom the land was not worth much. There are several possibilities one of which is to acquire land so he could expand for his children. This was not an especially good area to do that. A second reason was to get away from something. At the conclusion of the revolutionary war, those who were loyalists to the king were generally not treated kindly. Many chose to relocate to escape the stigmatism. The timing was right for Joseph to do this. It also appears that some of his children became or were Episcopalians (Anglicans). Finally, the family had close association to the pacifist Quakers and his brothers and sisters had gone with Quakers to Ohio. There were very few Anglicans in North Carolina but they took special interest in Valle Crucis. Anglicans were generally in favor of the British link. The Mast's sold land to the Anglicans and some of Joseph's children were Anglicans. It may well be that a loyalist could make a new life possibly among other like minded people up in the mountains. Some of his brothers, particularly David, were reputed to have been involved in the revolutionary war. His father was not and although not a Quaker, he associated with them. So another reason could be their pacifist nature being of Amish stock. Joseph's parents would have spoken English with a German accent and still had their Amish roots although John may have repudiated these when he parted with his brother. In addition Joseph did not go along with his siblings to Ohio preferring to remain in the mountains. Why? What set him apart. Joseph also had the ability to acquire a lot of land. He must have had some resources to do that. Where did that money come from?

It is reputed that Joseph bought over 1000 acres in Valle Crucis for a pair of leggings, a rifle and a dog. Only a man with more than one rifle would do such a thing. More importantly he was not the first owner of the land. The state did not give him free land as it had to others. In 1795 he acquired another 490 acres of river valley. A tax role for 1815 says Joseph Mast held 1390 acres. This included the best arable land in the center of the valley. The Baird and Shull families took the other ends of the bottom land in the valley. At first Joseph's name appeared as Moss then Most then finally settled corrected as Mast. There were eight children in the family, seven of them boys. Joseph either returned to Randolph Co. or maintained his connection there for it was there he died in 1809. It appears from the evidence that because Adam Mast had a bible with his name in it that he and likely his siblings were given some schooling. The careers of some indicated mathematical skills as well. So we can conclude the Masts unlike many pioneers of the time were literate.

~~~~

Joseph's eldest son **Adam** (gen 3) born Mar 6 1784 (died Oct. 18, 1857) in Randolph Co. married Elizabeth Cable born on the Uwharrie R. Mar 15, 1785 died July 31, 1859 (whose mother was Elizabeth Baker daughter of Daniel and Mary Baker.) They were married Mar 26, 1807 by Esquire Thornton a short time after her family moved to Dry Run, Baker's Gap. Her father, Casper Cable, was a former Hessian soldier who had fought for the British as a paid mercenary. About 3000 of the 30 000 Hessians decided to stay in America after the war rather than return to Hesse in Germany. Casper was born in Hanover, Germany and came to America as a British mercenary soldier. He was captured at Trenton Dec 26, 1776 by Washington. He changed sides and volunteered to join General Greene's army. He fought at Cowpens in the colonial service and was given a grant of land in Johnson County TN. Cable was very prosperous and lived at the Roan Creek Settlement. Adam and Elizabeth had 2 boys and 5 girls between the years 1808 and 1819. When Adam Mast came over the mountains from Valle Crucis to pay court to his daughter, Elizabeth, and they announced the wedding date, Casper saddled his horse and rode three days to Jonesboro TN to purchase a wedding trousseau for his daughter. So we have a German descendant marrying another German descendant. Adam must have been considered worthy to marry a Cable. Adam and Elizabeth, it is said, were poisoned by their slaves but he was 73 and she 74 so this may not be more than a popular folk story common in the south. He died Oct 18, 1857, she July 31, 1859. They lived at Cove Creek before moving to S.W. Virginia and then to Johnson County TN. Their children born at Cove Creek were Joseph Mast Jr. May 7, 1808 died 1862; Mary (Polly) Mast Aug 28, 1809; Elizabeth Mast Jr. May 29, 1811 died 1853; Eve Mast jr. June 20, 1813; born elsewhere were Susanah May 5, 1817 died Aug 18, 1881; Jacob Jan 12, 1819 died Oct 29, 1880 and Nancy Aug 20, 1819 Nov 29, 1908; Andrew J. 1830.

Adam Mast's bible (seen in 2002) was signed with his name on February 12th 1814. In what may be his own hand entries regarding himself it says *"Adam Mast son of Joseph and Eve Mast was born in Randolph County in North Carolina State on 6th March 1784."* and *" Elizabeth Cable dau of Casper and Elizabeth Cable was born in the county of Randolph near the Huwarre on 15th of March 1785."* And *" married by esquire Thornton of little Doe River at her fathers in Roan Creek Settlement Turnpike road Carter County and State of Tennessee March 26 1807."* In the same hand are recorded the children born at Cove Creek between 1809 and 1813. Another person has entered the births of the other 3 from 1817 to 1822. Yet a third person has entered various deaths of the above. The birth of Elizabeth Ann Mast daughter of Nancy on March 13, 1846 is yet another hand. Elizabeth Ann married William Butler McBride born 1849 (the older brother of Thomas Clark) December 11th 1870. It appears then the bible was in the possession of Elizabeth Ann Mast.

Minnie Belle, Lula Florence and James K. were born to Wm Butler and Elizabeth Ann McBride. Minnie Belle married Andrew Henderson Shoun and the bible passed to her from Nancy Mast on January 1ˢᵗ 1899. Minnie Belle held it until 1957 when it was given to her son Joe Clint Shoun in 1957. Adam built a fine brick two story house, one of three in the area, about 1820 on Dry Run road. It is on the west side of the road across from Wm. Butler McBride's farm. A family cemetery plot is nearby and away from the road. Adam, Elizabeth, and their children Jacob, Nancy, Susan are buried here as is Mary Mast Jones 1861 - 1950.

Joseph mast Jr. married Celia Campbell born Jan 1801 died Jy 3, 1887; Mary (Polly) married Alfred Slimp and had a child Jack. Jacob married Eveline Bradley.

Eve Mast, Adam's daughter married Elizah Dougherty and their son Thomas Jefferson Daugherty becomes related to the McBrides. He was born at Mill Creek in the Little Richmond house March 2ⁿᵈ 1837. The house was used as a confederate hospital in the war and the occupants defended it from Union raiders from the basement. Thomas Jefferson Daugherty married Polly McBride (Thomas Clarke's sister) at Cove Creek June 13ᵗʰ 1870. They lived at "little Richmond" for a time. In 1877 they bought land on Dry Run road from the Cables and Cable sr. a bachelor lived on with them until he died. Daugherty built a school and was its first teacher. He met a tragic end victim of an accident as he was killed by a cant hook in 1896. Polly wanted to continue educating the kids so she moved to Butler TN and opened a boarding house so her children could attend Holly Springs College. Her dormitory housed a number of students. Their children were quite close socially with their cousins, Thomas Clark McBride's children.

This section about the Masts and their McBride connections has much relationship to the Neva, Baker's Gap, Mill Creek, Dry Run area on route 67 along the Tennessee side of the state line. It is separated from Sugar Grove and Cove Creek by Stone Mountain ridge. By road it is some distance but about 10 miles in a direct line over the mountain. It seems remarkable that these two areas had so much interaction in earlier times as it takes 40 minutes on today's roads to go between them. Why Hiram McBride, for example, was buried in Cove Creek when he lived over the mountain needs some explaining.

More about John Mast, Joseph's second son later.

~~~~

David Mast, Joseph's third son, (1788-1830) married Mary Shull, daughter of Simon Shull and granddaughter of John Frederick Shull, descendant of Bavarian German stock. He stayed on the land of his father, Joseph.

David married Mary Schull and built a log cabin as it stands today on the Mast Farm Inn land. His children included William who was reputedly poisoned by his slave and Andrew who was born in the log cabin in July of 1827. Andrew married his cousin, Caroline, John's daughter and Finley P.'s sister. Andrew's son, also named Finley, married Allie Josephine Mast born May 8, 1861 - Feb 9, 1936. This Finley finished the house now known as the main building of the Mast Farm Inn in 1885. In the early 1900's he converted the house into an Inn. He died Jan 17, 1940. His sons were Claude who married Grace Moore and Joe C. who married Edna Abernathy (died Aug 1951) Over a 25 year time the Inn grew to 13 bedrooms, 1 bath. The water was gravity fed from a spring until a well was drilled in 1970. 13 of the 16 farm buildings still exist including the blacksmiths shop and the loom room, the original early 1810 cabin.

John A. (Jack) Mast, Finley P's brother, who was next child older than Finley had a son Noah T. He married Lucinda. Their son William Wellington took over the general store at Valle Crucis in the 1890's and expanded it in 1916. Masts ran the store until 1972. It was placed on the National Historic register in 1973.

I visited the store when it was still owned by the Mast family. The elderly fellow was not one to promote the business. When the store was sold to a promotion minded family, not connected to the Masts, it became the tourist attraction so well known today.

David Mast and Noah Mast, sons of Joseph both married Schulls. John Frederick Shull, wife Gertrude, son Simon and his wife Mary settled up river from the Masts. The Shulls were from Bavaria in Germany. John's parents Frederick and Maria arrived in Philadelphia in 1728, relocating after a time to Lincoln Co. NC Simon owned 150 acres in 1795. Later they would amass large amounts of property. The Baird, Mast, and Schull families interrelated for over 200 years and dominated the valley.

David's child Andrew Baker "Andy or Jack" Mast was born 1827 and died 1902 in a log cabin that was built in 1810 and still stands at the Mast Farm Inn, the site of David and his father Joseph's home. Andrew married Caroline Mast, his cousin, daughter of his uncle John and sister of Finley

Patterson Mast. They had 4 surviving kids: David Finley, William Harrison called "Billy", John Carroll, (Roy P. died as infant) and a girl Mary Elizabeth. After David died, his widow Mary stayed on the farm with son Andrew and wife Caroline.

Andrew's David Finley Mast 1857 - 1940 known by his second name Finley established the Mast Inn built in 1885. His wife was Josephine (Josie) Mast, also a cousin. She was very skilled at the loom. Claude Mast, child of Finley and Josie moved away from the valley while their other child Joe Carroll Mast remained on the farm but had no children.

Andrew and Caroline's second child William H. "Billy" Mast stayed in the valley dividing the land with his brother Andy. His children, if any, moved away. Another son of Andrew and Caroline, Andrew Jackson ("Andy") moved to Montana and a daughter moved to Washington.

William Mast another son of David,(not David Finley), was contracted to build the first bridge across the river in 1849 conveniently across from the family home. This was part of the toll road from Lenoir NC to Tennessee that other relatives had a stake in. In the same year William and his wife were having breakfast (oct 16 1849) when he and his wife fell violently ill as did all the children but one. The children vomited and recovered but the parents died in a short time from poisoned coffee. The slave cook Millie was suspected of the crime. The reason was fear that she would be sold to Williams uncle Jacob who was returning from Texas to marry Elizabeth Baker and take Elizabeth and a slave who Millie loved away. The case was never proved. But Millie was sold at Williams estate settlement to a Tennessee man.

The Masts were slave holders according to the records for Ashe county 1830. (The country was divided about this time so there is no 1840 or later record in Ashe.) Not many folk had slaves in 1820. No Masts are recorded. In 1830 this was the record of slave holdings: David 3, Joel 4, John 2, Joseph 7, Reuben 2. These numbers were consistent with other local folks. Very few owned more than 10. Most had 2 or 3 and thus rather than the image of the plantation these slaves were more in the image of domestic help or hired hand. The attempted poisoning of some of the Masts in the 40's and 50's by slaves also indicates something about the relationships.

~~~~

Jacob Mast, fourth son of Joseph and Eve , born Feb 24, 1790 - died Mar 10, 1878 in Melrose Texas, married the widow, Rebecca Robbins Fulcher in 1834 at Melrose, Nacogdoches Co. Texas. His arrival in Texas was about the time the first Americans began settling in East Texas and opposing the Mexicans. He appears to have gone there with his cousin Joseph Council. However Rebecca died in 1837 and he returned to Valle Crucis in 1849 to court and marry Elizabeth Baker. They went back to Texas with her slave Silas. He must have given a good account of life in Texas because Reuben and family went back there with him. Jacob was listed as a taxpayer in the tax list of 1837 for Nacogdoches. Small groups of settlers had been arriving at this Mexican mission outpost which became known as the cradle of Texas liberty. In 1832 the Mexican garrison was attacked here and was driven out clearing the way for settlement. In 1835 Sam Houston and Davy Crockett were here and the ill fated Almo group left from here. This area was peopled by Mexicans and Cherokees. In the census of 1850 Jacob age 60 was listed as a farmer and one of the oldest residents as he had lived there over 20 years. Milton and David and Lafayette J. were on the voters list in 1867. L.J. Mast had his will registered there in 1865. Masts were postmasters at Melrose. Milton Mast who had been in Co. K. 11th Regiment of Texas Volunteers (1862) during the civil war was the first postmaster after the war and he was appointed July 26 1870. Then Jacob Mast was appointed Feb 1, 1871, Also Jas W. in 1904 and Zachary T. at another time. A Mast married the granddaughter of the person who hosted the Alamo fighters before they left for the fight. Another Mast more recently endowed the S.F. Austin University Mast Arboretum and the Episcopalian Church. So Jacob's descendants are still among us.

~~~~

Joel Mast, fifth son of Joseph and Eve was born Nov 28 1792 (d 1850) in Ashe Co. (Watauga) never married. He built a home (between the 1990's elementary school and the Mast Store), and gained title to at least 784 acres of good bottom land, and built a mill of some significance. He sold 400 acres, including 100 under cultivation, a tannery and a grist mill to the Episcopalian mission in 1844 for 400 dollars. At this time the place was given the name Valle Crucis. A few years later the large landholdings of Joel were sold at public auction to Henry Taylor who had married Joel's niece Emmeline Mast ,born 1826, sister of Finley Patterson Mast. Taylor established the store that became Mast Store. In 1850 Joel owned 50 improved acres, 334 unimproved, 7 horses, 10 cows, 25 other cattle, 27 sheep and 30 pigs. He was an Anglican.

Reuben Mast, sixth son of Joseph and Eve, was born April 27, 1794 died April 18, 1862. He married first Nancy Webb (or Wheel) in 1839 (3 of his kids were born years earlier so this date is more likely about 1824) with whom he had Lafayette James Mast and William Penn Mast and also apparently Andrew Jackson Mast born Oct 27 1829 in Tennessee died Dec 22 1914 in Melrose Tx. Between Nancy and his second wife Jane Curtis he had 6 children.

Reuben's first child Charley was born April 16, 1819. According to his descendant Sharon Cranford, Joseph Mast bought a slave girl about 12 and her matron who were born in Ghana. In 1817 John Rhodes a slave trader sold him two black females for $500. The girl now 14 was of interest to Reuben. In 1818 Reuben about 24 years of age was reportedly engaged to be married when he conjugated a union with the young family slave. The young slave girl was soon sold farther south. Charley remained. The Masts whose religious background frowned on slavery went out of their way to disassociate themselves from this fact in later years. Charley was taught how to read and write and cypher and while he lived as a slave he was clearly part of the Mast family. He was a slave after Joseph died for Joseph's son John Mast for some time. At the age of 31 Charley married Mary Cloud a 14 year old Cherokee Indian apparently sold into slavery. Their children were Patterson 1851, Jacob 1853, Albert 1854, Louisa Caroline 1855, Patsy Irene 1857 and John Charles 1858. Other records identify Charley's sons also as Taylor and Bill Mast.

In 1859 Reuben informed Charley that he was buying him and his family back from John Mast for $5000 and taking them to Texas. The price Reuben paid for Charley was three times the going rate for a slave like Charley. Reuben clearly wanted Charley and his family. Charley Mast on April 17, 1862 was called by Reuben Mast his white father, now on his deathbed, and given his manumission papers thus ending his status as a slave and defacto acknowledging him as his child. Reuben also gave Charley a 240 acre farm to sustain himself and his family at Center Point, Nacogdoches, County. Charley and Mary had 3 more children, 9 in total, including Sarah, James and William. In 1869 Charley became the Reverend Charley Mast and help establish The Methodist Episcopal Church, Wilson Chapel in 1866. He also established a prosperous freight line business that enabled him to provide lands for schools for black children, a cemetery and two churches. His wife Mary died age 35 in 1871. He remarried and had a total of 15 children. Charley Mast died in 1901at the age of 82. A number of his children and grandchildren were highly successful people.

Read the novel about him "Kinship Concealed" by Sharon Cranford and Dwight Roth, 2013, Legacy Books. Roth is a descendant of Jacob Mast who remained in Pennsylvania as Mennonite when John left for North Carolina.

Reuben was an industrious, entrepreneurial fellow and by 1850 owned 400 acres 100 of which were improved. He had 6 horses, 10 cows, 20 other cattle,27 sheep and 31 swine. Reuben had bought from Benjamin Ward Sr. the river valley land Ward had earlier bought from Samuel Hicks the first settler. This is where the Watauga crosses Hwy 194. At the time Reuben was state representative and he built the house known as the Mast Baird House around a log cabin where he lived. Reuben Mast was elected representative to the North Carolina House of Commons for Ashe County in 1849. His cause was to get Ashe county divided because the county seat was too far away at Jefferson. He joined 2 others and by a 66% margin a law was passed January 27, 1849 creating Watauga County. Reuben and Charles H. Doughton were designated to survey and mark the new boundaries. The county seat was decided to be at Councill's store. 2 citizens donated 50 acres of land. Reuben's brother Noah and 2 others were appointed to lay off lots and designate what would be public land. 23 years later it became the town of Boone NC. Reuben's sister was married to Councill. Reuben was also a surveyor and responsible for the survey of the new county.

" *the first survey having been made by Reuben Mast, county surveyor when the county was first formed. It is said that Mast guessed that Deep Gap was south sixty degrees east from the mouth of Meadow Creek, but that when he got to the first high knob from which he could see Deep Gap he found he had been wrong. Instead, however, of turning back and running a new line, he continued the line to Deep Gap, leaving much land that legally belonged to Ashe in Watauga County. The court ordered a new survey, to be run on the true degree, and Rev. L. W. Farthing ran and marked it." (History of Watauga 1915)*

In 1852 Reuben was interested in the railway business and the NC assembly authorized Reuben and 2 others to open books for subscription and sale of stocks in the North Carolina and Western Railroad Company. Although planned for the mountains the railroad actually went from Salisbury to Hickory and Morganton. Reuben was appointed road commissioner and asked to select a route across the county for at least two roads in 1852 and 54. Reuben was present when the Episcopal Mission people arrived. He assisted them in crossing the river near his house and was well known to the Episcopalian Bishop in charge of the region who consulted with him. Thus Reuben and one brother Noah were known Episcopalians. Other brothers were known to be Methodists so the religious affinity of the family was divided.

Reuben was an influential force in the community. He was successful, but not an especially large landowner. It appears he must have had some education, The Masts, Shulls and Bairds were known to be supporters of schooling in the 1850's. When his brother Jacob returned from Texas something prompted Reuben to leave Valle Crucis and the county he helped create. In 1859, on the eve of the civil war he must have sensed the stress in the community. He sold 500 acres in the lower valley including his house to John Gragg of Globe NC.

On the first day of December 1859 Reuben Mast, 66 years old, his second wife Jane, and his kids crossed the ice on the Watauga River with 4 wagons, a surrey, his one family of slaves, Mary, Jake, Irvin, John, Len, Joe (who also became an Afro American Mast family) and headed for Texas with his returning brother Jacob. Jacob Mast had bought land at Nacogdoches many years earlier. They arrived at Melrose Texas March 12, 1860. For the first year they lived with Jacob and his family. Reuben had to return to Valle Crucis to settle up an estate where he had bought $5,000 worth of slaves, including his biological son Charley and all his children. Reuben went into the banking business in Texas. His son Lafayette James married Mary L? who had a child Will in Nacogdoches in 1859. Lafayette enlisted in the Texas Rangers and during the war Mary and the child mysteriously disappeared. Lafayette returned to find his family gone. After a time he married Mary Justina Procella the daughter of a Mexican family. Their son William Xavier Mast was born March 15, 1870 and died Feb 1, 1962 in Nacogdoches. Lafayette also had a daughter Mary L. Mast. For reasons unknown he set off for Oregon and died on the Oregon trail in 1871. Perhaps he was still a Ranger helping with problems in that area. Reuben had a son, William Penn "Bill" Mast who married Lottie Mast daughter of Leason Mast and Sally Dugger. So he married the granddaughter of his father's brother. They moved to Coquille, Oregon with 75 family members. (See Leason Mast) Reuben, according to legend, died of self inflicted poison which he drank on April 18, 1862. The day before he died he gave his black adult child his freedom from slavery. Was the reason he relocated to Texas done so he could bestow freedom and property to Charley? He certainly went out of his way to acquire Charley and his family. Reuben is buried in the Mast Cemetery, Melrose TX.

~~~~

Noah , 1797 -1850, seventh son of Joseph and Eve, appears to have been the most successful of the family although it is not clear how he became so. In 1850 he owned 2,900 acres in various places although only 90 of it was improved. He owned a few more animals except for sheep than any of his relatives and lived down river from Joel and Reuben. Noah married the sister of his brother David's wife, Elizabeth Shull. Interested in politics he was elected state senator in 1834 for Ashe county (included Watauga then). An Episcopalian he supported the church and educational work of the mission that was set up at Valle Crucis. Noah was appointed to lay out the lots for the town of Boone so he may have been trained as a surveyor. He later,1858, moved to Carter Co. Tenn. (Johnson Co. was taken from Carter Co.) where in 1860 he owned a house worth 8,500 dollars and had a net worth of $13, 000. Two of his sons were still at home in 1860. He possibly owned a slave family by the name of Mast for in the 1870 census a Rachel Mast age 64 lived with Buck Mast age 69 and several grown children. Rachel and Buck Mast were listed as being black. Noah's children included H. Patterson born 1837, Joel 1844 and others.

~~~~

Elizabeth Mast, born Dec 5 1800, Joseph and Eve's only daughter married Benjamin Council, who was a prominent citizen and large landowner. Councill's store became Boone and the county seat because of efforts of her brothers. The Council children were: Jacob married Sally Lewis, John; Joseph who married in Texas; Elizabeth who married Holland Hodges and Sally Council who married Ebenezer Smith (Rhoda Smith's brother.)

~~~~

We now return to the second son of Joseph and Eve, **John Mast** (gen 3) (born Feb 24, 1786 died Jan 6, 1868) and the story of him and his 14 children. John came as an infant to the mountains. This was not a very populated area but the Bairds and Shulls lived up and down the river from his family home. His father Joseph had a sugar camp on Davis creek and Frederick Shull and John Holsclaw also had camps on another branch of the creek which the young lad would visit. Some bottom land had been cleared for farming at what must have been near subsistence existence. However, his family did seem to prosper. Likely John had some schooling. It is possible he spoke some German as the family had contacts with other families of German background. His younger brothers were educated perhaps in accounting and survey work since they proved later to have some business skill. Not long after his brother Adam married, young John decided to court and marry. He was 22. His bride Susannah Harmon was 17 when they married.

Susannah Harmon was daughter of Mathias Cutliff Harmon (1748 - 1838). She was born Mar 5, 1791in Rowan Co. NC died July 15, 1868 of heart dropsy. Her father married Susan Fouts born 1761. Cutliff was the son of George Harmon born 1722(or born 1710 Mittlefranken, Austria died 1787 Rowan Co. NC) in Germany and Margaret Wiley born 1724 married 1744 in Maryland died 1789.

Susan Fouts born 1751- 1817 was the daughter of Theobald Pfouts born 1722 in Switzerland and Catherine Spergel born 1724. It will be recalled that the first John Mast, this John's Grandfather, had traveled with Harmons from Pennsylvania and the Fouts had been in North Carolina with the earlier Masts. So Finley Patterson had strong Germanic links on both sides. Cutliff sold 60 acres in Randolph Co. NC in 1798 and moved to Watauga.

John Mast (gen 3) **and Susan Harmon** were married July 14, 1808 and they built a home on Bushy Fork Creek ,Sugar Grove NC. During the next 22 years Susan had 14 children, seven boys and seven girls. The 14th and youngest child was Finley Patterson Mast. His father John lived to be 82 and was the postmaster at Sugar Grove for many years. A number of his children lived to their late 80's. Most remained in the area apparently marrying local people. A very complicated web of intermarriages and descendants takes place. Just try and sort it out! I will only recount some salient details and not try to replicate a complete who's who below.

Their first child, **Nancy Mast** (gen 4) was born May 18, 1809 and died Sept 22, 1882. She was married Apr 14, 1831 to Dudley Farthing 1810 - 1910. One record shows her as Jancy, not Nancy. The records contain a lot of Farthing relationships. Dudley's grandfather Dudley was born Apr 6 1749 in Halifax Co. Virginia of Welsh born parents. He became a brick mason building the first brick house in Richmond Va. Later in life he and his wife Anne Watkins moved to Wake Co. NC. He was drawn with rheumatism into the shape of a chair and before he died Feb 22, 1826 he asked he be laid straight. (couldn't be done). His son William Watkins Farthing was sent to Watauga in 1826 as a Baptist missionary but died the next year.

Nancy and Dudley had sons in the civil war. William Judson died in the Texas Rangers 1865 age 33. James Martin killed at Fredericksburg Va Dec 13 1862 age 27, Thomas Jefferson age 23 died in Lynchburg military hospital 1862. John Young age 22 was wounded at 2nd battle of Manassas Aug 1862 survived to age 80. Henry Harrison wounded twice. William J. went to Texas as a school Teacher before civil war and owned a section of land. There were other children including Wiley Hill born Mar 23 1850.

The second child, of John and Susan, was **David Mast** born July 21, 1810 died 1810

Noah Mast, Their third child, not to be confused with his uncle, born Feb 20, 1812 - died Feb 7, 1897 married Elizabeth "Katy" Roland and with their children Harvey, Mary and Joel they moved to Skidmore in the Missouri territory. They moved to MO around 1840 - 42 at the time that this territory was opening up. In the census of 1850 their children are listed as John age 7 and Susan age 1. Noah was 38 and his wife Katherine of TN was 31. So where were the other 3 kids? There were Shulls also in Skidmore and later Emmeline Mast Taylor's child Butler was postmaster at Skidmore from 1891 to 95. Masts still live around Skidmore and Nodaway Co. which is in northwest Missouri along the Iowa border.

Eli Mast , John and Susan's fourth child, was born Oct 31, 1813 and died Aug 26, 1902 married Celia Dugger on Nov 15 1845. It may be that Celia and Sally were sisters. The Duggers descended from William Dugger who came to Virginia before 1656, as that year he was a member of the Virginia House of Burgesses. Julius C. Dugger came from Virginia in 1766 and settled near Elizabethton, clearing land there. Julius C. Jr. and Mary Hall had 9 children. He served in Revolutionary War in Battle of Lookout Mountain. His son John served under Andrew Jackson in War of 1812. John had 20 children with Mary Engle. Abel Dugger owned the Cranberry Mines at Cranberry NC and was likely brother to Celia and Sally.
   Children: Sarah, Joseph Finley, Manuel Dugger, Mary Ellen, William Penn, John Calvin, Susan

Leason Mast, John and Susan's fifth child, born Dec 14, 1815 died June 22, 1884, married Sally Dugger and moved to Lee Oregon in 1873. The journey took from June 1872 to October 1873 and included as many as 75 persons in the entourage that went to Coquille and Coos Co. Oregon. Children: Charlotte 1838 - 1920; Eli 1848 -1941; Hester Hazel 1852 - 1937. Leason undertook this journey after spending nearly 60 years in Watauga. The homestead act of 1862 made free land available in Oregon. Roads and the railroad were just completing into the Coos County area along the coast in 1872. The population of Oregon skyrocketed in the 1870's . Today there is a Mast Cemetery east of Myrtle Point. Here are the remains of the pioneers: Leason Mast 1815 to May 23, 1885; Sarah his wife 1820 - 1909; Leason Harmon 1849 -1891; his wife Hester Hazel 1852 - 1937 died of a stroke after having been senile for 10 years; Charlotte H. 1838 - 1920; W.L. Mast 1864 - 1927 (Leason's son?); J.W. Mast 1866 - 1925 (also son?) ; W.P. Mast 1834 - dec 1899 - might be William Penn child of Reuben he married Lottie (Charlotte) daughter of Leason.; Hardee W. Mast 1873 -

1961 born in Oregon. In other area cemeteries are: J.C. Mast 1854 - 1891; Reuben Harrison Mast 1858 - 1949 - likely son of Reuben as he named his kids after famous Americans, also it appears that some of these people might have come from Texas to go to Oregon, thus accounting for the presence of Lafayette out there in 1871. Reuben's son Reuben Harrison was a doctor 1895- 1939; J. Finley Mast 1851-1923 died in an auto accident when his car hit the soft shoulder and went over an embankment while passing a team and another car. He was the son of Eli mast and his wife. Injured in the crash was daughter Alia Dugger; other children were Derinda Mast 1847 - 1920; Eli P. Mast 1848 -1941; Emeline Mast 1846 - 1921. So we can account for 15 Masts going to Oregon. Masts still live there and there is a Mast Hospital, Myrtle Point, Oregon.

Elizabeth Mast, John and Susan's sixth child, born Jan 19, 1817 married Joseph Shull on Oct 28 (?)   4 of their boys served in the confederate forces. They had 8 kids, 7 of whom moved west. Joseph was a postmaster for a time 1854-7. The youngest son James who married Allie Baird inherited the Shull farm. The Shulls were active Methodists.

Children: William F. Shull born Sept 18, 1836; Temperance Shull born Aug 7, 1838 married Wm Horton; Noah S. Shull Apr 15,1840; Phillip Shull Jy 20,1842; Ben C. Shull Oct 23,1845; John T. Shull Oct 27,1853; James Melton Shull may 23, 1859; "Addie" mary Adeline Shull Mar 28 ,1861

Mary Mast, John and Susan's seventh child, born Dec 25, 1818 married John W. Wilson
Children: Caroline Wilson married Dudley Seift; Sarah Emeline born Mar 1843; Hiram; John Andrew and Susan.

Charlotte Mast John and Susan's eighth child, born Nov 21, 1820 married Zepheniah Horton had seven children and moved to Yancy County NC
Children; Taylor Horton 1848, Finley, James, Nicholas, Emma, Jane, Jonathan who was killed by a runaway horse, Dave

Malinda Mast, John and Susan's ninth child, was born Sept 26, 1822 married Jesse Gragg whose family bought a Mast farm.
Children: William Finley Gragg; Peter Gragg

Caroline Mast, John and Susan's tenth child, was born Aug 21, 1824 married her cousin, Andrew Baker Mast son of David Mast, Joseph's son. Andrew was born 1827 in the existing log cabin at the Mast Inn. Andrew built the 1885 house that became Mast Inn which was the first place in Watauga placed on the National Historic Register, 1972 as one of the best preserved and complete groups of 19th century farm buildings in Western North Carolina.

Children: Billy (William?) married Polly Hayes (1855- 1938) Sept 17, 1874; David Finley Mast (died Jan 1940) married Josie Mast, Finley and Josie were the long time proprietors of the Mast Inn. Mary Mast married Robert McCoy.

Emmeline Mast, John and Susan's eleventh child, was born Jan 5,1826 died 1880. She married Henry Taylor. He had come to Sugar Grove from Davidson Co. NC as a salesman for Seth Thomas clocks about 1849. Being an opportunist he saw his future here. He obtained a contract to build part of the toll road from Lenoir to Valle Crucis and into Tennessee. Remember Reuben Mast? He was in on this also. Henry built a store, Taylor and Moore Company, on the new road across from the current Mast store after marrying Emmeline. They moved to Valle Crucis from Sugar Grove. The store drew people from a wide area. When Joel Mast died, Taylor bought all his land at auction. In 1860 he bought another 11acres which had been in part the Episcopal mission land. He bought other land by barter including trading clocks and guns for land and tax delinquent land. He built a brick house on the hillside which was expanded from time to time and still exists as a gift shop. Emaline and Henry had extra room, even after 4 boys, to rent out rooms to traveling salesmen (1872 rates, 25 cents a night, if driver and horse 40 cents) Henry by 1870 had 2300 acres of which 300 were farmable. He also ran a grist mill, brickyard. He was magistrate of Watauga Twp, and chair of Public Roads. Oh, he was also postmaster and a Methodist. When their second son was born, they named him James Patterson Taylor in honor of Jayhue Patterson the first circuit rider Methodist minister who had come to the area and who deeply impressed people. When Emmaline (various spellings of her name) died in 1880 Henry remarried and had 2 more children and in 1882 at age 63 built a new larger store across the road. This is the current Mast Store. His son Charles took over the store in 1890. William Wellington Mast after working at another Mast Store in Sugar Grove went to work in the 1890's at the C.D. Taylor General Store. In 1898 he bought a partnership, " Taylor and Mast" later he bought the entire business. W.W. Mast was a grandchild of John A. Mast, Finley P's next oldest brother.

Children: John Butler Taylor 1852-1931; James Patterson Taylor; Charles Davis Taylor; Thomas Hardison Taylor

Joseph Andrew Harrison Mast, John and Susan's 12th child, was born

Apr 9, 1827 married June 11, 1829 to Clarissa P. Moore. Clarissa was from Globe, the daughter of Daniel Moore and Elizabeth Hight. Their Daughter Josephine married first Cousin David Finley Mast.

Children: Sophrina Elizabeth Mast; Andrew Jackson Mast married Joanna King and had 7 kids, moved to Montana where he died.

Children were: Leona Angeline Mast; Martha Victoria Mast; John Hight Mast; Alice Josephine Mast; Sarah Caroline; Daniel Harrison Mast born 6/26/1866; and Joseph Carson Mast.

John Allen Mast, John and Susan's 13th child, (Sept 22, 1829 -died Feb 6, 1892) married Dec 5,1850 to Martha Elizabeth Moore (Apr 13, 1833 - Feb 15, 1905). Their son Noah T. married Lucinda Adams and their son William Wellington was born Apr 21, 1876. He became owner of Mast Store. John A. Mast joined the 58th NC carolina Regiment, 5th Sgt of D company. In 1862 he was a farmer at Laurel Creek and return to farming after the war. He died Feb 6, 1892 in Watauga Co.

Children: Elizabeth; Noah Tarlton; Charlotte Caroline; Virginia Ellen; Newton Lafayette; Julia Ann; Munsford Monroe; Mary Etta; Sussan Arrena; Martha Addie; William Hardy "Hard" Mast.

Finley Patterson Mast, (gen 4) John and Susan's 14th child, was born in 1832 and married Rhoda Smith (Ebenezer was her brother)

Children: David Charles (Charlie); Mary Elizabeth; Martha E. (Mattie); John Johiel (Jack); Emma Lenoir; Lillie Olympia. Now recall that Rhoda Smith's mother was a Dugger and two of Finley's brothers had married Duggers.

Finley Patterson Mast the youngest child was born March 30, 1832. He died Jan 12, 1924 age 92. Finley married Rhoda Smith (born Mar 22, 1839 died May 13, 1910) on Dec 21, 1865 a few months after coming home from the Civil War. Finley was a lean man with a long face and long fleshy nose. He wore an uncut beard and used a cane in later years. Rhoda was a fine featured woman with an oval face. She wore glasses. Whether he was named Patterson after the first Methodist circuit rider minister as at least one person was, is speculative. Finley was a popular name in the area. Other Masts were named Finley as were other families. There was a tendency to name a child after the most recently deceased relative but I can find none before him.

As a boy Finley would have had no shortage of cousins and siblings to play with. He came of age with family setting off to new places, deaths of his uncle Joel and the murder of William and the marriages of Emmeline to Taylor as well as others and finally the excitement of the Civil War. We don't know what he did as a young man. In an age of marrying young he was slow to chose. Probably he was needed on the farm. As a young man of 25 his father was over 70 and probably needed his help. Valle Crucis and Sugar Grove were Confederacy supporters but most of Watauga had opposed the war. Nearby Banner Elk was strongly Unionist. The Mast relatives especially the Cables were soldiering. Four Shull boys from the area signed up. Camp Mast was established, 4 miles northwest of Valle Crucis by the Watauga Home Guard under major Bingham. Their job was to look for draft dodgers and deserters, as well as protecting those left at home. Families were very often split in their sympathies. No evidence one way or the other of this with the Masts. There were some raiding parties in the area from time to time. Camp Mast surrendered to a detail of a hundred Unionists from Banner Elk in February 1865. In this environment it was hard for a single man not to do his duty. We don't know about his attitude over this event but he was certainly involved.

Finley enlisted in the 58th North Carolina regiment CSA, June 27, when it was formed in 1862.(Actual enlistment data: July 15, 1862, rank of 1st Sgt Co D age 20, day laborer, resident of Valle Crucis community in 1860). This thirty year old joined with his brother John A Mast (5th sgt Co D born 9, 22, 1829 age 30, farmer, resident of Laurel Creek) and cousin W.P. Mast son of Reuben Mast(1st Lt. Co D as of April 1st 1863)as well as others from Watauga, Mitchell, Yancey, Caldwell, McDowell and Ashe Counties.There were 57 soldiers on the post war roster in Co D. These mountain men went to Cumberland Gap in September of 62 to train. Finley was 1st Sergeant of Company D, 58th NC Infantry. Then they moved on to Big Creek Gap near Jacksboro Tn. for the winter of 62\3. During the war Co D 58th NC was assigned to Kelly's, Reynolds, Browns and Reynolds Consolidated and finally Palmers Brigade. At times this regiment acted as North Carolina Partisan Rangers, (guerillas or bushwhackers in those days). A part of the army of Tennessee, Finley saw action at Chicamauga where they had 46 killed and 114 wounded out of a total of 327 men and 186 arms. The unit was in the seige of Chattanooga, battle of Resaca where the 58th sustained the heaviest action with several wounded and killed. They were in the Atlanta campaign, battle at New Hope Church, Peach Tree Creek and in the battle of Atlanta (22 July 1864). Then he was involved in the defense of Atlanta. They fought at Jonesboro. When President Davis addressed the troops near Atlanta, they were there. They guarded prisoners at Columbia TN, during Hood's operations. Later they went to South Carolina and saw action along the Edisto River from February to April 65. Lastly, they fought at Bentonville N.C. The 58th surrendered April 26, 1865. Considering the destruction, privations and travails he went through Finley lasted in the army for 3 years of hell. The attrition through injury, death, desertion and capture meant that he was a dedicated soldier and very committed to the southern cause. The records show Finley, was captured March 28, 1865. This was a few days after the 58th and other remnants had retreated to Statesville NC after fighting at Bentonville, the last major effort in battle by the South. At the time of his capture

"the men of the 58th North Carolina and of Palmer's Brigade were nearly naked--each soldier only a single blanket--or less. Rations were very scarce. The Army of Tennessee passed the severe winter of 1864-65 in active field service. Despite severe exposure of the men and officers, there were no complaints. The men knew complaints would do no good and if they did complain, they did it with their feet and deserted."

The remnants were reorganized into new merged units. One suspects Finley may have finally decided the game was over and allowed himself to be captured although he may have been captured at Bentonville a week earlier and processed on the 28th. There were some men captured at Bentonville. Had he not been he could have simply gone home a month later. He was imprisoned at Nashville Military Prison and Camp Chase Ohio. Camp Chase was overcrowded and disease was rampant. Several of his relatives died in the camp. He was released June 10, 1865 after taking the oath to the USA. The pay, if he ever got it, was 1 Mexican silver dollar worth more than the 154 confederate dollars he would have gotten. From Camp Chase (now part of Columbus, Ohio) he and others walked back home. He likely arrived home by early July. Likely he had not been home in 3 years although by the time he got home others would have known he was likely still alive. He had seen direct action over and over in the war and did not seem inclined to discuss it later in life.

He didn't waste time in changing his life. Less than 5 months later he married Rhoda Smith and in 1868 when his father John died he took over the job of postmaster, the post office being in the family home at the corner of Mast Gap Road and # 319 Hwy.

Finley was well established in the community and he supported Cove Creek Baptist Church. His family was started rather late in life when he was 38 with the birth of Charles. Finley had a great interest in education, perhaps as a consequence of his travels in the war. He gave his support to building and maintaining the schools. This interest led to all six of his children being sent away to school at the Globe Academy in Caldwell county. Mary Elizabeth his oldest girl was the first girl in the county to go away to school. Charles went on to Lexington College. Emma and Lillie went to teachers' college at Greensboro UNCG. In 1878 Finley along with Tom Adams a colleague from prison camp and others in the community organized a masonic lodge at Sugar Grove. He held one of the positions in this lodge, now known as Snow lodge based in Boone.

Finley Patterson Mast's Children

Charlie (Charles David) Mast born Jan 30, 1867 died Nov 5, 1953 married 4/4/1899 (Lenora Mae) Nora Baird (born June 2, 1874 died Dec 14, 1947) both buried at Mast Cemetery. Children 2: David Patterson born 1901 married 1929 Grace Blaylock born 1905 and their children Pat 1931, Herndon 1934, George 1936.

Charlie and Nora's daughter, Johnsie Mae Mast born 1902 married 1923 Joe Phillips. They lived in Detroit on Nine mile road and their children Robert 1925 married 1945 Lois Kassnow (their kids Sandra Jean 1946, Rick 1950) Johnsie and Joe also had Nora Jean 1928 married Dale Whittbracht and their child Mark born 1949. Charlie's home was built in 1895 on Mast Gap Road 1/4 mile from the homestead.

Mary Elizabeth (gen 5)was the second child born Dec 19, 1868 died March 8,1947 and married Thomas Clarke McBride on Aug 19, 1887. More on her later.

Mattie (Martha E.) Mast born Feb 27, 1871 died Feb 13, 1952 married Wiley T. Laine and moved to Vero Beach Florida. It was a popular place to go visit. Her husband died early. They had no children. She took over the post office duties of her father when she was old enough.

Jack (John Johiel) Mast (born Mar 26, 1874 died May 31, 1948) buried at Mast Cemetery married Mattie Glenn born Dec 19, 1879 died Dec 29, 1908.

Their Children: Gilbert Carlton Jan 1902 died Apr 30, 1976 (Mast Cemetery) married Pauline Grimes Mar 28, 1909 died Dec 17, 1964 (Mast Cemetery), daughter Nancy; Lucy born May 20,1904 died 1964 (Mast Cemetery). She married Sept 1, 1924 Luther Bingham and their children are Geraldine married a Miller, Luther Martin Bingham, secondly Lucy married Clarence Watson; Henry born May 10, 1906 died Dec 17, 1986 (Mast Cemetery) married Mamie Henson (Mar 15, 1908 - Dec 16, 1982)(Mast Cemetery also Cty) on May 9, 1927 children: Billy; Peggy Ann (Jan 31, 1931- Aug 8, 1996) (mast Cty) married Charles Bryant Combs (may 29, 1925 - Oct 12, 1978) (Mast cty).

Several months after Mattie died Jack married Bessie Blanche Bingham on

Aug 7, 1909 (born Jan 21, 1892 died June 14, 1968). Jack and Bessie's children: Mattie Alice born June 9, 1910 died Sept 22, 1989 (Mast Cty); Dick born Dec 7,1911 died 1912 (Mast Cty); Louise born May 25, 1915 died June 25, 1988 (Mast Cty) married Bob Rahe (Feb 24, 1918 - Aug 1, 1986)(Mast Cty) children, Ron 1950; Ned April 20, 1917 died June 24, 1957 (Mast Cty) married Ruth Triplett on Sept 10, 1938 children Max 1940, Michael Joseph 1951; Evelyn born July 30, 1920 married Jr. Simpson June 1935 Children Jack 1936, Jim 1938; Tom born July 22, 1922 married Margaret Yates on Mar 9, 1940; Elizabeth April 25, 1925; Houston April 8, 1927; infant girl Nancy (Mast Cty) Aug 22, 1930. See Page 13 of Mast's and Mast Cemetery Plan. Jack and Mattie lived close by the Mast home place until mother Rhoda Died (1910) and Mattie married. They then moved in with Finley P. Alice and Elizabeth unmarried lived with their mother in the old home place until well after Jack died. They built a new small house and sold the old Mast home place which was moved.

Lillie Olympia Mast , Mary's sister, born Sept 19, 1882 married Oct 3, 1905 (Henry) **Floyd McBride** (father was Barzilla, Thomas Clarke's brother i.e. nephew) and at some point before 1914 went to Mexico with their kids; Henry Floyd, Francis Rachel, Allen Curtis, Rhoda and James survived .In January 1914 two died and February 6 and 8, 1914 two more died. All these kids had contracted scarlet fever. Lillie died and Floyd married Willie ? Floyd died May 9, 1952.

Emma (Emmaline Lenoir) Mast, married Thomas Carroll Baird and their children are Frank, Wilma, David (died in childhood) Frank and Wilma lived together as neither married. They lived across Mast Gap Road at Valle Crucis in the David F. Baird homestead about 2 miles from the Mast homestead.

The Masts of Finley P.'s generation were quit entrepreneurial. It was said that they were store keepers at a number of places in the area. Out of this comes the modern day fame of the Mast General Store and the Mast Farm Inn.

When Joseph Mast and his bride Eva Bowers moved from Randolph N.C. to Watauga they started a family of seven boys and one girl. John and Susannah Harmon raised 14 kids, 7 of each. Finley Patterson was the youngest.

Finley was even in hard times able to prosper. He was a member of Cove Creek Baptist Church. It was said he gave each of his children a farm when they married. When he died in 1924, he left $5000 to his daughter Mary Elizabeth which she used to buy her home near Scottsville Va.

Before Finley died he established a cemetery. A knoll at Sugar Grove was cleared and he and his wife and some direct descendants are buried there.

~~~~~~~~~~

Comment:

The McBRIDES

Thomas Clark McBride was born May 27, 1864 to Hiram McBride and Mary Hervey Farthing. Hiram at age 26 had married Mary Elizabeth Mast when she was 18 on Dec 1, 1844. Their first child Nancy was born in 1846 and by 1852 there were five children. Hiram arranged to purchase a larger home and 280 acres of land from James Brown (Nov 12, 1852). The house was either new or built by Hiram and was used for many years as the post office at Baker's Gap in the Neva Community. The rest of the children were born there. However on March 30th 1866 Hiram decided to sell the farm to R. L. Wilson.

Thomas Clarke was the youngest of eleven children. Nancy1846, Polly 1847, William Butler 1849 to 1943, Rachael 1850, Barzilla 1852, John 1854, Emily 1855, Martha 1857, Jane 1859, Carrie (Sis) 1862, Thomas Clarke May 27, 1864 which also was the birthday of Charles Eacott and his son John Frances Eacott.

William Butler McBride married Betsy Mast. Barzilla McBride's son, Floyd, married Lillie Mast, sister of Mary Elizabeth (our Mary). So Mary's sister married her husband's brothers son. John McBride married Carrie Mast, Emily McBride married John H. Mast and Thomas Clarke McBride married Mary Mast. Obviously this sequence of marriages related the two families very strongly. Four of Hiram McBride's 11 children married Masts and a fifth married a Mast son, Tom Dougherty (Elija Dougherty and Eve Mast). Tom Dougherty's brother Daniel was a war veteran, established businesses and was significant Boone landowner. Appalachian State University at Boone is on his former land. Thomas Clarke grew up near Mountain City Tn (originally Taylorsville) (Shouns, Tenn.).

Barzilla jr., Thomas' older brother of 12 years, lived till 1924. He had been a butcher. Thomas gave Barzilla, known as "Braz," 30 acres of land to move to Newmarket Tenn. where he had his farm. They had Indian rugs from Oklahoma at their home. Butler and John were farmers. Butler McBride lived at Newmarket and later Sweetwater TN. John, who lived at Sugar Grove, kept an orchard and every year would send others a barrel of apples. Nancy McBride, who married Lewis Farthing lived at Beaver Dam. Polly McBride, who married Tom Dougherty, lived in Johnson County TN where they raised 11 kids, one of whom married Carl Reese who became a senator. Emily McBride died at 22. Martha McBride, known as Mattie and Enoch Swift lived in Watauga with eight kids. Jane McBride also married a Swift (George) lived at Beaver Dam and raised 12 kids. Carrie McBride (Sis) and Andy Testor lived at Timber Ridge.

When Thomas was five years old, his mother Mary died at age 51 a day before his birthday. Ten months later in March of 1870 his father Hiram married again to Rachael Farthing Hayes, a relative of his first wife. Thomas's oldest sister Nancy McBride married Lewis Farthing Nov 24, 1870 and his oldest brother William Butler McBride married two weeks later 11th December. Rachael, Hiram's new wife, had eight children between the age of five and 19 to raise. When Thomas was 16, his father died at the age of 62. His childhood would have been rather confusing. Hiram was for a time the postmaster at Baker's Gap in the 1860's and at McBride's Mill in 1869. He was also witnessed the will of a Mary Ford in 1860 with R. Farthing.

Hiram was the second born child of Barzilla McBride and Rachael Wilson. Now the next generation back.

Hiram McBride was born Aug 9, 1818, died July 30, 1880 (age 62)
 - married Mary Hervey Farthing Dec 1, 1844. She died May 26, 1869 (51 yrs 3 mo).

At the age of 21 in the year 1840 Hiram and Asa Reese, Riley Wilson, plus two of Asa's uncles, a girl named Roland and two daughters of Jacob Reese went to the Platte Purchase which the US had bought in 1836 from the local natives. The Platte consisted of 5 counties in northwestern Missouri and includes Kansas city. A number of other Watauga pioneers went to this area. They stopped at the Platte river 300 miles west of the Mississippi and crossed it near New Market MO. Hiram got homesick and returned to Watauga. Then Asa returned in 1844. In 1844 Hiram married Mary Farthing daughter of William Watkins Farthing and Polly. William Farthing was ordained to preach by Eno Baptist Church in 1822 and came to Watauga to preach. He decided to settle in Watauga and moved from Wake Co. NC in 1826 with his family to a farm he bought from Mr. Webb near Bethel Church. However he died about a month after arriving. In the days after the civil war Hiram bought a farm from Albert P. Wilson at Cove Creek. Wilson was married to Elizabeth Councill daughter of Jordan Councill.

When his wife Mary Hervey died age 51, he remarried again but was divorced within months. Thirdly he married Rachel Farthing Hayes. Hiram and Rachel had no children together but she raised Hiram's.

Now it so happens that in this rural area the families were large and there were not a lot of them. This is a list of some surnames of families who married into each others family, with varying generations over a century or more. This was a repeating process of intermarrying cousins of differing distance.   Mast, McBride, Norris, Council, Dugger, Eggers, Farthing, Tester, Trivette, Wilson, Smith, Greene, Baird, Reese, Shull, Swift, Harmon.

As the pressure to find more land took place Watauga people choose to move to Ohio, then Missouri, then Texas and finally the far west.

Hiram McBride was the son of Barzilla McBride and Rachael Wilson.

~~~~

The next generation back.

Barzilla McBride (gen 2) was born Aug 9, 1818 and died July 30, 1880

Barzilla McBride was the son of the immigrants John McBride and Anne Baird. His obscure name was taken from the book of Samuel.

Barzilla McBride fought in the war of 1812 and at some point in time he became a preacher.

Barzilla enlisted in the 1st Regiment of the West Tennessee Militia and was a private in the company of Captain James Blakemore under the command of Col. Philip Pipkin on the 20th day of June 1814 when the regiment was formed. It was because of the eagerness of these volunteers in signing up that Tennessee became known as the "Volunteer State". For the next 6 days the newly enlisted men democratically elected their officers and underwent organizational training into 6 groups at Fayetteville Tn. Barzilla had signed on for 6 months and was to be paid $8.00 a month and 40 cents a day for the upkeep of his horse. He had to provide his own weapon and ammunition. On the 26th of June 1814 a thousand men began the march to Fort Strother, Jackson's headquarters near Ragland, Alabama which was reached in ten days. Then they marched on to Fort Jackson where on August 9, 1814 a treaty was signed in which 36 Creek chiefs agreed to cede to the United States half of their land. This was essentially the western half of Tennessee and parts of Georgia and Alabama. The Creeks had been beaten in battle in the previous several months by the regular army and the show of force by this militia army was enough to finally force them to sign.

Some of the men thought the 6 months enlistment was too much as 3 months was the usual enlistment and they wanted to go home. Some deserted and others spoke of mutiny. The work of the militia was garrison duty that proved to be unexciting and not what they had expected. However the militia marched on September 20th towards Mobile, Alabama which had been recently attacked by the British. There they remained until November 27th. The extension of their service proved unacceptable to some and a mutiny took place. During November six deserters were executed under General Jackson's order and others had their heads shaved and were drummed out of the militia. On November 27th the army marched north to Nashville and arrived there December 20th. Barzilla and the rest of his regiment were paid off and discharged on January 27, 1815. Barzilla was a militia volunteer, not a regular army volunteer and in his few months of service never saw any actual action. When Jackson fought the battle of New Orleans, Barzilla's militia was back in Tennessee.

The Reverend Barzilla's first wife Rachael Wilson was born Feb. 15, 1797 and died Aug. 18, 1839. Their children were Sarah, Hiram, Andrew Jackson McBride born Nov 27 1822 died 1891, Anne, Silas born Nov 18, 1827 died 1900, Eliza, Carol, Emily Amanda born Sept 1833 died 1915.

Rachel Wilson was the youngest child of John and Sarah Greene Wilson. He was born about 1750 in Rowan NC. Rachel had the following siblings. Mary born 1791 married Levi Heath and moved to Missouri. Isaac Wilson born 1774 married Mary McRary. George born 1775, Boyd born 1780, John Wilson born 1785 married Mary Fritts. Hiram Wilson born 1787 married Nancy Smith in 1812.

Rachel's mother **Sarah Green** was daughter of Jeremiah Greene.

Jeremiah Greene was the son of William Greene and Joanna Reeder. Joanna Reeder was daughter of John Reeder, John Reeder was son of John Reeder Sr.

John Reeder senior arrived in America in 1630 at Massachusetts Bay aboard the Arabella. (The Mayflower arrived in 1620). See Appendix C for details on this family.

In the 1830 census Barzilla had 3 boys and 2 girls. Barzilla's older brother Andrew McBride and his wife Rachael Dancey had 4 boys and 3 girls in 1830 under 5 up to late teens including John, James, Thomas, Hannah and Betsey. Thus 1 boy and girl are not known. John and Thomas went to AK, James to MO. Hannah married Thomas Dougherty and Betsey married Palmer Baird.

When Barzilla's first wife died, he married **Betsy Eggers** and their children were Rachael, Louisa, Martha, Nancy, Betsy, Manley, John. Betsy died in 1858 when Barzilla was 68. He was at least 48 when he married Betsy. So in order to bear him seven children she must have been much younger than he. His son Hiram was a grown man when his father remarried and his older children would have been of similar age to his father's second marriage kids. It would appear Barzilla created children over a 40 year period of time, 17 in all. He and Rachel are buried next to the Masoleum at Cove Creek Baptist Cemetery.

Barzilla's known siblings are Andrew (noted above), Billy McBride who married Eunice ? and whose children were: Jack, Rachael, Carolina who married a Barnes, Betsey who married a Hunt and Anne who married a Swicegood.

Barzilla's Sister Nellie married Landrine Eggers whose kids were: Barzilla Eggers who married A Kilby and a Reese; Ranson Eggers married Martha Issacs; Hugh Eggers married a Kilby; Landrine Jr married Anne Ward and Polly Potter; John Eggers who married Martha Stout; Sarah Eggers married John Issacs; Anne Eggers married Frank Reese; Ellen Eggers married Payton Davis

(Note: The McBride marriages to the Eggers makes a connection to Landrine Eggers born about 1757 who spent several years as a soldier in the revolutionary war and was sent from New York to Rowan county under Capt Smith, Col Thurston and General Clinton. This might have linked him to John McBride.

http://freepages.genealogy.rootsweb.com/~cchouk/ford/eggers/index0.htm for more on him. Also this :

There is living at this time of children of Landrine Eggers and Johannah (Silvers) Eggers five children Sarah Reece, Mary Ford, Hugh Eggers, Johannah Reece, Lydia Swift, which are now all the surviving children that is living. Sworn and Subscribed 30 Nov 1852. So Barzilla and his sister Nellie would have married grandchildren of Landrine and children of Hugh Eggers.)

Barzilla's sister Sally McBride married Will Wiseman and their kids were: John Wiseman and Calvin Wiseman

Barzilla's sister Betsey married a Goss and their child was Ephraim Goss

~~~~

John McBride (gen 1) (American generation 1)(probably born 1755-60) came to New Jersey from Ireland as a boy. He was a steerage passenger which was the lowest fare and for passengers living under the deck in the cargo area. At this time there was an exodus of people from Great Britain who had been supporters of Bonnie Prince Charlie and his cause. Also many Irish Protestants, especially Presbyterians, were disgruntled caught between the ruling Anglican church and the Catholics. In 1720 and again around 1740-50 many left Northern Ireland for America. Irish settlers were active in their antagonism toward Great Britain. The McBrides ancestrally came from county Donegal, northwestern Ireland. A rugged coastal area which was the last to be subjugated by England and where today some still speak Gaelic. McBrides moved down into county Down and county Antrim. Some, notably MacBride, originated in Scotland. The name, *Mac Giolla Bhrighde*, was from an Irish clan and is also known as McGilbride and Kilbride in English. The name means servant of St. Brigid or Bridget a monk from the 600's A.D. He was one of 3 patron saints of Ireland. The cult name spread in Donegal but in 1559 in County Down McBride was the principal name. From the 9th Century the cult was also active in Scotland and it is impossible to distinguish between the local and Scottish persons. However, the records of Scottish planters records only 1 McBride arriving between 1607 and 1633. McBrides are still to be found along the most northwestern coast of Ireland, a hilly land of rock strewn fields and peat bogs. Leaving Ireland in those times was an act of desperation and adventure. Prior to leaving, last goodbyes were said. These were usually final good byes as the departee likely could not read or write and likely would never set foot on his homeland again, never be heard from, or convey any news. It was a most final event. The departing ship might just as well have been a coffin. Likely John was a protestant and arrived in America between 1770 and 1777. In 1770 the chief Presbyterian minister in Belfast was John McBride who refused to conform to the king's law on using the Anglican service and was forced into hiding. In 1776 Captain John McBride led a landing party to claim the Falkland Islands for Britain.

In the year 1772-1773 more than 30,000 people left Ireland for England and America due to the breakdown of the linen trade, a food scarcity and rising food prices along with the religious conflict between Presbyterians and Anglicans. The land lease of the Earl of Donegal expired in 1770 and the rents were such that evictions and disturbances took place over the actions to raise rents. Whole families migrated.

In 1754 James McBride was the first to navigate the Ohio River to open Kentucky. In 1775 Daniel Boone lead the McGrady's, Harlands and

McBrides into Kentucky. Later Thomas McBride Morgan of Kentucky born 1842 went to Coos Bay Oregon on the advice of his relatives from Tennessee.

During the Revolutionary war Barnaby McBride was a private in Reid's 2nd New Hampshire Regiment until he was killed Sept 19 1777. At the same time a Pvt. John McBride served under Col. Hale in the 2nd New Hampshire. William McBride was private in the 2nd Regiment New York Continental line. On the other side Francis McBride a private in the 2nd UlsterCo. Rgt was killed Oct 6 1777 at Fort Clinton. Elsewhere Col. McBride was with the US army at Philadelphia where he led troops into New Jersey and Delaware. He was also at Yorktown according to an attestation of a certain Mr. Hardwick for a pension. John McBride of Tennessee was awarded a pension of $40.00 and an annual allowance of $120.00 which he received May 6th 1834 for having been a private on the North Carolina Line. His age was 82 according to the TN pension roll of 1835. This would mean he was born in 1752. Is this our John? In 1775 James McBride age 38, farmer arrived by ship in May in North Carolina with his wife and 4 kids. A James McBride of North Carolina was a private in Revolutionary war who was given a pension at age 84 presumably about 1832-4. This may have been his son or himself (pension could have been earlier).

In the North Carolina Deed book for those who served in the War, a deed from Boswell Pinkerton was given to John McBride in exchange for 40 pounds, to 180 acres on Allesus Creek adjacent to Root Elrode, Phillip Waggoner and Daniel Hoofhine in Surrey County. Then in the same County ten years later John McBride sold to John Truitt for 100 pounds, 180 acres adjacent to Allens Creek. This was signed by John McBride on 28 Sept 1789. In 1799 our John McBride bought 3 parcels of land, 3 more in 1801 and more again in 1806 all in Ashe county (before Watauga was created). Barzilla bought land in 1822 and 1823, Andrew McBride bought in in 1827, James McBride in 1840 and Hiram McBride in 1846.

Still at the time of the war in Monmouth New Jersey Mary McBride married Floyd Perry of the cavalry of the continental army now in the county of Hunterdon on 21 Feb, 1778. Since our John was in the Monmouth Militia it raises the question about this girl being his sister. Was Col. McBride the father? Are the sales above to our ancestor. Surrey county then was much bigger but the Waggoner name is associated with the same area as the Masts.

In May of 1806 in the first record of Ashe County Court Alexander Smith, Charles Toliison and John McBride were present. The reason is not known but John may have been interested in being elected Sheriff. This is likely our John as there were no other McBrides known in the area.

During the Revolutionary war John joined the New Jersey militia and served in Samuel Forman's regiment & under Captain John Copenhagen's (or Covenhoven or Conover) company, as of July 1st, 1780. (Note: In the Official register of New Jersey men in the war published by Wm. Stryker in 1882 there is one John McBride cross listed as milita and regular army. Samuel Forman led the 2nd Regiment of Militia at Monmouth. However John Conover of Monmouth militia can be confused with several Covenhoven family members also serving in Monmouth and elsewhere but none are John. See pg 386, 351, 242 of the Official Register. This is the only John McBride in the Official New Jersey registry of 1882. Another John McBride lived and died in New Jersey and was also proven to be a veteran. However other McBrides are known to have served but are not identified. North Carolina gave John McBride of Guilford county a pension for Revolutionary war service. His group became part of the continental army, a Monmouth regiment, where he was a private. He was required to provide himself with a musket or firelock, a ramrod, 23 rounds, 12 flints worm, wire and brush, knapsack, canteen and a cartridge box. If he had no musket, then a sword, cutlass or tomahawk would do. If he missed a muster call he was expected to pay two shillings fine. If he had not joined the militia he was liable to payment of 4 shilling a month as ordered by Congress. The New Jersey militia was quite active in the war because the state was very divided between loyalists and patriots and they engaged in many acts of sabotage to the other side. He was probably living in Monmouth County. His revolutionary war registration number was 189392. After the war he married Anne Beard or Baird in New Jersey in 1789. (Another version is they were married in 1786 in Rowan county) **Anne Beard/Baird** (probably born 1755-60). She came to America from Scotland with her father Barzilla Beard when she was about 16 years old. Her mother was born Susannah Bulman. They appear to have come to, and lived in, New Jersey. A story that she saw the battle of Bunker Hill from an old barn, and saw Washington rally his men from his white horse would have required her to have been in Massachusetts in 75. More than likely being in New Jersey what she saw was one of the number of battles in that state. Washington was there quite a lot and did win importantly there. A group of Baptists and former Presbyterians migrated to Rowan Co. NC to form the New Jersey settlement 1760 to 1790. Members of this group moved in the 1790's to Cove Creek area. So New Jersey might refer to this settlement elsewhere in NC.

The Baird family also went to Watauga. John Baird came from Scotland to New Jersey in 1683. His son Dr. Ezekiel went to South Carolina and then to the Baird Community in Valle Crucis in 1790.

In the 1790 Census for Rowan County there were the following Beards (Baird): John, Christina, Hannah, Lewis, Michael, Valentine. There were also nearby John Mash, (Mast) Joseph Shull, Michael Hlshouser, (Holtshouser) George Hoover.

John Preston Arthur in his book "History of Watauga County NC" 1915 says:

McBride Family.--*John McBride came from the north of Ireland and settled in New Jersey, from which place he moved to Rowan County with the New Jersey settlers. He married Mary Baird in Rowan, and their children were: Brazilla, who married Rachel Wilson in Rowan; Timothy, who went to Missouri, where he remained, and William, who married a Miss Swicegood in Rowan and died there. One of the daughters married Levi Heath; Ellen married Landrine Eggers, while another daughter married David Goss, who moved to Missouri. Brazilla was in the War of 1812 and named his first son for Andrew Jackson.*

Brazilla's (gen 2) children were: Andrew Jackson, who married Polly Green; Hiram, who married Mary Farthing; Silas, who married Emily Green; Brazilla Carroll, who married Catharine Brinkley, of West Tennessee; Sarah, who married Harrison Johnson; Ann, who married Squire Green; Mary Amanda, who married John Combs; Emily, who married Jonathan Green. Brazilla served in the war of 1812.

Brazilla's second wife was Elizabeth Eggers, and their children were: Manly, who married Martha Norris; John, who married Miss Greer; Rachel, who married George Hilliard; Ellen, who married Bruce Harman; Louisa, who married Jacob Younce; Martha, who died unmarried at the age of sixteen; Nancy, who married William Church; Elizabeth, who married Richard McGuire.

From the gravestones in the Cove Creek graveyard the following was taken; Rev. Brazilla McBride was born September 27, 1790 and died December 10, 1858; **Hiram McBride** (gen 3) was born August 9, 1818, died May 26, 1869; Rachel, wife of Brazilla McBride, born February 15, 1797, died August 18, 1839. (While the name is properly Barzilla it got altered to being Brazilla, reference was made of him as simply Braz McBride.)

From the A. J. McBride graveyard the following was taken: Rev. Andrew J. McBride was born November 27, 1822, and died November 12, 1891; Silas McBride was born November 18, 1827, and when he died he was aged seventy-two yeare, six months and twenty days; Elijah Green was born November 4, 1800, died July 15, 1882. His wife was born October 10, 1803, and died January 8, 1879."

A John McBride was living in Ashe county when it was created. He was the only McBride listed and he was between 26 and 46 years of age as was his wife. This John McBride had 2 boys under 10 and 3 girls according to the census of 1800. By 1810 this same person had 5 boys and 8 girls. In 1815 John McBride owned 1,200 acres all in one tract worth 1,100 dollars. This was a farm that was among the larger ones although the value was only average. He owned a lot of not especially good land. John McBride does not appear in the 1820 census. Moses McBride served in the War of 1812 in the 2nd Co. 5 th NC Militia. A check of the roster for the 5th regiment 2nd Co. says that William McBride was a 2nd lieutenant in 1814. So are William and Moses the same person? and in 1815 Moses has a farm of 320 acres worth 160 dollars. Moses in the 1820 Census has 2 girls and 1 boy under 10. Barzilla McBride appears in the same census with 1 boy under 10. Who was Moses and was this the same John McBride who died in Watauga county N.C. sometime after 1796 having moved over the mountains about the time Tennessee became a state. His wife Anne Baird died (unknown date) and their children were Barzilla, Andrew, Billy, Nellie, Sally, and Betsey. Either there are two John McBrides or there were more children than we know about. Who was Moses or William, an older brother of Barzilla? A cousin?

Comments:

The Farthings

Hiram McBrides first wife **Mary Hervey Farthing** was the daughter of **William Watkins Farthing and Polly White Halleyburton**. His second wife was the widow Rachel Farthing Hayes who had been married to Mary's brother Paul their cousin.

William Farthing 1782-1827, was born spiritually July 30, 1802, married Polly Feb 9, 1804 in Pearson Co., NC. In 1822 he became ordained to preach at Eno Baptist Church. He made two trips to the mountains to preach from his home in Wake Co. and liked them so well he bought a farm near the site of Bethel church. The missionary board of the Baptist Church sent him to Watauga. He moved to the farm in December 1826 and died the next month.

His wife Polly lived to be 90 years old. She was the daughter of **Thomas Halleyburton and Martha Humphries**, who claimed to be a descendant of Robert Bruce, the Scottish king. Both of her parents came from Scotland. When her mother died, her father remarried a Dieson.

The Rev. William Farthing and Polly's children were Dudley Farthing1804 -1895. He was county commissioner and chairman 1868 and he was also chairman of Watauga court of Pleas. Dudley married Nancy Mast, Finley's oldest sister. Their fourteen children included William Judson Farthing born 1832 a teacher who fought with the Texas Rangers and died of chills sept 1865. James Martin Farthing born 1835 was killed Dec 13,18 62 at battle of Fredericksburg, Thomas Jefferson Farthing born 1838 died of pneumonia at Lynchburg Military Hospital 1862, John Young Farthing born1840 was wounded at 2nd battle of Manasses. Henry Harrison Farthing born 1841was wounded twice once with his brother at Manasses, Wiley Hill Farthing born 1850 was state senator for Watauga 1895. Although the Farthings and Masts were Confederate supporters, the population in the area supported both sides in the war.

Rev. William and Polly's other children were: Martha Ruffin 1807 - ?; Rev. Reuben Pickens Farthing 1808 -1889. His son William born 1834 was killed at Brandy Station Va. June 18, 1863; Rev. John Atkinson Farthing 1809-1887; William Brown Farthing 1820-1885; Edward an infant; Thomas Halliburton Farthing 1813 -1863 was killed by bushwhackers. He had a son Robert who lost an arm in the Seven Day Battle of Richmond.

Another son Lewis born 1845 married his cousin Nancy McBride, Hiram McBride and Mary Hervey Farthing's daughter Ann Watkins Farthing 1814- 1883 married Wm Young who was killed near Winchester Va Nov 28, 1862. Her son Reuben born 1844 died as a POW at Camp Chase Ohio Apr 25, 1865 (Finley Mast was also at this camp); Harriett Newel Farthing1816 - 1897; Mary Hervey Farthing Feb 21, 1818 to May 26, 1860 married Hiram McBride; Rev. Abner Clopton Farthing 1819-1896; Paul Farthing1821- 1865 died at Camp Chase, Ohio Apr 11, 1865. His widowed wife eventually married Hiram McBride as his second wife. ; Rev. Stephen Farthing 1823 -1882. The marriages of Dudley and Nancy, Mary and Hiram tie the McBrides and Masts and Farthings quite closely. Four of William and Pollys sons were Baptist preachers.

The Civil War impacted greatly on the Farthings. Hiram and Mary McBride's children were too young for the war. Hiram and his brothers were probably too old for the war. Finley P. Mast , a brother John A. Mast and Mast cousin W.P. Mast were in the 58thNorth Carolina. Other relatives in D company of the 58th were: John Duggers, Joel Duggers (MIA at battle of Resaca in Georgia), Andrew J. Baird, Benjamin Franklin Baird (Captain) David F. Baird, John H. Baird (died Jackson TN) Empsey Gragg, Harvey Gragg, Solomon Green, Drewry Harmon (Captain) and perhaps others. During the war some illness prevailed in the community in the winter of 62/63 and a number of children died, several in some Farthing families. The Farthings of this time were also unique in that they very often married into their own families. First cousin marriages were very common especially among the ones who became preachers!

Going back a generation, William Watkins Farthings parents were **Dudley Farthing 1749 - 1826 and Anne Watkins** born July 4, 1747 -1812. Dudley was born in Halifax County (now Pittsylvania Co.1774), Virginia. It is not known when the Watkins family came to America, certainly before 1750. He was a brick mason and built, it was said, the first brick house in Richmond Va. He married Anne Feb 2, 1778. She was the daughter of William and Phoebe Watkins. They moved to Wake Co. NC.Feb. 13 1812 where they made a permanent settlement. Their children were Phoebe 1778 - ? and William Watkins, John 1784 - 1868, Reuben 1787 -1834, and Elijah 1790 who died an infant.

Dudley Farthings parents were William and Mary, they came from Wales about 1740 and settled in Halifax County Virginia. Richard Farthing was his brother.

William Watkins Farthing preached about 5 years after he was ordained Oct 21 1822. He had 4 sons who were preachers. They were all missionary Baptist. Some of their sons were also preachers. Wiley H. Farthing was senator for the state from Watauga Co. 1895. Winfield Farthing was state senator in 1899. The Farthings were involved with Bethel Baptist Church founded in 1851 and was constituted from Cove Creek Church. It had many Farthing members. Beaver Dams, Forest Grove and Timbered Ridge people were also involved in this church.

The Halliburtons (also Halleyburton)

David Halliburton was born Edinburgh Scotland in 1727 died in 1767 married Amey Humphreys (1735 - 1790) in Surrey Virginia. Their son Thomas Halleyburton born 1763 served in the revolution and married Martha Humphreys (who claimed descendancy from a cousin of King Bruce of Scotland). She died and he then married a Dieson. Their Children are Robert who married a Davie; Kemp Halleyburton who married Margaret Marony; Polly who married William Farthing and Patsey who married a Cozort. Their descendants founded the Halliburton energy and military supply company. Polly Halleyburton was mother of Mary Hervey Farthing who married Hiram McBride.

The Baird or Beard Family

John McBride the Irish settler married **Anne Baird** daughter of Barzilla Beard, More correctly Baird.

John Baird was born in 1665 in Scotland. It was said he was born in Limberton, Aldothian, Scotland. There is no Limberton although there is a Lamberton near Berwick. Aldothian is also a none place likely meaning old Lothian which was the district of Scotland around Edinburgh which is not far from Lamberton. The Baird Castle and family home however was in Aberdeenshire across the Firth of Forth.

John Baird departed Aberdeenshire on August 28, 1683 age 18. The date is significant because it indicates he was part of a colonization scheme by a group of Scots, mostly Quakers, who were granted land in East Jersey. This East, now New Jersey, colony was made up of English speaking Scots whose ancestry came from the ancient Angles of Denmark/Friesland and who had strong ties to England. Most Highland and other Scots were Picts or Celts. These Aberdeen Scots were also followers of a Quaker leader Robert Barclay. William Penn, founder of Pennsylvania, also a Quaker encouraged Barclay to set up this land filling scheme. The colony was an investment scheme and 250 people signed up including 22 young unmarried men who became indentured servants. As an indentured servant Baird was given free passage in return for 3 years labor as a tenant farmer after which he would be given 25 acres of land of his own. Thus so established he could endeavor to buy more land for himself from the sponsors who had acquired East Jersey.

This account about one of the proprietors (land owners):

"He soon settled 22 men servants and 3 boys on that property under three-year

indentures and had them furnished with 'corn, cattell, and matteriall.' The indentures of those servants expired in 1688"

These settlers were part of the very first effort by Scots to establish territory abroad, Scotland still being an independent nation. English gentry allowed them to do this as they were also part owners and it was desirable to populate the land taken from the Dutch only a few years earlier. Scots, unhappy with religious persecution for not being followers of the Established Church (Episcopalians), were happy to go although some who went were Episcopalians.

John Baird who was part of this project came to America with his brother on the ship Caledonia in 1683. He married Mary Hall in 1684 who he had rescued from a shipwreck on the coast. She later died. His second wife, mother of his children, was Mary Bedent (1675-1736) daughter of Thomas Bedient and Mary Osborne Bedient a widow from Staines, England. Thomas had a brother Morgan living in Monmouth NJ. Mary and her children came to Connecticut to claim an estate left them by her brother John Bernard near Fairfield CT in 1699. Thus Mary Bedent may have met Baird in Monmouth in 1799, married and subsequently Andrew was born in 1700.

Their children were Andrew Baird born 1700 -1773; John Baird Jr.; William Baird 1713-1792; David Baird; and Zebulon Baird 1715-1804. These people were born around Freehold, Monmouth Co. NJ and were buried in the Topanemus Episcopalian Cemetery at Marlboro, Monmouth Co.

Andrew Baird married Sarah Layton (1705- ?)

Their children were: Bedent Baird b. 1727 in Scholarie Co. NY. He married Hulda and his son Bedent went to Warren Ohio; Barzilla Baird born 1729 married Mary Bullman; Obediah Baird b. 1731; Jonathan Baird b. 1733; Samuel Baird b. 1735; and Ezekiel Baird b. 1737. He married Susan

Blodgett and went to Valle Crucis NC. Ezekiel had a son Bedent who was a magistrate.

John Baird Jr. went to Buncombe, North Carolina had grandsons Bedent and Zebulon. William his brother also had a son Bedent.

Here it needs to be explained that these people living around Freehold in Monmouth county ran into a major land title issue that meant they had not gotten clear title and thus were forced off their land. They joined those who migrated to North Carolina as part of the Jersey Settlement. Consequently several of the Baird families eventually settled in Watauga Co.

Barzilla Baird, a New Jersey shoemaker, paid for a substitute to represent him during the Revolutionary war as he was nearly 50 years old. This man Parker went on a number of tours of duty during the war at Barzilla's expense. Barzilla had at least one son, Thomas Bulman Baird who married and moved to Paris, Kentucky. He also had a daughter Anne. After the Revolutionary war Baird relocated to Rowan Co. NC as part of the Jersey Settlement.

It was Anne the daughter of Barzilla Baird and Susan Bulman, who married John McBride in Rowan NC. (or in New Jersey)

Comment:

Thomas Clarke McBride and Mary Elizabeth Mast family

The marriage of Thomas Clarke McBride (gen 4) and Mary Elizabeth Mast (gen 5) on Aug 11, 1887 at Sugar Grove joined these family lines even more closely. Thomas 23 and Mary 18 shared 34 years together before he died as a result of an infection from stepping on a rusty nail.

They first lived at Sugar Grove on a farm given to them by Mary's father Finley who gave each of his children a farm when they married. Thomas built a house up a small valley around 1888. It was off Ivan Trivett Road. This house was framed in chestnut and used square nails which were still made in that area at that time. The floors were of Tulip poplar. Mary thought it would be too big a house as she expected to have only 5 kids. It was a mile or so nearer Boone, and down across the fields from Finley's house. Mary would walk across them to visit her family. Once she met an old woman lying in the snow with a cloth around her head. The woman complained of a toothache and Mary told her to go inside and get warm if she wanted to help it get better. It snowed a lot in the high mountain country and often one could walk over the fences filled by snow banks. This farm was sold to Dr. Bingham reportedly in 1899 but might have been around 1904/5 as their son Finley was born at Sugar Grove or they may have lived in another place for a time. (in 2001 this house was owned by M. Stolberg)

Thomas bought land at Washington College TN where he built a large house along the railway track. He joked that he had moved out of the mountains because he didn't want his girls to grow up and marry Binghams. Mary didn't like the house along the tracks because the house was too large and because hobos and tramps would come along the railroad. With young children about, she was concerned. In 1905 Thomas bought 425 acres of land below a ridge on rolling land at Rocky Valley just East of Newmarket TN. Mary was not consulted until after the farm was bought. They did not relocate to this farm until about 1908 as Nelle and Jim were both born at Washington College. The Rocky Valley farm was good productive farmland consisting of a main farm house and three tenant houses. The house had a main fireplace that opened into the kitchen and on the other side into the living room. Every room had a fireplace. It was a two story, of a style typical in Carolina, with a center hall going upstairs and bedrooms on either side. The kids slept 2 to a room with boys on one side of the hall and girls on the other. The farm grew corn, oats and wheat and they kept cattle, geese, guinea hens, and ducks. There was an outdoor vegetable storage bunker. Thomas prospered well enough. He became active in the cattle business and bought and sold and moved herds of cattle to market. Records of T.C.'s life here are at the Jefferson County archives, Dandridge TN.

He was a short, stout man known to everyone as Captain McBride. The reason was not clear. He was active in the community and was the county commissioner for Jefferson County. His work took him away from home a lot and the day to day management of the farm was the task of his wife Mary who also raised 11 children born between 1888 and 1910. There were three or four hired hands at the farm including a black man called Ike who lived with them. Thomas was a progressive man who arranged to get the roads improved and graveled while commissioner. He bought the first automobile in the county, a vehicle frequently used by Grey, the eldest boy.

The house at Rocky Valley is on the left as approached from Newmarket. My mother, Rhoda, said their family knew the Ford family, of the same area, whose son was singer Tennessee Ernie Ford.

Daughter Rosalie (gen 5 and 6) born 1888 had grown up at Sugar Grove and went to school at Watauga Academy at Boone for a year. Then she went at the age of 15/16 to Greensboro Normal and Industrial college for a year and a half to become a teacher. With the family now living near Jefferson City, Rose entered Carson Newman college in 1905. She graduated first in her class with an A.B. degree 1909. She was the class valedictorian and was a literary major having studied Latin, Rhetoric, French, Classic literature, Physics, Algebra, Chemistry, Sallust, Psychology, Ethics and other courses, 30 in all. She had 9 A+, 12A, 2B+,2B a 96 in Trigonometry, 96 in advanced Algebra, and 97 in Latin. She was fluent in French (3 years) and had 4 years of Latin, as well as 2 years of German. The college president regarded her work as somewhat irregular, with some subjects being in the preparatory department. He said in respect to a job application *"She is an unusually bright and capable young woman. You will find her thoroughly reliable and able to carry the work for which she is applying."*(April 17, 1912).

After graduating she continued to do post graduate work at Carson Newman.

In March of 1912 Rose was teaching grade school in Forest, Idaho. She decided to apply to Radcliffe College in Massachusetts because *"I wish to take up work in English Literature, French, German and Spanish. This year I shall complete the course for the M.A. degree at Carson Newman College in the subjects English literature and French. I have had two years work in German, but no work in Spanish. I have taught for three years in the graded*

The McBride homestead was a busy place in the early years of the 20th century. By the time Rhoda (gen 5 and 6) was born in 1910 there were 11 kids and all were at home. Katherine Rosalie (Rose) was 22 and teaching after graduating from Carson Newman College. She had become interested in photography and had her own dark room to do her own developing. William Grey was 20 and helping at the farm and possibly courting Mamie Mann daughter of William and Addie Mann who lived just up the road. They married in October of 1912,the first of the children to be married. Annie Boone, 18, was just finishing school. Lucy Imogene was 16 and in high school. Wiley Preston Brown was a vigorous 11 year old, while his sister Carrie May was just a little over a year younger. Emily, a frail girl troubled all her life by heath problems had just turned eight. The little ones around the house were Thomas Finley 6, Nellie Ashburn (Nelle) 4, and James Kenneth (Jim), age 3 and the newborn Rhoda. Also living at the farm was a black hired servant man Isaac Hensley. Thomas was 45, Elizabeth 41 and they had been married 22 years.

When Nelle was two (1908), she went with sister Rose to see her Grandmother. On the trip Nelle was introduced to the ice cream cone. When she got home, she said she even ate the dish.

Since Thomas was away a lot on business, Mary ran the farm. In addition to the black man Ike, they had a black cook who would put manure on her face for her complexion. Rose, when she was home, would babysit the younger children. She taught them to some degree including instruction on penmanship. Rose had said she would have been happy to stay at home forever but as there were so many kids she felt she needed to go to make room for the others. An old horse on the farm was called Nell, a fact that did not sit well with the young Nelle.

Grey married Mamie Mann, the daughter of a family who had a little farm nearby, in 1912. The death of Emily was the first of two great tragedies. Emily, always frail took ill and died, August 8, 1913. The funeral service was held under the large trees in the front yard. She was 11 years old. After her death her mother would go and sit among Emily's things. This persisted for a time until Thomas, her husband finally gathered up Emily's things and gave them away. Emily, her father Thomas and her brother Grey are all buried at Piedmont Cemetery, Newmarket Tn.

After the funeral Rosalie set off to enter Radcliffe college in Mass. She was an unclassified student, one of 19 out of a college registration of 586. Rosalie had applied for entrance to an A.M. degree and was admitted to residence. She was 25. Her financial aid was listed as Union Room. She had hoped to get recognition for her work at Carson Newman but the graduate admission committee dean said" *In view of such information as I can gather regarding the standing of Carson and Newman College, I believe Miss McBride should register as an unclassified undergraduate student. If her work as an undergraduate should show unusual quality, she might later be admitted to graduate standing without necessarily having to take her A.B. We should not however admit the ordinary graduate of Carson and Newman College to registration in the graduate school of Arts and Sciences*" C.H. Hoskins May 15,1913 The quality of Southern colleges was poorly regarded in elite northern schools as the treatment afforded Rosalie bears out.

Rose took 2 full and 4 half courses in English obtaining Bs and Cs in all. Mr. Hoskins, Dean of Harvard Graduate School was not impressed. He wrote a letter to a Miss Harriet Buckingham, "*It seems to Mr. Robinson and me, after looking over Miss McBrides papers, that she is not yet ready for admission to candidacy for the A.M. on the minimum period.*"They suggested she be admitted to graduate registration and do two years more work for her masters but suggested it would be preferable to get an undergraduate rating and an A.B. in one year more. "*I should advise taking up her case as a case of advanced standing in college. If it appears that she cannot be admitted to the Senior Class in September as a candidate for the A.B. next June, I shall then be glad to give a definite ruling upon her status as a graduate student.*" July 17, 1914. Radcliffe graduated 89 students with an A.B. in 1914. Rosalie went back home.

Braz McBride (Barzilla was Thomas' older brother by 12 years) and his wife Emma came to live at Rocky valley at the urging of Thomas who gave them 30 acres off of the farm. He was a butcher by trade. Emma his wife always wore a lace collar and cap. She wore slippers not shoes and she always had flowers in the house. His son Jesse and his wife Maud lived just down the road in later years. Braz and Emma kept a home which featured Indian made rugs from Oklahoma.

Another older brother, William Butler, lived for a time at Newmarket before moving on to live at Sweetwater Tn. William Butler married

Elizabeth Anne Mast descendant of Adam. They farmed at Mill Creek along Dry Run Rd. where they had an apple orchard. They had twins Minnie Belle and Lula Florence born Nov 23, 1873 and James Cauley McBride born Nov 16, 1875. Minnie Belle married Andrew Shoun. Thomas Clark's other brothers and sisters lived in Johnson County TN, Sugar Grove and in Watauga Co. John, 10 years older than Thomas lived at Sugar Grove where he also kept an orchard. Every year he would send a barrel of apples and some chestnuts to his brother.

Thomas' sister Polly married Tom Dougherty and their children kept in contact with their cousins. Maggie (born1882) married Carol Reese who became a U.S. senator from TN. Hunter Daugherty (born 1885) worked at a federal hospital and kept in touch with several of his Mc Bride cousins. Polly married well and had 11 kids including a set of twins. They began married life on Mill Creek living with the Dougherty Srs. In 1877 they bought their own farm of 700 acres in the Dry Run Settlement along the Watauga R. This was his great-grandfather Cables land given for his service in the Revolutionary War. His grandmother was Eve Mast. The Dougherty's lived in the original log house with his grandfather until he died in 1880. They organized the Baptist church at Sugar Grove. They opened a school where Thomas was the teacher. He sat as a member of the court of Johnson County for many years. After his death, Polly having limited means, rented a large house at Butler TN and converted it to a boarding house for the school. Her kids thus were able to live there as well and get an education. Other relatives boarded with them also. Many of their children went to University. Polly's wool winder is in the Mountain City museum. Rosalie McBride(born 1888) and Annie Boone McBride(born 1892) went with cousins Maggie and Minnie Dougherty (twins born 1883) led by the older Cora Dougherty (born 1878) to Flowerlee, Montana to homestead and teach school in 1918. All these girls had gone to Carson Newman College.

Nelle recalls several adventures growing up in Rocky Valley. They would go to visit their grandfather Finley at Sugar Grove. To get there they would take the trains, the Southern RR to Johnson City then the narrow gauge railway known as Tweetsie. People would come meet the train known for its shrill whistle to get things that the conductor had bought at their request in town. This included thread, salt and other things needed by the mountain folk. Finley's wife Rhoda died May 13,1910, three weeks after the birth of her daughters last girl, who was named Rhoda. Nelle recalls Finley as an old man, quiet, with a long beard. He was looked after by his son Jack Mast and his wife Bess Bingham, who after Finley died inherited the home. Jack Mast was a friendly man given to drink to much. He would invite passersby to stop in for a meal. Once when Nelle was there, Judge Bingham was visiting his daughter Bess and Nelle's query to Jack about whether he would invite a passerby in for a meal resulted in his comment that no one would go by his door hungry. Nelle opined that he must have a lot of stars in his crown. His wife responded that for everyone that was added to his it was taken out of hers. The old Finley Mast home has been relocated since those days where it stood on a ridge. It eventually burned down.

As the 1st World War ended the life of the family began to change greatly. Rose and Annie had gone to Montana about 1915. In 1918 Rose was 30, single and well educated. She homesteaded 640 acres of flat prairie near Rosebud, Montana. Rose built her own cabin, a small one story affair later added to with more rooms and a porch. She was interested in photography and did her own developing in her dark room. She taught at Laredo school and had a class of about 20 kids. At some point in time Finley her brother came to help her with the farm. There is a photo of him building the fences. While there she met John Glass, a farmer, who had grown up in Maryland. They were married in December of 1918. Rose had no luck bearing children and after losing three babies they decided to adopt. In 1922, having recently lost an infant she was able to nurse a child from the orphanage. The story is that she and John went and picked out the most forlorn infant there, the one which seemed to be the most lonely. He was renamed David. It was many years before David learned that he had been adopted. The news was given to him when he was in the army and about to leave for Panama. Rose and John farmed for a time but in successive years the crops failed due to drought and John packed up and headed back east with his family. He recalls taking his team and wagon to the bank as he was on his way east. He went in and told the banker the farms were his and he was leaving the horses to help pay off the debt. The family drove the model T Ford to Maryland (about 1924) where John began general farming and kept some dairy animals. Rhoda and Jim visited them there and Jim stayed to help on the farm. A cow kicked John and broke his leg seriously injuring him so he could not manage this place. The farm was sold and in 1924/5 they drove the Model T to Florida to visit aunt Mattie near Vero Beach. This was a popular destination as everyone at some time or other went there for a time. Once recovered John and Rose went to Detroit where Rose ran a boarding house (about 1925/6). In 1933 they once again took up farming and moved to Scottsville Va. to raise chickens and sell eggs.

Annie Boone, a graduate of Carson-Newman College, married Fred Curtis September 16 1916. (possible dates for him 05/08/1890 to 04/10/1957) He had served as a private in the Marines during the First WW. He is buried in the Los Angeles National Cemetery. After the war he went to Minnesota and by 1930 was a carpenter in Los Angeles. In 1930 Annie was working as a saleslady. That year they owned a house at 852 Orange Grove. He was a successful contractor whose buildings were well known in Hollywood. Their son was Thomas Grey Curtis. He married Jean ? and divorced after a few years later he married Fran ? Thomas Grey had two children with Jean, Dan and Stuart who went to live with their mother. They were not babies at the time of separation. They may have changed their surnames. Contact has been lost with this family. Annie was born April 4 1892 and died Feb 27 1958.

Grey was living in a tenant house on the farm before his father built him a new home in 1918. Here Grey's daughter Emily was born. Everyone came to call her Topsy because like Topsy in Uncle Tom she just "grewed". Topsy 4 and Rhoda 8 were children together in these days along with Jim. Nelle was 12 and Thomas Finley (Finn) 14. In those days, Rhoda was nicknamed Tom because she was a Tomboy. Nelle decided to become Bob. Carrie known as Kiz was 18 and probably at college learning to become a teacher. She may have at this time also been living with her Uncle Butler McBride at Sweetwater Tn. where she dated Estes Kefauver who went on to become a famous senator. Grey was working for the Virginian Railway. Lucy was 24 and had attended Woman's College at John Hopkins University in Baltimore to become a nurse. Later she joined the Army where she was a nurse possibly in South Carolina where she met Dan T. Hix whom she married in 1923. He owned a shoe store in Columbia SC.

Wiley was 19 and had already had several rough and tumble adventures. At 15 or 16 he had gone to business college to learn to be a bookkeeper. Because of a fight and an accidental death with an acquaintance, he left home to join the navy and avoided repercussions. At the same time Jesse Clark McBride 18 his cousin also joined the navy. At 17 he found himself involved in the first great war and must have lied about his age to do so as he is listed as age 18 in the Tennessee Veterans records. He was aboard a minesweeper on duty in the North Sea when the ship struck a mine and was blown up. Suffering only minor injuries to his hand he was able to remain in the navy as a store keeper.

Thomas Clark McBride, all 5'5" of him, was having some business problems. As county commissioner he had arranged for the roads to be graveled to accommodate the new automobiles. He had purchased the first vehicle in Jefferson County. He was a dealer in lumber and cattle and had arranged a large shipment of cattle to go to South Carolina. On the way the herd contracted hoof and mouth disease and had to be destroyed. The financial setback was considerable. Three years later as a result of a rusty nail infection he died although he had some health problems earlier.

His death May 2, 1921at age 54. seriously disrupted the family, resulting in a dispersal of them all over the place. At first Mr. Mann whom the kids knew as Uncle Henry although he was Grey's father-in- law, came to help run the farm. It was soon apparent that the debts incurred over the loss of the cattle and other misfortunes could not be met and now they were bankrupt. Mary had to sell the place. Rhoda the youngest was 11 and went to live for a year with her sister Carrie who had just married (June 1921) Tom G. Dunn and was teaching in Osakis Minnesota. Nelle 15 went to Fort Pearce, Florida to live with her Aunt Matt (Mother's sister Mattie Laine) and sister Lucy where she dated several of the Fort Pearce cadets. The next year Nelle went to boarding school at Lincoln Memorial in Harrowgate Tn. For some reason people in Valle Crucis and Sugar Grove developed an interest in Vero Beach, Fort Pearce and a community of them went there to live.

Jim 14, after some high schooling went to Detroit to work and lived with Rose and John Glass. Finn was 17 and perhaps now in Montana.

Wiley was somewhere at sea in these times. Rose and John Glass were in Detroit where Rose operated a boarding house on 4th street. In 1922 Grey had moved to Mullins, West Virginia with the railroad.

Nelle went with Grey's wife Mamie and the kids to help them move. While there Nelle met Royce Collins who was also working in Mullins with the railroad. He was from coastal North Carolina.

In early 1923 Lucy Imogene married Dan T. Hix. During the summer Nelle married Royce Collins at Knoxville. Royce was the only son-in-law of Mary McBride to meet her before marrying. All the other girls husbands met her after they were married.

The final time of living at Newmarket was during 1924. Nelle's daughter Betty was born there in 1924. Rhoda, Jim, and Finley were there with their mother. That winter Mary went to Detroit to stay with Rose. Rhoda 14 went to Central High in Detroit. Finley was now 20 and was about to leave to go back to to Montana to teach school at Niehart. Later he got a job at a smelter in Ely, Nevada.

Royce and Nelle and Betty also went to Detroit. Rose ran her boarding house, full of relatives, on 4th Street. Royce and Nelle lived on 61st St. off of West Grand near the Henry Ford Hospital where Rhoda was to do nursing training.

When Mary's father Finley Mast died in early 1924, he left his daughter a sum of 5,000 dollars. Mary, having lost the farm after Thomas' death, was now able to purchase another home. Finn got a cross country real estate book and a listing near Scottsville Va. told that the property of a recently deceased Mr. Seay was for sale. At his urging she decided to check it out and bought the 27 acre property from Belle Seay in 1925 for $1,900. That fall Rhoda enrolled in Scottsville High School where she graduated in 1927. In May of 1926 Royce was in Detroit and Joyce tells the story that Nelle, her mother, had been in Scottsville. She wanted to go back to Detroit. She was 6 months pregnant with Joyce and had no money. She got on the bus and said she wanted to go to Detroit so the passengers took up a collection to buy her ticket. Joyce was born in Detroit but in the fall of 1926 was back in Scottsville with her mother. Nelle said this was not a true account of the event.

Royce tells of how he got a job in Detroit. Having worked on the railroad he was seeking other opportunities. He went to an employment centre and stood in line waiting for work. As people went forward most were sent away without any help. A few were given slips with addresses. When the person ahead of him said he was a pipe fitter they gave him a slip to report to work. Royce anxious for work identified himself as a pipe fitter also and was given a slip. When he reported for work he was asked where his tools were and he said they had not yet arrived as he had just moved there. In this way he entered the plumbing and heating trade which was to be his life avocation.

Royce and Nelle did not have any easy marriage. During the fall of 1926 they were staying at Scottsville with Mary and Rhoda. Nelle was working at the braid factory. Rhoda, a popular girl whose year book said she was to become a Hollywood star, had a date with Hugh Stamp for a Halloween dance and Royce was expected to join them. Nelle's babies were being looked after by Grandma. Royce did not appear and it was assumed he had gone off drinking and forgot. After a time Nelle, Rhoda and Stamp went with another boy who owned a car to get a hamburger in Charlottesville. As they went along, they spotted a car along the road and yelled and hollered at the poor unfortunate standing by a flat tire. The person was Royce and he recognized his wife. Later that night he confronted Nelle and her mother and got so mad at a remark made by Mary that, then and there, he ordered his wife to get in the car with the kids. They went to Watauga Co. NC, where Nelle's uncle Jack loaned them $100.00 to buy a house at Sugar Grove. Here Harriet was born and for 15 years Royce operated a plumbing and heating business. Nelle left him in early 1940's to work in the war effort in Washington. Her children were looked after for a time by her mother. She worked in war shipping recording losses of ships and contents. However after a couple of years Royce and Nelle came together again and bought 8 acres next to her mother's land with $179.00 Royce had won at poker. It was difficult to build a house during the war but he could build a chicken barn. The so called chicken barn became the house. Later in the 50's when grants were available to build bomb shelters Royce built a fine underground bunker which was great for poker sessions. Royce took great pride in raising cattle and clearing land to make it productive although his main income was from his plumbing and heating business. Royce died in his 80's and is buried at Scottsville. Nelle and Royce were well know in Fluvanna and Albemarle Counties of Virginia.

Wiley met Doris Collins while he was stationed at Norfolk, Virginia. They married in 1932. He was 33 and she was 16.He enlisted in the Navy in May of 1917 and was aboard the minesweeper the Pelican when it was blown up. He was given a commendation as a result. Later Wiley was storekeeper aboard the Wisconsin in 1934. Then he was posted to shore duty in California at Long Beach and Chulla Vista where his daughters were born. Doris's three girls were all born before she was twenty years old. Mary (Aug 1933), Anne (Dec 1935) and Carrie (Dec 1936)

In 1938 Wiley become a reservist for a short time. From a real estate catalogue he found a nice place in Arkansas and moved there. It was a pretty backward community with the school being opened for only 3 months a year. Needing education for his kids he went around with a petition and organized the local parents. A full time teacher was hired. He was not retired for long when events in Europe caused the navy to call him back to active duty in 1939. He was appointed to be the storekeeper for the new USS Essex. In this capacity he was in charge of outfitting the entire ship from cutlery to furniture. He sailed on her maiden voyage and expected to be a part of the crew. Unfortunately back in port he had to have his teeth removed. His dentures were not ready when the ship sailed to war and he was left behind. At this time it was discovered he had circulatory problems as well and could not go back to sea. He was posted to Maryana Florida, then to Birmingham Ala. This was Dec. 1941. Royce had come for a visit and was with them when the bombing of Pearl Harbor was announced. The shore patrol came and picked up Wiley, escorting him away. The 3 girls were frightened about this mysterious disappearance. For the next three days and nights Wiley was manning the navy recruitment office signing up volunteers.

Wiley was next sent to Durant, Oklahoma where his task was to close up a small navy base. Later he went to a navy base in Burns Flat OK and was there when the war ended. After the war he went to New Orleans to escort recruits to California. On Dec 10 1946, after 27 years in the U.S. navy, he was put on inactive service. His family relocated to Norfolk Va. and then to Scottsville and then back to Branch, Arkansas. When Jim died in early 1947 Wiley sold the Branch Arkansas house and moved into Mary Masts home near Scottsville. She was staying next door with Nelle at this time. However, the day before she was to move back home she died. Wiley remained in her house until 1950 doing some work as a bookkeeper for some construction people.

He moved to Mamie NC and took a job as a guide at Kitty Hawk site of the first powered aircraft flight. During his time in the navy he developed some sort of heart problem. Being the longest surviving of the boys he was, like his brothers, to die of a heart attack. He died at age 63 in 1962. Wiley is buried in Arlington National Cemetery. He may have been namesaked after three relatives. Wiley Farthing a Senator 1895, Preston?, and Brown Farthing. (While it is odd all 4 boys died young of a heart attack, there is no evidence of an inherited factor). Wiley's daughter Mary joined the military, married and finally settled in Oklahoma. Ann became a nurse and had a career in North Carolina she had a special affinity to her aunt Rhoda. Carrie joined the military and married a naval officer and lived in San Diego, Scotland, Connecticut, Nova Scotia, and Newfoundland before reconditioning a boat to live a nomadic life. They finally settled in Maine. All have children. Carrie lived near Baddeck, Cape Breton, Nova Scotia for some years. Her children live in Canada.

In 1933 Rose and John and their son David bought a tract of 200 acres near where her mother lived. It was the depths of the depression and the land was bought for 5 cents an acre, the same price as a dozen eggs. John Glass went into the egg business and built a house and barns as his farming business prospered. As a small boy I clearly remember she introduced me to Cheerios and also the old English narrative book "Beowulf" which she read to me. Both were kept above the refrigerator. Rose was much better educated than her husband. John Glass learned to drive in the days before a licence was needed. A ride with him was an adventure. Rose was 69 sitting on her sofa reading a mail order catalog, she exclaimed that she could not see and was shortly dead of a stroke. Her husband John outlived his 2nd wife and died at age 96 leaving a 3rd wife. Their son David married Alice Black who he met in the service. Both were stationed at Dayton, Ohio and one afternoon David asked two girls to go for a ride. One of them was Alice. Dave worked for many years at Sperry in Charlottesville, retired early, as he suffered from arthritis. He became an invalid, had a stroke and died at age 61. They had three children, Stewart, Connie and Clayton all of whom live in Virginia. Rose is buried at Scottsville Cemetery, Scottsville Va.

Rhoda after graduating from high school at Scottsville in 1928 went to Savannah Georgia to go to business college. She lived there with her sister Lucy, who was now a nurse, and her husband. After business college she worked for a time in Savanna for the Edison Company. She decided to enter nursing and went to Detroit to live with Rose and train at the Henry Ford Hospital. She changed the dressing on an infection on Henry Ford's toe. Rhoda graduated as an R.N. in Nov. 1934. She chummed with a girl from Highgate, Ontario who introduced her to John (Jack) Eacott (gen 4 Eacott of Canada) of Highgate, a cabinetmaker. They were married Feb. 14, 1935 in Detroit. They eloped and informed their families afterward. This did not go down well with Jack's mother so they were not welcomed to Highgate. Seeking work Jack found employment at Dunnville, Ontario for 25 cents an hour. On his way back from his first day of work he met an unemployed neighbor who was looking for work at 10 cents an hour but could not find anything. Jack would not tell him what he was getting paid. They lived briefly at Dunnville Ontario before going to Timmins in 1936. Here Jack worked first for a lumber company Hill Clark and Francis and then found a job at the Dome Mine as an underground construction foreman. Their first child John (gen 5,6,7) was born in 1937. On the way to the hospital for the delivery the taxi cab had to wait for a bear to cross the road. In 1941 Jack joined the air force and was stationed in Nova Scotia and Newfoundland. Rhoda and her son Jackie (John) went to live at Scottsville with her mother. After the war they went to live in Tillsonburg ON where her daughters were born. She was active in the community being an organizer of the school parents association, active in the hospital auxiliary, a Commissioner in the Girl Guides, ladies president of the golf club, and the fair board. In 1967 she was named citizen of the year. She collected antiques and did weaving, knitting and other crafts. In 1969 she moved to the St. Petersburg Florida area. Later she and Jack had a summer home at Highgate ON. This was a house Jack had helped his father build. During her last summer there she organized a family reunion. Wiley's daughters came. Ann who had never traveled much marveled at how rural Ohio was since she had been taught it was an industrial state and expected wall to wall factories. Rhoda lived to age 69 and died in Florida of bowel and liver cancer. Her remains were scattered at sea. Her husband remarried and died age 78. They had 3 children including me, John McBride (July 19 1937), Jill McBride (May 7 1946) , Janifer Lee (Nov 28 1948).

Thomas Finley (Fin) decided to go to college at the Montana school of Mines in 1930 (age 26) where he excelled and was involved in the yearbook where he was editor one year. He was also on the debating team and was Montana State tennis champion. After graduation he married Louise Lilly (July 2, 1934). He was hired by the American Smelting and Refining Company of East Helena Montana. Later he was transferred to Barber, New Jersey. At one point in his career he went to Cuba where, according to Ron L. Hubbard the founder of the Church of Scientology, he met Finley who he found to be a most remarkable person as in a space of 6 weeks Finley learned the Spanish language. In 1942 he went to work for the Metalurgica de Mexico as General Manager at Tlalnepantia Mexico. He began suffering from heart problems and had two heart attacks before dying of a third Nov 4 1944 at the age of forty. He is buried in Mexico City. He had two daughters, Dorothy and Virginia both of whom went on to become university teachers. A scholarship donated by them in his name has been established at the University of Montana for women in engineering.

William Grey had a heart attack and died at the age of 47 in the year 1937. He and Mamie Mann had four children all of whom were raised in West Virginia Emily (Topsy), Mildred, Thomas (Jack), Wayne. Grey is buried at Piedmont Cemetery, Dandride TN. His descendants now live in Florida and North Carolina as well as West Virginia and Virginia. One grandson is the only family line to carry this McBride name in 2001.

Jim eventually married Anita Seay, served in the army during WWII, and suffering from kidney problems had a heart attack and died January 10, 1947 at the age of 39. No children. He and Anita are buried in Fluvanna County. Anita was in a car accident and spent her last years paralyzed at the waist. The McBride men died exceptionally early in life. There has been no genetic evidence for this but each of these men may have had rheumatic fever as children and had heart damage. The women on the other hand lived longer lives some into their 90's.

Annie Boone lived in Los Angeles California after marriage. Her husband Fred Curtis was a building contractor and built a number of large office buildings in Hollywood and Los Angeles. Their son was Thomas Grey Curtis. Annie died age 66 in 1958. Thomas Grey Curtis was born 1920 in Minnesota and died 1978 in Los Angeles was married twice. His sons lived with their mother Jean and took new names when she remarried. Thomas graduated from California Institute of Technology with B.S. in 1942 and M.S. in civil engineering in 1944. He died in Los Angeles. All trace has been lost of his children. Annie is buried in Los Angeles.

Lucy outlived her husband and died at Scottsville age 75 in 1969 after having lived many years in Columbia SC. During the war she was an army nurse. They had no children. Lucy spent her last years with Nelle. As a hobby she painted. She is buried in Columbia SC.

Carrie May lived out her life at Osakis Minn. farming and teaching. After her husband Tom Dunn had a serious stroke, she tended him daily at the nursing home for several years. She had a very quick wit and a sunny disposition. In her 80's she continued to volunteer at the nursing home. At the age of about 90 she decided to go to Washington on the train and recalled they hadn't improved much in 70 years. She died age 94. They had a son, Bob who died at an early age in Hamburg NY and a daughter, Kathryn. Carrie Dunn is buried at Osakis.

Nelle and Royce Collins lived at Scottsville where he conducted his plumbing and heating business, played a weekly game of poker, improved the land he owned, engaged in raising cattle and grandly expressed his views on the world from behind a Churchillian cigar. He admired Roosevelt and the New York Yankees. A large photo of Roosevelt hung in his office. As a younger man he had a serious drinking problem and after an ill advised fishing trip off the North Carolina coast, the small craft was caught in a major storm and all but capsized. During this trip he swore to god that if he was spared he would never touch another drop and never did. He did enjoy drinking huge volumes of Coca Cola. After his death Nelle moved first to Charlotte NC then to Orlando, Florida. They had three girls, Betty, Harriet, Joyce.

Mary Elizabeth Mast McBride lived at her home at Scottsville until her death March 8, 1947. She had suffered for some time from circulatory problems. She had outlived 3 of her boys and after her youngest boy Jim died in January of that year she became very distressed over this and suffered a stroke, dying at the age of 79. Thomas and Mary had 19 grandchildren, 13 of them girls. She is buried at Scottsville. Their descendants are scattered all over North America from the Maritimes to British Columbia, from California to Florida.

The diaspora of the McBrides during the 20th century has broken the links of family. Some of the 19 first cousins have never met. Some are now dead. Their children are not only mostly strangers they are unaware of each other. I have written this so those who want to know may build onto their own family history.

This is an incomplete work and I welcome any information to enlarge on it.

John Eacott

465159 Curries Rd, Woodstock, Ontario N4S7V8   eacott@execulink.com

519 424 9762 or 941 747 4585   July 2018

Longevity Records

The genetic background is always a point of interest. Items surface over the years. Things are inherited. I have unusually stubby fingers and feet like a duck with high arches. I find some others have similar traits. Fine features appears to be a Mast trait. Some have broad foreheads which is likely a McBride trait. What seems of greatest interest is the fact that the sons of Mary Elizabeth and Thomas all died exceptionally early of heart disease. So the chart below shows the age of death of as many as I could locate in the direct lines. It includes the year of death so a person 72 years 3 months is 73. There is a longevity streak of sorts in the Masts given the odds in the 1800's. Note also the untimely deaths of women at relatively early ages. Would that we could know why.

So dear reader you have a 50% , 25% , 12.5%, 6.2% or 3.1% or 1.5% or less chance of having genes from the above depending if you are 1 to 6th generation after the children of John and Barbara Mast. Grandchildren of Mary and Thomas McBride are generation 6 and 7, (the first cousins sharing 3.1% with John McBride and 1.5 % genes with John Mast), Great grandchildren are Generation 7 and 8, Great great grandchildren are generation 8 and 9 etc.

~~~~

John Mast 66 (generation 1)

his kids:

Joseph 71 David 75, Nancy 102, Elizabeth 71 Mary 36, John 70, Jacob 39, Mollie 78, Catherine 41, Susannah 55 Stephen ?

Avg age 63.8 tears

Joseph's kids: (Gen 2)

John 82, Adam 73, David 42, Jacob 88, Joel 57, Reuben 68, Noah Elizabeth 39

Avg age 64.1 years

John 82 and Susan Harmon 77 kids: (Gen 3)

Finley Patterson 92, Nancy 73, David 1, Noah 85, Eli 89, Leason 94, Elizabeth 80, Mary 87, Charlotte ? ,Malinda 20,

Caroline 63, Emeline 54, Joseph Harrison 88, John A. 63,

Avg age of adults over 20   78.9 years

Finley Patterson 92 - wife Rhoda Smith 71   her mother Elizabeth Dugger 95, Father Johiel ?,   grandparent Abner Smith 85

Finley's kids: (Gen 4)

Mary Elizabeth 78, David Charles 86, Jack J. 74, Lillie ?, Mattie 81, Emma 89

Avg of adults 81.6 years

Mary and Thomas Clarke McBride (Gen 5)

John McBride ?, (Gen 1) son Barzilla 68 (Gen 2) his wife Rachel Wilson 42

Barzilla's Kids:(Gen 3)

Hiram 67, Sarah ?, Andrew ?, Anne ?, Silas 73, Eliza ?, Brazilla Carol ?, Emily ?, Amanda 82,

Hiram McBride 67 and Mary Farthing 51 kids: (Gen 4)

Thomas Clarke 57, Nancy 85, Polly ?, Wm Butler 94, Rachael 75, Barzilla 72, John 84, Emily 23, Martha ?, Jane 62, Carrie 79

average of adults 70.1 years 76 if Emily is taken out.

Mary 78 and Thomas 57 kids: (Gen 6)

Rose 69, Annie 66, Wm Grey 47, Lucy 75,Wiley 63, Carrie 94, Emily 11, Thomas Finley 40, Nell 92, Jim 40, Rhoda 69

Avg of adults 65.5 years

Mast and Harmon Relationship

The following are notes copied from the internet about the Masts and the Harmons showing their relationships. This collection of information shows the problems of actual identities and some other background about the earliest Masts and Harmons in our line.

Barbara HARMON [1709]

_____ - _____

Father: Cutliffe HARMON
Mother: Sarah FOUTS
Family 1
: John MAST
+John MAST
+Hannah MAST
+Mary MAST

The one thing I have never been able to find is the wife of John Mast Sr. It has been given as Barbara Harmon, daughter of Cutlif Harman . But this is untrue, one of those myths that continues to circulate. There was a marriage of John Mast and Barbara Harman but a generation or two later. (From Mary Cassel Case Wcase22@aol.com)

George Harmon
Born: 1710, Wurttenburg, Germany
Died: 1787, Randolph Co., NC, USA
General Notes:
George's father originally left Moravia in what is now either Slovakia or the Czech Republic due to religious persecution. As far as we know he lived in Germany near the Danube River while raising his seven known sons. These sons traveled to Pennsylvania on the "Charlotte" in 1726. Brother Heinrich Adam purchased land in Philadelphia Co., PA in 1734. George moved to Maryland next where he met and married his wife. He and his brothers then traveled down the Shenandoah Valley, some settling in Virginia (West Virginia) with a few continuing south to live in Rowan Co. (now Randolph Co.) North Carolina. They could have started this move from Pennsylvania as early as 1737 when Heinrich Adam's son Henry was age 11 as passed down in family tradition. The first written evidence of their settlement in the New River German Settlement was in 1745 when Adam's ford is mentioned to exist at the end of the "Indian Road" in an Orange Co. Road order.

He is listed as the 4th brother in age, younger than Mathias and older than brother, Daniel of these original Harmon immigrants. He is also the possible parent of Cutliff Harmon who married Susan Pfoutz.

In his will, George Harmon (Hermann, Harman) lists his executor as John Mast, a "family friend", who could have been the husband of possible daughter, Barbara Harman. He names five of his children and a son-in-law, Daniel Waggoner. Daniel is married to an Elizabeth Harmon who was not named in his will. I suspected the same of Barbara but wondered why he wouldn't use the term son-in-law for John Mast also. The will was written at a point where George's granddaughter, Susanah, who married a John Mast, had not even been born yet, so the John Mast is likely to be the husband of Barbara. However, because he is listed as a "family friend" I suspect that he's simply the husband of Barbara Harmon who is related to George in some way. Below is an attempt at transcribing George Harmon's will. The xerox copy sent to me by Kathy Schoen is very difficult to read. Original capitalization, punctuation and spelling will be maintained.

"Randolph County, North Carolina, Will Book Vol.1, 1773-1793. Salt Lake City, Utah Microfilm 475,245.

In the name of God (amen) (Whereas) I George Harman of Randolph County, North Carolina am weak of body but of Sound mind and memory do make this my Last Will and Testament in (manner) (and) (form) following (To wit) First I give to my loving wife Mary one third parte of the Plantation I now live in (during) this life Including the house Barn and Orchard with the (affictures and Servants) Belonging to (As) (Laid) off if the (ss) (Cass) in Order to (Divide?) (part) or Otherwise and also the third parte of my (Still) and also the Stove (or Store) in my house as ( ) where (as) ( ) (came) (during) her life and also one Good Feather bed and (furniture) with the good one third part of my personal Estate with my (Passing) and What may be therein for Ever. I also give to my son George the Plantation whereon I now live Everything as before & at his death to him and his heirs for ever and ( ) for Ever. Also to Cutliffe and George I give the wood Work of ( ) and the (Tin) of an Old One (Stove or Store?) and (Sk) alike. Also to my son (Phillip) I give Twenty Shillings (Apiece) and the (remainder) of my Personal Estate in Goods and (Chattels) I (give) to my (five or fine) Children (To Wite) Mathias Cutliffe (Catrin?) (Allex or Ulics) & George after my wife's third parte is (divided) to be equally Divided Between Them. Also my Son in Law Daniel Waggoner I give the (team) of (five) (ponies) And I Do hereby Nominate & appoint my (trusty or family) friends, John Maste and Adam (Bowers) Executors to this my Laste Will and Testamente To ( ) the ( ) (transferred) according to the (true) intent & meaning thereoff in Witness whereof I have (herewith) set my hand & Seal this twentieth Day of August on the year one Thousand Seven hundred & Eighty (five or six) Signed Sealed & (Acknowledged) in the presence of us who (..........) (Witnesses) (Godfrey) ( ) George (Bowers) William (Motholm) Signed in Death George Harmon (Seal)

Events:
1. Will; 20 Aug 1786; , Randolph Co., NC, USA.

Marriage Information:
George also married Mary Margaret WILEY. (Mary Margaret WILEY died after 1785.)

The following extensive information comes from .... Coate Dudick "Ancestrees"

John Mast Sr.
(Abt 1740-Abt 1800)
Spouse: Catherina Barbara HARMON

Children: Nancy MAST, Elizabeth MAST, Captain David MAST, John MAST Jr., Joseph MAST, Hannah MAST, Mary MAST
Jacob MAST, Mary Magdalena (Mollie) MAST, Catherine MAST, Susanna MAST, Stephen MAST

General Notes:
"John Mast, Sr. was born in Switzerland in 1740 and died in Randolph Co., N.C. in 1800. Orphaned John, brother, Jacob Mast, and 4 sisters immigrated to the Schuykill River in Pennsylvania under the care of their uncle, Johannes Mast" on the ship Botherhood, John Thompson, Captain which arrived in Philadelphia from Rotterdam on Nov. 3, 1750. This account from a 2nd hand history, although the best info we have, has not yet been supported by first hand records. Supposedly the only copy of the passengers from this ship's arrival included 119 persons out of the 300 who were on board and no Masts are on it to verify the data above.

If his wife was born in 1725 or 1733 as now suspected by me, then his birthdate is likely to be earlier than the 1740 date often given also. I am making this assumption until I find first hand information otherwise. Around 1760 they moved into the Conestoga Valley (in Lancaster Co.?) of Pennsylvania due to Indian uprisings. It is here that his brother Jacob Mast became a Bishop of the Mennonite Church. Although Jacob is usually listed as the older brother, there is no first hand evidence of this. Brother John married and had several children before Jacob began having children and could easily be the older brother.

Before 1763 John Mast, Sr. drifted on foot from what is now Elverson located west of Philadelphia, Pennsylvania in what appears to be the border of Chester Co., PA and Bucks Co. It was the home of his brother Jacob. He traveled through Virginia to what is now Randolph Co., NC. In one account, he moved south because he and his brother had a falling out. He and his family of wife and about 4 children migrated with the Beiler and Fisher families leaving Malvern, Chester Co., PA which is even closer to Philadelphia, PA to go to Watuaga Co., NC and then to Rowan County, NC. He along with several Fouts and Hoover families bought land on Feb. 17, 1763 in Rowan Co., NC. It became part of Guilford County, NC when Guilford Co. was formed and is currently a part of Randolph County, NC. John's sister, Magdalena moved to what became Randolph Co., North Carolina also. Their other three sisters are supposed to have died unmarried.

John Mast Sr. is often listed as a Revolutionary War soldier. This is based on the fact that John Mast Sr. with his son John Mast Jr. (and David Mast) supposedly appear in the records of the Siege of Charleston in the 1797 Yearbook of the City of Charleston, SC on pg. 405. However, when the original records are checked the names are for a family of Mash's not Masts. This makes sense that John Mast Sr. and relatives were not a part of the Revolutionary War because John Mast, along with Andrew Fouts, Jacob Fouts, Frederick Waymire and Andrew Hoover, are shown on the 1779 Randolph Co, NC tax list of William Cole as having refused to take the Oath of Allegiance because they were pacifists. The other families listed in this group were Quakers suggesting that Jacob Mast had similar feelings.

John Mast Sr. and Barbara Harman had 12 children, ten of whom came to Ohio, seven daughters and son's David, John and Jacob, about 1801. They settled in Miami and Montgomery counties. Many of their children attended Quaker meetings and married Quaker spouses although they were never official members of the Quaker church.

Many of the Harmans also settled in Ohio, but not in Miami Co. This info. is from Brien's Vol. I of Quaker Genealogies, a section entitled: The Mast Family.

HISTORY OF WATAUGA CO., NC, p.330 and info from Mrs. McIntosh (*NOTE: The dates on this family group sheet should be taken as opinion only. They are often contradicted between sources, especially birthdates. Birth order of John and Barbara Mast's children has not been the same in any two records I've seen.)
Events:

1. Immigration; 3 Nov 1750; Rotterdam, South Holland, Netherlands. From Switzerland.

Marriage Information:

John married Catherina Barbara HARMON, daughter of Jacob HARMON and Maria Catherina PAUSCHEN, about 1756 in , , PA, USA. (Catherina Barbara HARMON was born about 1733 in , , , Germany 11 and was buried in , , NC.)

Marriage Notes:

Sources

1. Alan D. Shearer to Linda Coate Dudick Letter dated 23 Jan 1996 at 185 Katy Lane, Englewood, OH 45322 In possession of Dudick at 648 Ulverston Dr., Gahanna, OH 43230.

2. Grace Arabelle Coate Wilson to Albert and Marcena Coate Letter dated Oct. 195? In L. Dudick files.

3. Judge Evan P. Middleton, History of Champaign Co., Ohio, It's People, Industries, and Institutions, Vol. II, (Indianapolis, Indiana, B.F. Bowen and Company, 1917).

4. Glen Gallagher to Linda Coate Dudick Letter dated 1984 at P.O. Box 1592, Decatur, AL 35602 In L. Dudick files.

5. Mast Family History.

6. Pemberton, Mary Helen, Historian, West Milton's Sesquicentennial, 1807-1957, Quarterly Meeting, (West Milton, OH: c1957).

7. Lambert, Ellen, Family Tree database at www.familytreemaker.com/users/l/a/m/Ellen-Lambert/COL17-1143.html, (7/23/2000).

8. Vaught, William McDonald, Tennessee, The Volunteer State, 1769-1923, Vol. 2, (in electronic version at www.ancestry.com).

9. Mast, James, Email, 2000 at jmast1@yahoo.com.

10. Sutton, Jordan, Email dated 2000 at jordan65@peoplepc.com.

11. Pennsylvania Foreign Oaths of Allegiance, (at www.ancestry.com).

Jacob Harmon emigrated with his wife and family of 6 children sometime in the summer of 1733, arriving in Sep, 1733 in Philadelphia according to "Immigrants into Pennsylvania, Vol. 1" at www.ancestry.com. Specifically they came on the ship: Brigantine RICHARD AND ELIZABETH, Captain: CHRISTOPHER CLYMER, Place: ROTTERDAM, on SEPT. 28,

1733.

He is the only Harmon I have found who has a daughter named Barbara in this time period. She is however, 7 to 12 years older than we had estimated the age of Barbara Harmon married to John Mast of PA and NC. Since we truly have no first hand information giving us their exact ages though, this seems still to be within a possible age range for our Barbara. They most definitely have the right names - as her parents and 3 out of 4 of this Barbara's siblings are her children's names. They also are living in the right place for Barbara and John to meet. If this is not our Barbara, I still highly suspect that this Jacob and Catherina are her parents or possibly grandparents because the naming pattern is so accurate to this exact family. It might have been that she was the Catherine Barbara Harmon who was age 6 months in 1733 instead -- or she could be the child of one of their sons David. In any case, I feel confident that these are her direct relatives as no other Harmon families I've found in this time period had the same naming patterns as our Barbara until now.

In the Ancestry World Tree submissions at www.ancestry.com, Jacob's parents are listed and in one source he is listed with a 2nd wife but he apparently had no children. She was Maria Elizabeth Lachen. Several other submissions give his first wife's name as Maria Catherine... so I suspect that this is a mixup with the 2nd wife's name.

His birthplace at ancestry.com is listed as Kunsel, Rhineland Palatinate, Germany. This is listed as Kunsel, Pfalz, Bayern on an IGI record at www.family search.com. Another IGI record there gives an alternative birthplace as Rotterdam, Zuid Holland, Netherlands and he was married to a Catherina that could be him instead. This last record likely was guessed at by the ship he came on, whereas the Kunsel, Bayern place of birth is based upon his "German" origin which was stated when he took the oath of allegiance.

They likely first lived in the Philadelphia area. By 1738 they had moved to Lancaster Co., PA via the Reading Lancaster Road, the only route at the time. On Aug 7, 1738 he received warrant number 170 which gave him permission to hold 200 acres of land at or near Quintapolhilla, Lancaster Co., PA for which he paid 15 pounds, 10 shillings for each 100 acres. He never got a patent on this land. We know that he continued to live in the Quitapahilla-Swatara area of Lancaster Co., PA because of the baptisms of his two daughers in 1739 and 1742 which are published in Stoever's Baptisms and Marriages. Quitapahilla is a small stream that flows west into the Swatara Creek which is basically where they would have lived. The Swatara flows through the Tuscarora Mountains into the great Susqehanna River at Middletown.

Sometime after 1742 Jacob and his family traveled south to Virginia. He appears in Augusta Co. VA land records on Apr 15, 1749 when he purchased 220 acres, lying on a branch between Shanando and the Peaked Mountain..

On May 13 1764 his will was probated in Augusta Co., VA (now Rockingham Co.).. I give and Bequeath... To My wife Catrina Harman,...To my daughter Elizabeth Harman...; amoung my four daughters and two grandchildren, Phillip William and Madlina Price....

Elsewhere it appears a Barbara Harmon married in Augusta county Va. thus discounting this link.

Catherine Barbara Harmon

General Notes:

The parentage of Barbara Harmon has been stated in various sources to be Cutliffe and Susan Pfoutz Harmon. (C-205) This has proved to be an error in confusion as a Susan or Sarah, daughter of Cutliffe did marry a John Mast. However, these were a full generation younger. Cutliffe and Susan were of the previous generation and almost of the same age as our Barbara.

Until recently, I suspected that George Harmon (one of the 7 brothers that went to the Shenendoah Valley in the 1740's) was the father of Barbara. This was based upon the fact that the administrator for his will was John Mast called a "family friend" , and likely husband to Barbara Harmon. Even though this suggests some likely relations in their ancestry, three points suggest it's not so: 1) There seem to be no Barbara's in the naming of this families siblings in this or any close time period 2) If he was a son-in-law, wouldn't John have been called that like son-in-law Daniel was in the will, 3) Barbara is not named as his daughter in the will and 4) George's migration pattern places him out of PA before 1747, years before John Mast and Barbara Harmon marry and have children in PA. It has been my experience that almost always a daughter lives where her parents live when she marries.

I have finally found one Harmon family that had two known daughters with the name Barbara. Both are older than we have estimated her to be, but in reality we have no first hand proof on the age of her or her husband and both would still be in a reasonable age to be having the children. They did. So my newest theory on her parentage is that she is the daughter of Jacob and Catherina Harmon who emigrated from Rotterdam in Palatine in 1733 to Philadelphia, PA. If it's true, all but one of her siblings has been repeated as a name in her children. She'd also be living in PA where she and John Mast supposedly met and married. I have connected her with the one named Catherine Barbara Harmon born 1733, though it might still be possible that she was the older sister named Barbara Harmon, born in 1725 instead. Both these Barbara's are listed in a 1733 PA Early Census

Index deriving from these ships lists.

We have one extra piece of evidence to support this theory that is provided by Mike Bate. In the "Westbranch Monthly Meeting Records of Marriage Certifications" Book No. 1, A.D. 1835, under the "Notes" section, there is the following: "Molly wife of John Wagoner was born Mar 20 1772 and was the daughter of John Mast born c. 1740 in Switzerland and Barbara his wife. After this someone had written "(Harman)" and "c 1730". This indicates to both of us that someone in an earlier generation had known that Barbara was older than her husband by a number of years.

Catherine Barbara Harmon is listed at age 6 months in the Philadephia passenger lists and she seems to have a brother named Johanne Peter who is listed at 9 months. It is likely that the transcription of one of the two of them dropped a 1 from the front of their age, meaning one of them was 16 or 19 months of age..... but that remains to be figured out. She is also listed at age 6 months when she was listed with the members of her family who took the Oath of Allegiance to the Province and State of Pennsylvania.

Comment:

Appendix C

McBride - Reeder connection

Thomas C. McBride

son of Hiram McBride

son of Barzilla McBride and Rachel Wilson

Rachel was daughter of Sarah Greene

Sarah Green was daughter of Jeremiah Greene

Jeremiah Greene son of William Greene and Joanna Reeder

Joanna Reeder Daughter of John Reeder

John Reeder son of John Reeder Sr.

John Reeder Senior   arrived in America in 1630 at Massachusetts Bay aboard the Arabella. (The Mayflower arrived in 1620)

John Reeder Sr.
b. 1618, d. before 9 March 1659/60, #5809

Appears on charts:
Pedigree for Lieutenant Colonel John Robert Stewart

John Reeder was a Dutch-Englishman, his family having immigrated to Protestant England (Kent County) from Holland when it was invaded by Spain. The earliest Reeder wills in the Canterbury Courts show that the Reeder family first settled on the southern branch of the Thames River estuary at Sittingbourne, Kent County (which village was north of the Pilgrim's Path to Canterbury.) From Sittingbourne, the younger generations of Reeder gradually spread south and east to Canterbury where Thomas Reeder was an Alderman, and finally down to Dover and Folkestone. John Reeder is a qualifying founder for the Founders of New Haven Colony. John Reeder Sr. was born in 1618 in Kent, England. He emigrated from Yarmouth, Isle of Wight, England, leaving 8 April 1630. He departed England on Winthrop's flagship the Arabella. In the passenger list he is referred to as "... Reeder." He immigrated to Salem/Boston, Massachusetts Bay Commonwealth, arriving 13 June 1630. He was a young passenger on the "Arbella", flagship of Governor Winthrop's 1630 fleet to Boston. He was a schoolboy and was addressed as "Reeder" by Winthrop's personal list of 76 passengers aboard the ship. He was taken, after the first dreadful winter in Massachusetts (Cambridge) during which so many of the passengers died, into the household of William Pynchon (another on the first five of Winthrop's 1630 fleet), who was sent by Winthrop to found Roxburg (today part of Boston) on the other side of the Charles River in 1632. He accompanied Pynchon and his company, and moved to the Indian town Agawam on the Connecticut River, where the company founded "Springfield" across the river in 1636. He relocated to Massachusetts, in 1636. Being now eighteen years old, he received his first grant of land from Massachusetts Bay Colony, ten acres of land bounded by neighbor John Cabell, in 1636 in Springfield. He immigrated to Kent, England arriving 1637; He sold his 10 acres and returned to England on Captain Henry Smith's ship (Smith was the son-in-law of William Pynchon). There he visited relatives in Kent County, but decided to return to America again. He emigrated from London, England, leaving circa April 1637. "In Nov. of 1633, [John] Davenport fled to Amsterdam to escape increasing disapproval of the Crown where the group organized their move to the New World. The group included: John and Elizabeth Davenport (left infant son in care of noble lady); Theophilus Eaton, Anne Eaton, dau. of George Lloyd, Bishop of Chester, and widow of Thomas Yale, the second wife of Theophilus Eaton; old Mrs. Eaton, his mother; Samuel and Nathaniel Eaton, his brothers; Mary Eaton, the dau. of his first wife; Samuel, Theophilus and Hannah, the children of his second wife; Anne, David and Thomas Yale, the children of Anne Eaton by her former marriage; Edward Hopkins, who on Sep. 5, 1631 had married Anne Yale at St. Antholin's in London; and Richard Malbon, a kinsman of Theophilus Eaton. Also many inhabitants of the parish of St. Stephen, Coleman St. Nathaniel Rowe (son of Own Rowe who intended to follow); William Andrews, Henry Browning, James Clark, Jasper CRANE, Jeremy Dixon, Nicholas Elsey, Francis Hall, Robert Hill, William Ives, Geo. Smith, George Ward and Lawrence Ward."

"Others (probably from the neighborhood, but not members of St. Stephens): Ezekiel Cheever, Edward Bannister, Richard Beach, Richard Beckley, John Brockett, John Budd, John Cooper, Arthur Halbidge, Mathew Hitchcock, Andrew Hull, Andrew Low, Andrew Messenger, Mathew Moulthrop, Francis Newman, Robert Newman, Richard Osborn, Edward Patteson, John Reader, William Thorp and Samuel Whitehead. The group chartered the "Hector" of London. On June 26, 1637, John Winthrop recorded the arrival of the group from London at Boston."

He immigrated to Boston, Massachusetts Bay Commonwealth, arriving 26 June 1637. He returned to America aboard the "Hector" accompanied by William Tharp/Thorp and his daughter Hannah, who became his first wife. On June 26, 1637, John Winthrop recorded the arrival of the group from London at Boston. He settled then in Hartford. He married Hannah Thorpe, daughter of William Thorpe and Garthered Blithe, circa 1639 in New Haven, Connecticut. He relocated to New Haven, Connecticut, before 4 June 1639. He and his father-in-law moved to Connecticut, because William Pynchon had moved there as the first magistrate, where Reeder opened and maintained an inn on the river (Reeder's lot was #10 in the village). He was one of the free planters who assented to the Fundamental Agreement of the Colony on 4 June 1639 in New Haven Colony, Connecticut. He was not a Puritan, but a "Separatist" rather (much like the Plymouth Pilgrims). He lived in 1641 in New Haven, Connecticut; John Reeder is described as a resident of New Haven, but not within the "Nine Squares" of the town. His father-in-law, William Thorpe, is found within one the the nine. He lived between 1643 and 1650 in Connecticut. He relocated to Stratford, Connecticut, circa 1651. After his father-in-law's death, he and his wife Hannah and their children moved to Stratford, Connecticut at the mouth of Housatonic River and Long Island Sound. (Stratford is now the river port of Bridgeport, Connecticut on Route #1.) He was operator of a trading post and inn in 1651 in Stratford, Connecticut.[1] He relocated to Middleburgh (now Newton), Queens County, New York, in 1652. He left his children with friends at Stratford and moved across the Sound to Long Island, where Henry Feake of Massachusetts and his company of 12 men were building a new town named "Middleburgh" in 1652 in Long Island, New York. He married Margaret Isackes in 1652 in Middleborough, Long Island, Queens County, New York; His 2nd or a different John Reeder? One of Connecticut, another of New York? This too explains why mother is variously Hannah Thorpe, Margaret Thorpe, and also Margaret Isackes. He died before 9 March 1659/60 in Newton, Queens County, New York.

Children of John Reeder Sr. and Hannah Thorpe:

> Elizabeth Reeder b. c 1644
> John Reeder Jr.+ b. c 1645, d. b 18 May 1710
> N. N. Reeder+ b. c 1647
> Joseph Reeder Sr. b. 1647, d. a 1702
> Jacob Reeder Sr.+ b. c 1649
> Jeremiah Reeder b. c 1651, d. 1722
> Isaac Reeder+ b. c 1653

Interview with Ernestine Siegel (John Reeder Family Association, Tampa, Florida). Unknown repository. Wes Reeder corresponded with Ernestine Siegel, Director of the John Reeder Association, whose members are descendants of John Reeder. This is the information they provided..

Founders of the New Haven Colony website, online http://www.tyner.simplenet.com/NEWHAVEN.HTM. Hereinafter cited as New Havan Founders.

Francis Bazley Lee, *Genealogical and Personal Memorial of Mercer County, New Jersey* (New York, Chicago: The Lewis Publishing Company, 1907), 2:604. Hereinafter cited as *Genealogical Memorial of Mercer*

County.

Isabell MacBeath Calder, *The New Haven Colony* (Yale, Massachusetts: Yale Univ. Press, 1934). Hereinafter cited as *New Haven Colony*.

FamilySearch®® International Genealogical Index™™, *International Genealogical Index (IGI)* (unknown repository address: Internet), film # 1985719 - "1635".

Rollin G. Osterweis, *Three Centuries of New Haven, 1638-1938* (.: Yale University Press, 1953), information from a copy of the 1641 Brockett map. Hereinafter cited as *New Haven, 1638-1938*.

International Genealogical Index (IGI), batch # 2260254 source call # 1553407 sheet 1.

William Thorpe

b. 2 July 1589, d. circa 1650, #19856

d . c 1 6 5 0 | p 3 2 7 . h t m # i 1 9 8 5 6 | J o h n Thorpe|b.8Aug1564|p327.htm#i19865|||||BryanThorpe|b. c1537|p327.htm#i19866|||||||||');"Pedigree

Appears on charts:
Pedigree for Lieutenant Colonel John Robert Stewart

1639 in New Haven Colony, Connecticut.6 He lived in 1641 in New Haven, Connecticut. William Thorpe was shown in the top right square, on 1/16 of the block (a smaller lot). His son-in-law, John Reeder, is also mentioned as resident, but not in the nine squares. He died circa 1650 in New Haven, Connecticut. He died at his son-in-law, John Reeder's Inn and home. There are three William Thorpes born in London 1589-1591. William, son of Francis, was christened in St. Dunstan, Stepney, Parish 27 Aug 1592. William, son of William, was christened in St. Andrew by the Wardrobe Parish 28 Aug 1591. William, son of John, was christened in St. Andrew, Holborn, Parish 2 Jul 1589. Given there was no Francis or William grandchild (or decendant even) I'll give the nod to John being the father of William who was the father of Hannah. Neither St. Andrews parish is very far from St. Giles. If we had a William christened in St. Giles ... William Thorpe was christened on 2 July 1589 in St. Andrews, Holborn, Parish, London, England.3 He was the son of John Thorpe. He married Garthered Blithe on 19 November 1615 in St. Giles without Cripplegate Parish, London, England.4 Associated with the church of St. Stephen's, Coleman Street. St. Stephen's parish was directly neighboring to St. Giles Without

Cripplegate parish. He married in St. Giles without Cripplegate, had one daughter christened there, and then joined with people of the neighboring parish as they fled religious persecution.2 He emigrated from London, England, leaving circa April 1637; "In Nov. of 1633, [John] Davenport fled to Amsterdam to escape increasing disapproval of the Crown where the group organized their move to the New World. The group included: John and Elizabeth Davenport (left infant son in care of noble lady); Theophilus Eaton, Anne Eaton, dau. of George Lloyd, Bishop of Chester, and widow of Thomas Yale, the second wife of Theophilus Eaton; old Mrs. Eaton, his mother; Samuel and Nathaniel Eaton, his brothers; Mary Eaton, the dau. of his first wife; Samuel, Theophilus and Hannah, the children of his second wife; Anne, David and Thomas Yale, the children of Anne Eaton by her former marriage; Edward Hopkins, who on Sep. 5, 1631 had married Anne Yale at St. Antholin's in London; and Richard Malbon, a kinsman of Theophilus Eaton. Also many inhabitants of the parish of St. Stephen, Coleman St. Nathaniel Rowe (son of Own Rowe who intended to follow); William Andrews, Henry Browning, James Clark, Jasper CRANE, Jeremy Dixon, Nicholas Elsey, Francis Hall, Robert Hill, William Ives, Geo. Smith, George Ward and Lawrence Ward."

"Others (probably from the neighborhood, but not members of St. Stephens): Ezekiel Cheever, Edward Bannister, Richard Beach, Richard Beckley, John Brockett, John Budd, John Cooper, Arthur Halbidge, Mathew Hitchcock, Andrew Hull, Andrew Low, Andrew Messenger, Mathew Moulthrop, Francis Newman, Robert Newman, Richard Osborn, Edward Patteson, John Reader, William Thorp and Samuel Whitehead. The group chartered the "Hector" of London. On June 26, 1637, John Winthrop recorded the arrival of the group from London at Boston."5

He immigrated to Boston, Massachusetts Bay Commonwealth, arriving 26 June 1637; He came to America aboard the "Hector", accompanied by his future son-in-law, John Reeder and his daughter Hannah. He settled in Hartford.1,5 He relocated to New Haven Colony, Connecticut, before 4 June 1639; He and his son-in-law, John Reeder.1,6 He one of the free planters who assented to the Fundamental Agreement of the Colony on 4 June

Child of William Thorpe and Garthered Blithe:

    Hannah Thorpe+ b. 6 Sep 1616, d. bt 1650 - 1652

Interview with Ernestine Siegel (John Reeder Family Association, Tampa, Florida). Unknown repository (PSC 94 BOX 2538, APO, AE). Wes Reeder corresponded with Ernestine Siegel, Director of the John Reeder Association, whose members are descendants of John Reeder. This is the information they provided..

- "My Theories", Robert B. Stewart (unknown author address), to unknown recipient (unknown recipient address); unknown repository, unknown repository address. Hereinafter cited as "My Theories".

- FamilySearch®® International Genealogical Index™™, *International Genealogical Index (IGI)* (unknown repository address: Internet), batch # C010511, source call # 0374348, film # 6901256.

- *International Genealogical Index (IGI)*, batch # M022431, source call # 0380199, film # 6903743.

- Isabell MacBeath Calder, *The New Haven Colony* (Yale, Massachusetts: Yale Univ. Press, 1934). Hereinafter cited as *New Haven Colony*.

- Founders of the New Haven Colony website, online http://www.tyner.simplenet.com/NEWHAVEN.HTM. Hereinafter cited as New Havan Founders.

Hannah Burroughs[1]

b. circa 1657, #5815

Pedigree

Also called Joanna.[2] Hannah Burroughs was born circa 1657. She was the daughter of Jeremiah Burroughs.[1] She married John Reeder Jr., son of John Reeder Sr. and Hannah Thorpe, circa 1674.[1] She was co-executor for her husband's will on 1 March 1710 in Newtown, Long Island, Queens County, New York.

Children of Hannah Burroughs and John Reeder Jr.:

Joseph Reeder b. c 1677
Isaac Reeder+ b. 1678, d. Mar 1763
John Reeder III b. a 1692
Jeremiah Reeder b. a 1692
Hannah Reeder b. a 1692
Mary Reeder b. a 1692

- Francis Bazley Lee, *Genealogical and Personal Memorial of Mercer County, New Jersey* (New York, Chicago: The Lewis Publishing Company, 1907), 2:604. Hereinafter cited as *Genealogical Memorial of Mercer County*.

- FamilySearch®® International Genealogical Index™™, *International Genealogical Index (IGI)* (unknown repository address: Internet), film #

2078052 - mother called Joanna Burroughs.

- M. D. Amos Canfield, "Abstracts of Early Wills of Queens County, NY, Recorded in Libers A and C of Deeds, Now in the Register's Office at Jamaica, NY," in *Long Island Source Records, From the New York Genealogical and Biographical Record*. (Baltimore, MD: Genealogical Publishing Co., Inc., 1987), pg. 139-140. Hereinafter cited as "QCo Wills".

John Reeder Jr.

b. circa 1645, d. before 18 May 1710, #5814

d. b 18 May 1710|p89.htm#i5814|John Reeder Sr.|b. 1618
d. b 9 Mar 1659/60|p89.htm#i5809|Hannah Thorpe|b. 6 Sep 1616
d. bt 1650 - 1652|p89.htm#i5810 |William Thorpe|b. 2 Jul 1589
d. c 1650|p327.htm#i19856|Garthered Blith |p327.htm#i19864|');"Pedigree

John Reeder Jr. was baptized circa 1645 in New Haven, Connecticut. He was the son of John Reeder Sr. and Hannah Thorpe.1,2,3 He and Joseph Reeder Sr. were assigned part of a bill by Thomas Robinson, a "brother," on 12 September 1667 in Newtown, Long Island, Queens County, New York.4 He married Hannah Burroughs, daughter of Jeremiah Burroughs, circa 1674.1 He left a will on 1 March 1709/10 in Newtown, Long Island, Queens County, New York; "To wife Hannah all moveable estate, except a negro boy who I give to my daughter Mary. Lands & buildings to sons John & Jeremiah when of age. ££50 each to daughters Hannah and Mary Reeder, when of age. Executors wife Hannah and my brother Isaac Reeder. Witnesses: John Smith, Samual Reed, and John Gancel.5 He died before 18 May 1710 in Long Island, New York.6,3,5 His estate was probated on 18 May 1710 in Queens County, New York.5

Children of John Reeder Jr. and Hannah Burroughs:

Joseph Reeder b. c 1677
Isaac Reeder+ b. 1678, d. Mar 1763
John Reeder III b. a 1692
Jeremiah Reeder b. a 1692
Hannah Reeder b. a 1692
Mary Reeder b. a 1692

Children of John Reeder Sr. and Hannah Thorpe:

Elizabeth Reeder b. c 1644
John Reeder Jr.+ b. c 1645, d. b 18 May 1710

N. N. Reeder+ b. c 1647

Joseph Reeder Sr. b. 1647, d. a 1702

Jacob Reeder Sr.+ b. c 1649

Jeremiah Reeder b. c 1651, d. 1722

Isaac Reeder+ b. c 1653

- Interview with Ernestine Siegel (John Reeder Family Association, Tampa, Florida). Unknown repository (PSC 94 BOX 2538, APO, AE). Wes Reeder corresponded with Ernestine Siegel, Director of the John Reeder Association, whose members are descendants of John Reeder. This is the information they provided..

- Founders of the New Haven Colony website, online http://www.tyner.simplenet.com/NEWHAVEN.HTM. Hereinafter cited as New Havan Founders.

- Francis Bazley Lee, *Genealogical and Personal Memorial of Mercer County, New Jersey* (New York, Chicago: The Lewis Publishing Company, 1907), 2:604. Hereinafter cited as *Genealogical Memorial of Mercer County*.

- Isabell MacBeath Calder, *The New Haven Colony* (Yale, Massachusetts: Yale Univ. Press, 1934). Hereinafter cited as *New Haven Colony*.

- FamilySearch®® International Genealogical Index™™, *International Genealogical Index (IGI)* (unknown repository address: Internet), film # 1985719 - "1635".

- Rollin G. Osterweis, *Three Centuries of New Haven, 1638-1938* (.: Yale University Press, 1953), information from a copy of the 1641 Brockett map. Hereinafter cited as *New Haven, 1638-1938*.

William Thorpe[1]

b. 2 July 1589, d. circa 1650, #19856

d. c 1650|p327.htm#i19856|John Thorpe|b. 8 Aug 1564|p327.htm#i19865||||Bryan Thorpe|b. c 1537|p327.htm#i19866|||||||||');"Pedigree

Appears on charts:

Pedigree for Lieutenant Colonel John Robert Stewart

There are three William Thorpes born in London 1589-1591. William, son of Francis, was christened in St. Dunstan, Stepney, Parish 27 Aug 1592. William, son of William, was christened in St. Andrew by the Wardrobe Parish 28 Aug 1591. William, son of John, was christened in St. Andrew, Holborn, Parish 2 Jul 1589. Given there was no Francis or William grandchild (or decendant even) I'll give the nod to John being the father of William who was the father of Hannah. Neither St. Andrews parish is very far from St. Giles. If we had a William christened in St. Giles ...2 William Thorpe was christened on 2 July 1589 in St. Andrews, Holborn, Parish, London, England.3 He was the son of John Thorpe.3 He married Garthered Blithe on 19 November 1615 in St. Giles without Cripplegate Parish, London, England.4 Associated with the church of St. Stephen's, Coleman Street. St. Stephen's parish was directly neighboring to St. Giles Without Cripplegate parish. He married in St. Giles without Cripplegate, had one daughter christened there, and then joined with people of the neighboring parish as they fled religious persecution.2 He emigrated from London, England, leaving circa April 1637; "In Nov. of 1633, [John] Davenport fled to Amsterdam to escape increasing disapproval of the Crown where the group organized their move to the New World. The group included: John and Elizabeth Davenport (left infant son in care of noble lady); Theophilus Eaton, Anne Eaton, dau. of George Lloyd, Bishop of Chester, and widow of Thomas Yale, the second wife of Theophilus Eaton; old Mrs. Eaton, his mother; Samuel and Nathaniel Eaton, his brothers; Mary Eaton, the dau. of his first wife; Samuel, Theophilus and Hannah, the children of his second wife; Anne, David and Thomas Yale, the children of Anne Eaton by her former marriage; Edward Hopkins, who on Sep. 5, 1631 had married Anne Yale at St. Antholin's in London; and Richard Malbon, a kinsman of Theophilus Eaton. Also many inhabitants of the parish of St. Stephen, Coleman St. Nathaniel Rowe (son of Own Rowe who intended to follow); William Andrews, Henry Browning, James Clark, Jasper CRANE, Jeremy Dixon, Nicholas Elsey, Francis Hall, Robert Hill, William Ives, Geo. Smith, George Ward and Lawrence Ward."

Child of William Thorpe and Garthered Blithe:

Hannah Thorpe+ b. 6 Sep 1616, d. bt 1650 - 1652

- Interview with Ernestine Siegel (John Reeder Family Association, Tampa, Florida). Unknown repository (PSC 94 BOX 2538, APO, AE). Wes Reeder corresponded with Ernestine Siegel, Director of the John Reeder Association, whose members are descendants of John Reeder. This is the information they provided..

- "My Theories", Robert B. Stewart (unknown author address), to unknown recipient (unknown recipient address); unknown repository, unknown repository address. Hereinafter cited as "My Theories".

- FamilySearch®® International Genealogical Index™™, *International Genealogical Index (IGI)* (unknown repository address: Internet), batch # C010511, source call # 0374348, film # 6901256.

- *International Genealogical Index (IGI)*, batch # M022431, source call # 0380199, film # 6903743.

- Isabell MacBeath Calder, *The New Haven Colony* (Yale, Massachusetts:

Yale Univ. Press, 1934). Hereinafter cited as *New Haven Colony*.

- Founders of the New Haven Colony website, online http://www.tyner.simplenet.com/NEWHAVEN.HTM. Hereinafter cited as New Havan Founders.

- Rollin G. Osterweis, *Three Centuries of New Haven, 1638-1938* (.: Yale University Press, 1953), information from a copy of the 1641 Brockett map. Hereinafter cited as *New Haven, 1638-1938*.

Hannah Burroughs[1]

b. circa 1657, #5815

Pedigree

Also called Joanna.2 Hannah Burroughs was born circa 1657. She was the daughter of Jeremiah Burroughs.1 She married John Reeder Jr., son of John Reeder Sr. and Hannah Thorpe, circa 1674.1 She was co-executor for her husband's will on 1 March 1710 in Newtown, Long Island, Queens County, New York.3

      Children of Hannah Burroughs and John Reeder Jr.:

      Joseph Reeder b. c 1677

      Isaac Reeder+ b. 1678, d. Mar 1763

      John Reeder III b. a 1692

      Jeremiah Reeder b. a 1692

      Hannah Reeder b. a 1692

      Mary Reeder b. a 1692

      - Francis Bazley Lee, *Genealogical and Personal Memorial of Mercer County, New Jersey* (New York, Chicago: The Lewis Publishing Company, 1907), 2:604. Hereinafter cited as *Genealogical Memorial of Mercer County*.

      - FamilySearch®® International Genealogical Index™™, *International Genealogical Index (IGI)* (unknown repository address: Internet), film # 2078052 - mother called Joanna Burroughs.

- M. D. Amos Canfield, "Abstracts of Early Wills of Queens County, NY, Recorded in Libers A and C of Deeds, Now in the Register's Office at Jamaica, NY," in *Long Island Source Records, From the New York Genealogical and Biographical Record*. (Baltimore, MD: Genealogical Publishing Co., Inc., 1987), pg. 139-140. Hereinafter cited as "QCo Wills".

John Reeder Jr.

b. circa 1645, d. before 18 May 1710, #5814

d. b 18 May 1710|p89.htm#i5814|John Reeder Sr.|b. 1618
d. b 9 Mar 1659/60|p89.htm#i5809|Hannah Thorpe|b. 6 Sep 1616
d. bt 1650 - 1652|p89.htm#i5810|||||||William Thorpe|b. 2 Jul 1589
d. c 1650|p327.htm#i19856|Garthered Blithe||p327.htm#i19864|');"Pedigree

John Reeder Jr. was baptized circa 1645 in New Haven, Connecticut. He was the son of John Reeder Sr. and Hannah Thorpe.1,2,3 He and Joseph Reeder Sr. were assigned part of a bill by Thomas Robinson, a "brother," on 12 September 1667 in Newtown, Long Island, Queens County, New York.4 He married Hannah Burroughs, daughter of Jeremiah Burroughs, circa 1674.1 He left a will on 1 March 1709/10 in Newtown, Long Island, Queens County, New York; "To wife Hannah all moveable estate, except a negro boy who I give to my daughter Mary. Lands & buildings to sons John & Jeremiah when of age. ££50 each to daughters Hannah and Mary Reeder, when of age. Executors wife Hannah and my brother Isaac Reeder. Witnesses: John Smith, Samual Reed, and John Gancel.5 He died before 18 May 1710 in Long Island, New York.6,3,5 His estate was probated on 18 May 1710 in Queens County, New York.5

Children of John Reeder Jr. and Hannah Burroughs:

Joseph Reeder b. c 1677
Isaac Reeder+ b. 1678, d. Mar 1763
John Reeder III b. a 1692
Jeremiah Reeder b. a 1692
Hannah Reeder b. a 1692
Mary Reeder b. a 1692

Appendix D
The McBride Irish

McBrides live in both Northern Ireland and in the Republic. The telephone directory for the west and north of the republic has a little over a full page of McBrides. The vast majority live in the northern and northwestern edges of Donegal county in an area that still speaks Gaelic as the first language. In northern Ireland there was also about a page and a half living mostly in northern Derry (next to Donegal) County Antrim and County Down. Now Antrim is an area that is heavily protestant and many of these people have strong roots to Scotland. Although there is a MacBride name of Scots ancestry, some MacBrides could be Scots descended as well. Northern Ireland is not far from Scotland. It was a day trip by row boat in the old days so there was a lot of interaction. Settlers came to Ireland from Scotland over many centuries but especially in the 1600's and were Protestants at that time. These were the Covenanters The Covenant was introduced in 1638 to the Church of Scotland to change it to a presbyterian form of government. In 1660, however, episcopacy under the Church of England was restored. In the years afterward, the struggle over a presbyterian vs. episcopal form of church government was partly regional, the episcopalians being in the North and North East, the presbyterians being strong especially in the Southwest of Scotland (Galloway). In the 1680s, armed struggle broke out and in the Southwest this period was known as the "killing times." As a result, many Covenanters from this area left Scotland for nearby northern Ireland. Some MacBrides may have come changing the spelling to McBride.

The ancestral home of the Irish McBrides is an area of Donegal county known as the Gweedore which is the northwest corner of Ireland and Donegal, sea on 3 sides and Ireland's biggest mountain on the 4th side. It also included the offshore island known as Tory island. The McBrides took their name from the sept of Mac Giolla Bhrighde which became McBride in English. The name means "servant of St Brigid". They were an ecclesiastical or priestly clan allied with the chief O'Donnell in the middle ages and lived at Ray.(short form name). They lived in the last area of Ireland to submit to English rule. In Irish mythology Gweedore was the home of the Formarians, a race of evil tempered devils whose leader, Balor had one eye. Anyone on whom he gazed would turn to dust. In a great feat he was killed by Lugh who became god of light. Gweedore is where the majority of Mc Brides live today as well.

Irish emigration to America began as a trickle in the 1600's and in the 1700's small spurts occurred, mostly by disaffected presbyterians from the North. At the time all governance was only by persons who were members of the established Anglican (Episcopalian) church. Presbyterians, and other Protestants could practice their beliefs while Catholics at certain times were all but forbidden to do so. After Cromwell there was a strong sentiment for freedom in the north of Ireland and dislike of English control. Land holding was also in the hands of the establishment. A significant number emigrated and subsequently were deeply involved with the revolutionary war which was an extension of their religious and political beliefs. They either paid their own way or got passage and worked off the fare as indentured servants which took about 7 years. One wave came in 1740's. The next wave of emigrants was in 1770 to 1774 when nearly 30,000 emigrated to America, almost all from northern Ireland. The reasons were 1. a population increase and no available land. 2. Strong dissatisfaction with their lack of rights resulting in riots in Belfast. 3. An economic downturn. 4. An attempt to raise land rents

A large number of these people were young, under 24 years of age and unmarried. John McBride fit the mold perfectly. Whether he came from Donegal or Antrim or Down is not known. In the 1800's many McBrides lived in Country Down. In America he was in good company seeking not only his fortune but also eager to distance himself from being a second class citizen. His participation in the war and subsequent relocation to the interior to take up land is in common with many who sought the same goals. Up until the great famine of the 1840s most Irish immigrants were from the protestant north, thereafter from the south.

What did emigration mean to a young man in the 1770's? Leaving Ireland was an act of great finality. It was a one way trip by a person who likely could not read or write and even if they could, mail was next to impossible. Saying goodbye to family was as final as death. Whether John McBride ever knew when his parents died, or his cousin married or if they knew he arrived in America is not known. But in those times the answer was probably not. He could not think about the past. He had to look forward because his life in Ireland was over. This in part explains why we shall never know more about our ancestors. When he emigrated John McBride might as well never had any relatives because they lived in another world.

The McBride coat of arms ...which may or not be authentic... is red and white. Three rows of alternating red and white squares , 6 across, like a checkerboard. Then two small red fish facing left. Under them a red inverted chevron ^ with a 6 pointed star in the axis and under that a large red fish facing left..

There are 4 million people in Ireland today and between 50 and 75 million people in America, Canada, Australia, England and elsewhere with Irish ancestry.

Appendix E

Background on the Smith family

The ancestors of Rhoda Smith Mast, some additional information on her lineage:

Parents: Jehiel Smith (b. 9/16/1806; d. 1/10/1885) & Elizabeth Dugger (b. 1807); m. 9/15/1835

Grandparents: Abner Smith (b. 7/4/1781; d. 5/20/1850) & Mehetable Fairchild (b. 2/15/1771; d. 3/5/1855), dau. of Asa Fairchild. Mehetable is the "Meuetaba" you made reference to, but Mehetable is the correct spelling, and she was not a Cherokee Indian.

Great-Grandparents: George Smith (b. 3/11/1747 on the Rappahannock River, Culpepper Co., VA; d. 4/30/1838 in Ashe Co., NC after an illness of 2.5 days) & Elizabeth Earls (b. 9/10/1749 in Granville Co., NC; d. 3/8/1842 in Ashe Co., NC); m. 6/8/1775 in Granville Co., NC. They moved to Cove Creek, Ashe Co., NC in 1791, and both are buried in a graveyard at Cove Creek.

Great, Great-Grandparents: Robert & Polly Smith; Gamaliel & Martha Earls

The preceding information was taken from a booklet "George Davis, Archibald McElroy, George Smith, and Their Families 1765-1890." It was written in 1990 by Edna C. Davis of Laguna Hills, California.

Rhoda Smith Reese is, in fact, the aunt of Rhoda Smith Mast. Bennet Smith was Rhoda Mast's uncle, and his wife was Elizabeth Moody.

Here is breakdown on the Smith descendants:

Children of George & Elizabeth Earls Smith:

1. Mary Smith (1777-died in infancy)
2. Elizabeth Smith (1779-1853); m. Archibald McElroy
3. Abner Smith (1781-1850); m. Mehetable Fairchild
4. Susannah Smith (1783-1862); m. Nathaniel Daugherty
5. Martha Smith (1785-bef. 1852); m. _____ Isaacs
6. Absalom Smith (1787-1814); m. Nancy Vanderpool
7. John Smith (1788-1793)
8. Sarah Smith (1789-1857); m. Hugh Eggers
9. Nancy Smith (1795-1823); m. Daniel Flannery

Children of Abner & Mehetable Fairchild Smith:

1. Rhoda Smith (1799-1829); m. Hiram Reese
2. Elizabeth Smith (1801-1851); m. Jacob Reese
3. Bennet Smith (1802-1844); m. Elizabeth Moody
4. Jehiel Smith (1806-1885); m. 1st, Rachel Adams; 2nd, Elizabeth Dugger
5. Susannah Smith, m. Jacob Moody
6. Rebecca Smith, m. Jacob Norris
7. Mary Smith, m. William Roland

Children of Jehiel Smith:

(1st marriage - by Rachel Adams)

1. Ebenezer (Eben) Smith (1828-bef. 1870); m. Sarah (Sallie) Councill, dau. of Benjamin & Elizabeth Mast Councill
2. Bennet Smith (1835-?); m. Jane Greene (Their son, John C. Smith, m. Sarah Caroline Mast, dau. of Joseph Harrison & Clarissa Moore Mast)

(2nd marriage - by Elizabeth Dugger)

3. Wiley Smith (1836-?)
4. Carolina Smith (1838-?)
5. Rhoda (1839-1910); m. Finley Patterson Mast
6. Henry Smith (1841-?)
7. William Smith (1842-died as a child)
8. Mary M. Smith (1845-?); m. John Tillett Combs
9. Martha Smith (1847-?); m. D. J. Lowrence
10. Jehiel Smith, Jr. (1849-?)

Appendix F
Commentary by Terry Harmon

Finley Mast's son Joe did marry, but I show her name as Edna Deberry. She was from Mt. Gilead, NC and married Joe in either 1931 or 1932. She died in August, 1951. They had no children.

John Mast, Sr.'s wife is stated by many sources to have been named Barbara. I have never seen her name recorded as "Catherine Barbara." Some sources have said she was a Harmon. Others say her maiden name was Yoder. Some have claimed that she was a daughter of Cutliff Harmon & Susan Fouts, but this is impossible because Cutliff was not born until 1748. Some sources have recorded Cutliff's name as "Mathias Cutliff," but this is incorrect. He had a brother named Mathias, but he himself was only known as "Cutliff." He was the son of George Hermann/Harman/Harmon & Mary Margaret Wiley. I am pretty confident that George & Mary Margaret were not the parents of Barbara (Harmon?) Mast. I have a copy of George's will and he does not name her among his children. It is true that the Harmon and Mast families were closely associated and intermarried, so perhaps Barbara was a relative of some sort to Cutliff Harmon's family. Also, Cutliff's wife Susan is believed by some to have been the daughter of Theobald (or Dewald or David) Pfautz/Fouts & Catrina Spengel (not Spergel). Others say she was the daughter of John Michael Pfautz, Sr. & Katarina (Catherine) Varner. I tend to agree with the latter. John Michael's sister, Anna Margaretha (Margaret) Pfautz, married Andreas Huber Sr.(Andrew Hoover), Their son, John Hoover, was the great, great-grandfather of Herbert Clark Hoover, 31st President. John Michael Pfautz, Sr. was the son of Jacob Mast, and Jacob was supposedly a first cousin to Theobald (Dewald or David) Pfautz.

The story of Joseph Mast trading a pair of leggings, rifle, and dog for land at Valle Crucis is mentioned. Only in recent years have I heard that story in reference to Joseph. Always before, it referred to Benjamin Ward, and in John Preston Arthur's 1911 History of Watauga County (p. 213), it states that Samuel Hix "sold his holdings [at Valle Crucis] to Benjamin Ward for a rifle, dog, and sheepskin, Ward selling it later on to Reuben Mast...." I believe this information is likely more accurate, and that this transaction never involved Joseph Mast. (Incidentally, both Samuel Hix/Hicks and Benjamin Ward are also ancestors of mine.)

Regarding the story of the poisoning of William Mast and his wife Myra, I have never seen anything that indicated his children were poisoned too. The same History of Watauga County (p. 200) states that William and Myra were poisoned by drinking wild parsnips in their coffee. My personal belief is that only the parents were poisoned. This story is also mentioned again in John Preston Arthur's History of Western North Carolina.

Reuben Mast's 1st wife was Nancy Webb (not Wheel) and she was a sister to my 4th great-grandmother, Sidnea Webb Horton. His 2nd wife, Jane Curtis, was the daughter of Thomas Curtis & Nancy Harmon, and a granddaughter of Cutliff & Susan Fouts Harmon.

Reuben's children were:

(1st marriage)

1. Eliza Mast
2. Jennie Mast
3. Ellen Mast (never married; lived in the household of her Uncle Jacob Mast)
4. James Lafayette Mast, m. Mary L. Shull
5. Andrew Jackson (Jack) Mast. m. Jemima Clementine (Clemmie) Stallings
6. William Penn (Bill) Mast, m. Charlotte Helen (Lottie) Mast

(2nd marriage)

7. David Crockett (Crock) Mast, m. Mary Leona Teutsch
8. Nancy Ann (Nannie) Mast, m. Milton Mast, son of Jacob Mast & Rebecca Robbins Fulcher
9. Reuben T. Mast
10. Zachary Taylor Mast, m. Martha Elizabeth (Mattie) Teutsch
11. Sarah Baxter (Sally) Mast, m. Elwood N. Seale

#4, James Lafayette Mast married Mary L. Shull (not sure of her relationship to the Watauga County Shull Family). They had a daughter, Mary L. Mast, (b. ca. 1859). Supposedly both Marys died during the Civil War. James Lafayette did not remarry, but had a child out of wedlock by Mary Jaustine Antonia Procella -- William Xavier Mast.

The children of Jacob Mast & Rebecca Robbins Fulcher were:

1. Milton Mast, m. Nancy Ann (Nannie) Mast, dau. of Reuben Mast & Jane Curtis
2. Leona Mast, m. William Teutsch
3. Madison Mast
4. Jacob Marion Mast

As a note of interest, one of Milton & Nannie Mast Mast's children was Mary Emma Jane (Mollie) Mast. She married James William (Dick) Mast, a son of Jack & Clemmie Stallings Mast (see above).

Noah & Elizabeth Shull Mast's son H. Patterson was "Harry Patterson."
Also, Noah & Elizabeth had a daughter, Mary Pauline (Polly) Mast, who married John Shearer, and they have descendants in Washington Co., VA.

John & Susan Harmon Mast's oldest daughter was definitely named "Nancy" and not "Jancy."

The children of William Penn (Bill) Mast & Charlotte Helen (Lottie) Mast were:

1. Reuben Harrison Mast (1858-1949), m. Lola M. Leabo
2. William L. (Will) Mast (1863/1864-1926)
3. James W. (Jim) Mast (1866-1925); never married
4. Leason Webb Mast (1868-1951); m. Bessie Durnberger
5. Hardee Walton Mast (1873-1961); m. Maude Dora Brown

This information might help sort out the Masts buried in Oregon.

Regarding Mary Mast Wilson (dau. of John & Susan Harmon Mast), I don't show that she had a daughter named Caroline. I'm assuming this Caroline married Dudley Swift (rather than Seift), as Swift is a Watauga County name.

I don't show that Charlotte Mast Horton had a son named Dave. He is not listed in the Horton Family History that was written in the 1930's. There was a David Filmore (Dave) Horton who was a brother to my great, great-grandfather, James Washington (Jim) Horton. These Horton brothers were the sons of John E. (Jack) Horton & Rebecca Mast (dau. of David & Mary Shull Mast). Dave Horton married Susan Arrena (Sue) Mast, daughter of John A. Mast & Martha Moore. Jim Horton married Mary Sophina (Polly) Councill, daughter of Benjamin Councill & Temperance Shull. Benjamin Councill was first married to Elizabeth Mast (dau. of Joseph & Eve Bowers Mast), but they were divorced. He married secondly, Temperance Shull, a sister to Mary Shull who married David Mast. Jim & Polly Councill Horton's daughter, Addie Horton, married Newton Lafayette (Newt or N. L.) Mast, son of John A. Mast & Martha Moore, and a brother to Sue Mast Horton mentioned above.

Referring to Benjamin (Ben) Councill, here are his children:

(by 1st wife, Elizabeth Mast)

1. Jacob Mast Councill, m. Sarah (Sallie) Lewis
2. John Councill
3. Joseph Carson Councill, m. Martha W. (Mattie) Gilbert
4. Elizabeth (Betsy) Councill, m. Holland C. Hodges
5. Sarah (Sallie) Councill, m. Ebenezer (Eben) Smith, a half-brother of Rhoda Smith Mast

(by 2nd wife, Temperance Shull)

6. Jordan Councill, m. Polly Melinda Horton
7. Benjamin J. (Ben) Councill, m. 1st, Susan Alice Adams; 2nd, Cordelia (Delia) Bradley

8. Mary Sophina (Polly) Councill, m. James Washington (Jim) Horton
9. James Patterson (Jim) Councill, m. Sarah Evelyn (Sallie) Horton

Malinda Mast Gragg's children were: Susan Moore Gragg, Carroll Pinkney (Pink) Gragg, Sophronia Emeline (Fronie) Gragg, William Finley Gragg, & John Boone Gragg.

Emeline Mast Taylor also had two daughters who died in infancy and are buried in the Mast-Taylor Cemetery at Valle Crucis: Lenora A. Taylor & Mary E. Taylor.

Joseph Harrison Mast's name did not include "Andrew" as part of his name. You had him listed as "Joseph Andrew Harrison Mast," but it was actually just "Joseph Harrison Mast." His daughter Josephine (Josie) did marry Finley Mast, but they were 2nd cousins rather than 1st cousins.

Just as a note of interest, John Johiel (Jack) Mast's son Henry married Mamie Henson. Mamie was my great-aunt, a sister to my grandfather, Jack Henson. Another sister, Nell Henson, married Robert Mast, son of Newton Adam (Newt) Mast. This Newt Mast was a son of Robert Bower Mast & Leona Angeline Mast. Robert Bower Mast was the son of Joseph Cable Mast & Cecelia (Celia) Campbell. Leona Angeline Mast was the daughter of Joseph Harrison Mast & Clarissa Moore. My grandfather Henson and his siblings were the children of Watt Henson & Maggie Horton, Maggie being the daughter of Jim & Polly Councill Horton who I referred to earlier.

As mentioned, Mary Shull Mast was the daughter of Simon Shull. Her mother was Mary Sheiffler, daughter of Philip Sheiffler & Mary Ormatenfer.

Simon Shull was the son of John Frederick Scholl & Gertrude (Charity) Merckel, and the grandson of Frederick Scholl & Maria Barbara.

DUGGER and SMITH FAMILY TREE - Relatives of Rhoda Smith

1. **David[1] Dugger** , born 11 Nov 1777 in Wilkes Co, NC; died 30 Jul 1850 in Vilas, Watauga Co, NC, son of Benjamin Dugger and Elizabeth (---) . He married in 1800/07 in Ashe Co, NC **Margaret Ernest** , born 11 Jun 1787 in NC; died 9 Mar 1835 in Ashe Co, NC, daughter of Henry Ernest .   David Dugger's brother was Joel Dugger who married Hester Ann Primer. Their daughters Cecelia 1825 and Sarah 1818 married brothers of Finley P. Mast

Children of David Dugger and Margaret Ernest were as follows:

+ 2 i **Elizabeth[2] Dugger** , born 1806/07 in Ashe Co, NC (now Watauga Co, NC). She married **Jehiel Smith** .

3 ii **Mary "Polly"[2] Dugger** , born 1800/10 in Ashe Co, NC (now Watauga Co, NC). She married bef 1840 in Ashe Co, NC (now Watauga Co, NC) **David Howell** , born 1800/10.

+ 4 iii **Henry[2] Dugger** , born 14 Jun 1809 in Ashe Co, NC (now Watauga Co, NC); died 30 Mar 1863 in Civil War. He married **Sarah Green** .

+ 5 iv **William H[2] Dugger** , born 29 Jun 1814 in Ashe Co, NC (now Watauga Co, NC); died 30 May 1899 in Watauga Co, NC. He married **Eunice Munday** .

Generation 2

2. **Elizabeth[2] Dugger** (David[1]), born 1806/07 in Ashe Co, NC (now Watauga Co, NC). She married on 11 Sep 1833 in Ashe Co, NC (now Watauga Co, NC) **Jehiel Smith** , born 16 Sep 1806 in Ashe Co, NC; died 10 Jan 1885.

Children of Elizabeth Dugger and Jehiel Smith were as follows:

+ 6 i **Ebenezer[3] Smith** , born 3 Mar 1828 in Ashe Co, NC (now Watauga Co, NC). He married **Sarah (---)** .

7 ii **Bennett[3] Smith** , born 29 Jan 1835 in Ashe Co, NC (now Watauga Co, NC). He married on 6 Dec 1856 in Watauga Co, NC **Jane Green** .

8 iii **Wiley[3] Smith** , born 27 Jun 1836 in Ashe Co, NC (now Watauga Co, NC).

9 iv **Carolina[3] Smith** , born 5 Jan 1838 in Ashe Co, NC (now Watauga Co, NC).

10 v **Rhoda[3] Smith** , born 22 Mar 1839 in Ashe Co, NC (now Watauga Co, NC). She married **Finley P Mast** .

11 vi **Henry[3] Smith** , born 3 Mar 1841 in Ashe Co, NC (now Watauga Co, NC).

12 vii **William[3] Smith** , born 18 Sep 1842 in Ashe Co, NC (now Watauga Co, NC); died bef 1850 in Ashe Co, NC (now Watauga Co, NC).

13 viii **Mary[3] Smith** , born 15 Jun 1845 in Ashe Co, NC (now Watauga Co, NC). She married **Tillett Combs** .

14 ix **Martha³ Smith** , born 15 Jun 1847 in Ashe Co, NC (now Watauga Co, NC). She married **D J Lawrence** .

15 x **Jehiel³ Smith** , born 27 Oct 1849 in Watauga Co, NC.

4. **Henry² Dugger** (David¹), born 14 Jun 1809 in Ashe Co, NC (now Watauga Co, NC); died 30 Mar 1863 in Civil War. He married bef 1829 in Ashe Co, NC (now Watauga Co, NC) **Sarah Green** , born 29 Dec 1811 in Ashe Co, NC (now Watauga Co, NC); died 12 Jan 1882.

Children of Henry Dugger and Sarah Green were as follows:

+ 16 i **John W³ Dugger** , born 15 Dec 1829 in Ashe Co, NC (now Watauga Co, NC); died 2 Feb 1914. He married (1) **Mary H Rector** ; (2) **Catherine M Bean** ; (3) **Julia Ann Clinton** .

17 ii **David A³ Dugger** , born 28 Jan 1832 in Ashe Co, NC (now Watauga Co, NC); died abt 1885/90 in Kingfisher, OK. He married on 10 Jun 1853 in White Co, TN (now Cumberland Co, TN) **Rachel Frances Pollard** , born 1833 in White Co, TN; died 1893 in Wichita, KS.

18 iii **Eliza E³ Dugger** , born 4 Mar 1835 in Ashe Co, NC (now Watauga Co, NC).

19 iv **Wiley T³ Dugger** , born 30 Oct 1837 in Bledsoe Co, TN; died 25 Dec 1862 in Civil War.

20 v **Hardin G³ Dugger** , born 16 Mar 1840 in Bledsoe Co, TN.

21 vi **Enoch Arden³ Dugger** , born 23 Feb 1843 in Bledsoe Co, TN.

22 vii **Benjamin F³ Dugger** , born 21 Aug 1845 in White Co, TN (now Cumberland Co, TN); died bef 1850 in White Co, TN (now Cumberland Co, TN).

23 viii **Finley P³ Dugger** , born 7 Apr 1848 in White Co, TN (now Cumberland Co, TN); died aft 1850 in White Co, TN (now Cumberland Co, TN).

24 ix **Margaret E³ Dugger** , born 22 Jul 1850 in White Co, TN (now Cumberland Co, TN).

5. **William H² Dugger** (David¹), born 29 Jun 1814 in Ashe Co, NC (now Watauga Co, NC); died 30 May 1899 in Watauga Co, NC. He married on 2 May 1835 in Ashe Co, NC (now Watauga Co, NC) **Eunice Munday** , born 13 Oct 1818 in Ashe Co, NC; died 18 Jan 1894 in Watauga Co, NC.

Children of William H Dugger and Eunice Munday were as follows:

25 i **Henry C³ Dugger** , born Apr 1836 in Ashe Co, NC (now Watauga Co, NC).

+ 26 ii **Benjamin Franklin³ Dugger** , born 4 Oct 1837 in Ashe Co, NC (now Watauga Co, NC); died 10 May 1921 in Watauga Co, NC. He married **Martha M Presnell** .

27 iii **David Crockett³ Dugger** , born 13 Apr 1838 in Ashe Co, NC (now Watauga Co, NC); died 26 May 1920 in Watauga Co, NC. He married **Mary E Munday** , born 13 Oct 1854 in Watauga Co, NC; died 9 Apr 1911 in Watauga Co, NC.

28 iv **Elizabeth M³ Dugger** , born Apr 1841 in Ashe Co, NC (now Watauga Co, NC).

29 v **John Wesley**[3] **Dugger** , born 1842/43 in Ashe Co, NC (now Watauga Co, NC); died 1863 in Civil War.

30 vi **Margaret C**[3] **Dugger** , born 1848/49 in Watauga Co, NC.

+ 31 vii **William Eben**[3] **Dugger** , born 4 Feb 1856 in Watauga Co, NC; died 15 May 1919 in Watauga Co, NC. He married **Nancy Wilkerson** .

32 viii **Mary Jane**[3] **Dugger** , born 1859 in Watauga Co, NC.

Generation 3

6. **Ebenezer**[3] **Smith** (Elizabeth[2] Dugger, David[1]), born 3 Mar 1828 in Ashe Co, NC (now Watauga Co, NC). He married abt 1849/50 in Watauga Co, NC **Sarah (---)** , born 1831/32 in Ashe Co, NC.

Children of Ebenezer Smith and Sarah (---) were as follows:

33 i **Elizabeth**[4] **Smith** , born 1850 in Watauga Co, NC.

16. **John W**[3] **Dugger** (Henry[2], David[1]), born 15 Dec 1829 in Ashe Co, NC (now Watauga Co, NC); died 2 Feb 1914. He married (1) in 1840/49 in White Co, TN (now Cumberland Co, TN) **Mary H Rector** , born 1828/29 in TN; died 1850/60 in Cumberland Co, TN; (2) in 1850/55 in White Co, TN (now Cumberland Co, TN) **Catherine M Bean** , born 1833/34; (3) **Julia Ann Clinton** .

Children of John W Dugger and Mary H Rector were as follows:

34 i **Sarah E**[4] **Dugger** , born 1848/49 in White Co, TN (now Cumberland Co, TN).

Children of John W Dugger and Catherine M Bean were as follows:

35 i **George William**[4] **Dugger** , born 18 Sep 1854 in White Co, TN (now Cumberland Co, TN); died 17 Apr 1918.

36 ii **Mary E**[4] **Dugger** , born 1855/56 in Cumberland Co, TN.

37 iii **Emily J**[4] **Dugger** , born 1856/57 in Cumberland Co, TN.

38 iv **Frances M**[4] **Dugger** , born 1857/58 in Cumberland Co, TN.

39 v **David M**[4] **Dugger** , born 1859 in Cumberland Co, TN.

40 vi **Willis Monroe**[4] **Dugger** , born 9 Dec 1871 in Nashville, Davidson Co, TN; died 19 Jan 1925 in Independence, Polk Co, AR.

26. **Benjamin Franklin**[3] **Dugger** (William H[2], David[1]), born 4 Oct 1837 in Ashe Co, NC (now Watauga Co, NC); died 10 May 1921 in Watauga Co, NC. He married abt 1860 in Watauga Co, NC **Martha M Presnell** , born 4 Jul 1834 in Ashe Co, NC; died 10 May 1921 in Watauga Co, NC, daughter of Elijah Presnell and Elizabeth (---) .

Children of Benjamin Franklin Dugger and Martha M Presnell were as follows:

41 i **William E**[4] **Dugger** , born 14 Nov 1861 in Watauga Co, NC; died 14 Nov 1861 in

Watauga Co, NC.

42 ii **Alice C⁴ Dugger** , born 12 Jul 1863 in Watauga Co, NC; died 1879 in Watauga Co, NC.

43 iii **Savanah E⁴ Dugger** , born 20 Nov 1865 in Watauga Co, NC; died 2 Feb 1917 in Watauga Co, NC.

44 iv **Sarah Caroline⁴ Dugger** , born Dec 1867 in Watauga Co, NC; died 1943 in Watauga Co, NC.

45 v **Lula C⁴ Dugger** , born Apr 1869 in Watauga Co, NC; died 1952.

46 vi **John Hardin⁴ Dugger** , born Sep 1871 in Watauga Co, NC; died 1943 in Watauga Co, NC.

47 vii **Lucinda S⁴ Dugger** , born 28 May 1876 in Watauga Co, NC; died 30 Apr 1908 in Watauga Co, NC.

31. **William Eben³ Dugger** (William H², David¹), born 4 Feb 1856 in Watauga Co, NC; died 15 May 1919 in Watauga Co, NC. He married **Nancy Wilkerson** , born 10 Oct 1859 in Watauga Co, NC; died 4 Oct 1938 in Watauga Co, NC.

Children of William Eben Dugger and Nancy Wilkerson were as follows:

48 i **Benjamin S⁴ Dugger** , born 17 Jul 1877 in Watauga Co, NC; died 1 Sep 1950 in Avery Co, NC.

49 ii **Adelaide Virginia⁴ Dugger** , born 21 Jun 1882 in Watauga Co, NC; died 28 Oct 1978 in Avery Co, NC.

50 iii **Infant⁴ Dugger** , born Jan 1886 in Watauga Co, NC; died Jan 1886 in Watauga Co, NC.

51 iv **John Gray⁴ Dugger** , born 7 Apr 1890 in Watauga Co, NC; died 25 Jul 1979 in Asheville, Buncombe Co, NC.

52 v **Annie Laura⁴ Dugger** , born 15 Apr 1893 in Watauga Co, NC.

53 vi **Ruth E⁴ Dugger** , born 3 Apr 1900 in Watauga Co, NC; died 25 Aug 1901 in Watauga Co, NC.

Details as at 2005

Appendix H

BARZILLA MCBRIDE and RACHAEL WILSON

Their children ...All dates are from 1850 to 1950 so add 18 or after 1900 add 19

-A- Sarah McBride - married Harrison **JOHNSON**

-johnson-   - children

       -i-   -Emily Johnson married William **WILLIAMS**

       Sarah m. Moses Dyson

       Don Williams m. 2 kids , he killed in WW1

         Bill Williams m. 92 Nora Harbin b 71 d 46   (married 1892, born 1871, died 1946)

         3 kids died in childhood

         Beeler m. Johnsie ?

         Earle m. Jake **Lowe**

         Mattie m. Grady **Davis**

         Lessie m. Jethro **Wilson**

         Jessie m. Dean **Lawrence**

         Tom Williams m. Eliza Henson

         Grady m 36 Pearle Bunte

         Arlie d 26

         Doris d. 1919

         John Williams m Charlotte Greene

         Dorothy 05   (Born 1905)

         Blanche 08

         Paul 10

         Zilla m 1. Nora ? 2. ?

         Ben (twin)

         Bob (twin)

- Mary Johnson married Thomas **STEPHENS**

         Ben m. Sarah May

         Joe m. Julia Stephens

         Mollie m. Filmore Hilliard

         Lizzie M. Elbert Hutton 1872-35

         Arlie

         Ruth

         Spencer Eggers (may not go here)

- Rachael Johnson married Jack Henson

         Robert 1871/29 m. 08 Lillie McBride

         Eliza d. 41 m. Tom Williams d. 43

- Barzilla-

- Clarissa married McKender Johnson died March 19, 1927

- John Johnson married 1. Sarah Day 2. Rhetta Greer

         Lewis m. Dora Winebarger

Elizabeth   m.1936 Worth Combs
                                    Henry Lewis 1939

Ruth m. John Henson 38
Henry
Sarah
-Maggie Johnson m. Walter Johnson

- Joe Johnson   -Jan 31,1860 -Nov 1916 married Nan Day Nov 20,1881
Jack   82 d 19 m. 15 Hattie Swift
Arthur 85 m. Mattie McBride 06
Alice 88 d. 29 m. 06 Charles Lewis
    Wiley 07 m.
    Bonnie Jean   m. Robert Rivers
        Lucendia Jane 35
    Blanche
    Clara m. Glenn Davis
        William Howard 38
    Bess 90/17 m. 39 T.D. Heafner
    Robert d 47
    Carl
    Ernest b 23
    Louise 25
    Alice d 29

Hiram McBRIDE - born Aug 9, 1818, died July 30, 1880 (62)
    - married Mary Hervey Farthing Dec 1, 1844
    she died May 26, 1869 (51 yrs 3 mo)
      SEE SEPARATE FILE ON HIRAM's descendants

Andrew Jackson McBRIDE b. No 27 1822 m. Polly Greene Jn. 18 1854
               d. Nov 12 1891   Polly b.No 7 1836 d. Apr 28 1927
    Children
    Mattie McBride 1856 m. 1883   Finley **HOLTZCLAW** b. 57 d 1904
        Minnie 85/85
                May 88 d. 45 m. 08 **Jack Smit**
                Grace 09 m. 30 Ira **Fox**
                Forrest 10
                Erin 13 m. 30 Ward **Billings**
                      Jack 33
                Alma 17 m 34 Homer **Shoemaker**
                Susie 21/23
                Jean 26
                Essie 93 m. 10 Lewis Hayes
                Mabel 11 m. Luther Floyd

Liza McBride 1857 m 74 Ben **HOLTZCLAW**   d. 86
        Hattie m. Will **Sherwood**
        Berdie m. Joe **Sherrill**
        Hillie m. Jack **Huggins**
        Lena m. Roy **Osborne**
        Benny b86 died
        Mary and Mattie (twins) one died one married

Anne McBRIDE   m. Squire **GREEN**
      Children
       Silas Green - killed at Fredericksburg
-Greene-   Carrol - die d in the war between the states
or Green   Polly - twin m. Calhoun Davis
     Silas m. Rose Cooke
    Richard twin died
    Preacher Dave m. Betty Brown
       Ida m. Seemore Jones
         David
         Loyd
       Richard Green m. Etta Dougherty
         David m. a Hughes
         Mae m. Cleve Johnson
         Roy

     Henry Green m. Martha Goodman
         Emma   m. Mark Holtzclaw
       Allie   m. a Williams

     Hiram Green b.59d. 36 m. Elizabeth Lawrence d. 14 m. Rachael Issacs
        Callie d. age 2
       Laura 81/82
       Jack b83 m. Polly Warren
         Ralph 08 m. Lura Shoun
           James29
           John Keith 37
           Maxie 09 m Claud Edmiston
           Billy 36
            Doughton 10 m. Joy Glenn
            Tommie
           Gerald
           David P. b12d12

       Nan 85 m.02 Andy **GREER**

-GREER-

Fred Greer 03 m. 26 Ruth Presnell
Jaunita 28
Louise 30
Ted 32
Ned 39
Dora Greer 05 m. 23 Clay Greene
Iva Lee 24
Mabel 29
Clay Verne 36
Ted 38

Mary Greer 07 m. 24 Grady **MINTON**
Dora Lee 25/33
Richard 28
Anor 30
Ray 32
Ralph 34/36
Roy 38
Nannie 40/40
Gertrude 09 m. 26 Ronda Earp
boy 27/27
Raymond 28
Robert 30
Dewey 34
Dean 36
Jacky 39

Henry Greer 12 m.31 Marylyn Love
Dorothy 32
Maxie 34
`   Lee 37

Stanley Greer 15 m 40 Susie Belle Moody
James 17 m. Ruth Thompson
Robert Wynn 43
Madge 21 m. 38 Archie Dancey
Archie 38
Bobby 40
Mae 23 m. 40 J.W. Barnes
Barbara Anne 41

Faye 25
Billy Andrew Greer 33

Emily Green m. Aldrin **ISSAC**

Sarah Issac m. Joe **Mast**

-ISSAC- Julia m. George Johnson

Becky Issac m. 97 A.N. **Mast** (little Newt)

Mae 98 m.24 Hildrey Hobby

Mary Elizabeth Hobby m. 51 a Boone

- MAST- Emma Mast m. Tom Taylor

Ray Mast m. Pauline Greer / 2nd wife also

Daisy Mast m. Raymond Greer

Rebecca

Mary Lee

Robert Mast m. Nell Henson

Bobby

Gordon

Carolyn

Teddy

Joe Clay Mast

Clint Mast m. Gladys Glenn

Betty Joe 32 drowned 36

Leslie Glenn

Pearle m. 38 Joe Page

Grace

Fred Mast m. Jewel Hagerman

J.D.

Mildred m Frank Cornelius

Sue

Johny Issac   m. Nancy Greer

Lennis m. Larkin **Pennell**

Annie Lee m. Ralph **Beach**

Gardener

Iva Dean 38

Emma m. 35 Max Hagaman

Emma Jean 36

Hazel

Alonzo Issac m. Lossie Shook Norris Parlier

Don Issac m. Dora Eggers

Sarah Issac m. Joe **Greene**

Reese

Mae

Ann

Maggie m. Roy Stansberry

Eva

Inez

Manley Green m. Eliza Brown

Linny Green m. Bessie Wilson (linny died 1936 age 59)

Verne Green m. Nellie Crawford
                Kenneth 32
                Catherine 35
Frank Green
Rayfield Green m. Luclle Hayes
Woodrow Green   m. Ruth Wilson
Burl
Emma Green 80 m. a Sitzer or Setzer
      Emma Jean m. Ernest Hicks
      Louise

Silas McBRIDE b.Nov 18 1827 d.No 12 1891 m. Emily Greene b.1826 d.1916
Jackson McBride   m. Emmeline Wilson he d. 33 she d 32

Carroll McBRIDE m. Catherine Bringle and Molly McIntyre
    Minnie
    Ellen
    Sarah Ann
    James McBride d. 1948
        William Clarence McBride d. 1928 m. Bertha Snider
            Bessie m. a Walker (in St.Louis) n/c
        Egbert McBride m. Ina Davidson
            Eugene McBride
            Ferris
            John Roy
            Robert McBride

        James Thomas McBride m. Hattie Hicks
            Herbert d.19 34m. Ruth Hightower
                Herbert Jr
                Birdie
      Lillie Mae d. 1930 m. a White
          Lillie
          Violet
      Annie Myrtle McBride m. Mr. Dragon   n/c
      James Woodrow McBride (Rev) m. Georgina Smith
         James Jr.
      Melvin Eugene McBride m. Virgie Goode
         Eugene d. 1910 age 2
                James McBride m. Bessie Taylor
         Leslie Raymond d. 1917
         Walter McBride m. Edith Miller
              Edith Maxine
        Dorothy m. Arthur Max

                        Carylon
                        Kenneth
        David McBride m. Virgie Cothran
                        David jr.
        Hazel m. Calvin McNott
                        Melba
        Willie McBride m. Lanthan Powell
        Knoble McBride 1919 d. 1939
         Charlotte
        Paula
        Evelyn
         Ruby
        Gail
        Shirley Ann

(The records do not clearly identify where the following fit in. They are descended from Carroll and James but after that the records are unclear.)

Norman Lafayette and Clara Mae Burlson's children and Grandchildren are Curtis Lafayette Burlson,married Hazel DeLancy. Their Children are Nathan and Shirley Mae. Mary Josephine Burleson married Robert Delancy. Their Children are Mary Helen, Robbie Sue and Jr. Clara Myrtle Burleson married Douglas Bomar. The Children are Betty Joe, Mary Lulia, Gordon, David and baby born April 6 1941.

Daisy Theo Burleson married Chalmer Gillehan. their Children are Norris Eugene, died at birth 1935, Frances and Doris Ann

Fannie Lee McBride married Willis Winn. Their Children are Mary Frances, Winn married John Peyton. Austin Winn not married and 2 sons dead

Wesley Albert McBride married Lillie Mae Blackmon. They have a girl Doris and a son Huey. Leon McBride died 1921 1yr old.

Amanda McBRIDE (Barzilla and Rachels Dau--remember them!)
        b. sep 1833 d. 15 m. 52 John **COMBS** 1825-80
        Children
        Newton Combs 53 m. Hannah Church d.42
                        Will 81 m. 05 Mag Burkett b. 89
  -COMBS-   Charles 07 m. Viola Eggers
                        Marie 30
  -COMBS-   Blanche 31
                        Tomie
                        Roberta 35
                        Sarah 37
                        Nora 39

                                    Magaline
                                    Mary Louise
                    Myrtle   m. Dixon **Sherwood** d. 38
                         Faith
                         Ruby
    -SHERWOOD_   Olen
                         Lonnie
                         D.M.

                         John E. Combs   m. Mattie Eggers / Carolyn Belcher
                                    caroline children
                              John Edward
                              Frank
         Daily Combs 1858-40 m. Sally Adams b. 58
                         Mag m. Preacher McSwain
                         Emma m. Tom King
    -Combs-   John Combs m. Etta Eller
                         Harvey Combs m. Mary ?   and Mollie Burkett
                                    Delmar
                                    Olen
                                    James
                                    Mary
                                    Myrtle
                                    Hazel
                         Lily m. Lester Seegraves
                         Mae m. 1911 Will **Campbell** 89-45
                                    Ralph
                                    Clifford
                                    Luther
                                    Ned
                                    Mrs. Nile Eller
                                    Mrs. Mattie Waddell
                                    Edward
                                    Imogene
                                    Jack
                                    Lilly
                         Ola m. Spencer Miller
              Rachael Combs b. 1855 d. 58
              Jack Combs b. 1860 m. Mollie Fletcher b 62 / Bertha Smith*
                         Mollie's children
                         Rhetta 81 m. 01 Shober **Rogers**
                                    Mary Gwendolyn m. Ernest Justine
                                    Millie
                         Robert 88 m. 08 Laura Hall
                         Flora 90 d. 20 m. 08 James **Woods**

George

James

Blanche 96

Charles Combs 98 d 43 m. 21 Rose Mast

Velma 21 m 41 Jack **Burnoley**

Boy 28/29

Carolyn 25

Ruth 01 m. 20 John **Dugger**

Shelton 21

James 28

Winnie Combs 07 m. 24 Dallas Hodges

Ruth 25

Robert 27 m. Jean Banner

*Bertha's Children with Jack Combs

Pansy

Tillet Combs 62 d 30 m.1. Elizabeth Church 2. Mary Smith 3. Adeline Henson 4. Zora Keller

Children via Elizabeth

Maggie m John Presnell

Ernestage 20 killed in war France Dec.1.17

Ralph fell off truck died

Glenn

Bynum

Conrad

Mrs. L.C. Miller

Oscar m. Mary Greene

Walter m. 1. a Greene 2. Ida Wilson

Filmore Combs m. Nannie Wooten

Alice 91 m. 08 Bill Banner

Ethel 08/13

Blanche 10 d 50 m.34 Emory Phillippi

Jim 12 m. 33 Gladys Harper

Susie 13 m.34 Don Henson

-Combs-

Joe 16

Helen 18 m.37 Ralph Williams

Ruth 22 . m. 40 Glen Warren

Robert 20 m. 39 Nina Hayes

Josephine 24 m Miller then Joynes

Sophronia 28

Charlotte 30

Edith Catherine 31/31

Eva Nell 32

Martin Luther 34

John 35

Billy 37

Children via Zora

Vance

Marvin

Edna

Rufus Combs 64 d. 42 m. Missouri Matherson

Sophia m. Walter Davis

Hattie m. Dave Arney

Ed

Daisy m. Scott

Rilla m. Joe Slimp

Bess m. Will Greene

Maud m. Joe Wilson

Alma Combs m. Willard **Phillips**

Kate

Gladys

Lloyd

George

Blanche m. Dean Wilson

Crathia m. a Wilson

Lee Combs 90 m. 12 Bertie Storie

Eula 12 m. Dennis Norris

Beryl 29

Betty Lou 30

Arnelle 34

Mary

Billy Combs

Ida Combs 14 m 33 Ray Norris who committed suicide

Greer 33

Robert 18 m. 37 Myra Arrant

Lois 38

Roger 40

Velma 16 m. 36 Don Johnson

girl 52

Rufus 20

Rex 22

Kathleen 24 m. 41 Jim Adams

Norman 26

Josephine 29 m. 51 Paul Issacs

Carlton 1930

Laura Jean 1934

Clyde Combs d. 36 m. Vic Guy

Dolp m. Bess Perkins O'Donnell

Jesse m. Lula Farthing

                              Mary Kate
            P aul m. Bonnie Love
                                  Jean
                                  Mary
                       Earl m. Lizzie Ward
            A lbert m. Frances Trivette
                             Rachel
                             a boy
            G enevieve m. Edgar Farthing
            Ralp h m. a Presnell he killed Se 44 Holland
            W illard m. Etta Faye Harmon
            W alter
            A lice and Dallas dead
            Raleig h
            Kerm it
            Merl an d Berl born
        W iley Combs
        Clau d Combs m. Arvilla Ward
     Isabella Combs b. 56 d. 23 m. 74 Abner **Adams** 49-34
        A llie Adams m. Sam Norris
                       Troy Norris   m. 40 Mattie Seat
                       Grace 99/35 m. Hamptom Blackburn
                                       Pauline Blackburn
                                       Ruth
                                       Charles Blackburn
                       Hubert Norris
                       Mabel Norris m. Waldo Tugman
   -ADAMS-   Alfred Lee Adams 87/41
            Jo hn Hopkins Adams 89
            A manda Alvertia 81 m. ? Barlowe
            W illett Adams 76 m. 1927 Allie Elizabeth Norris b. 77 2. Bessie
                                          Eg gers
                       George
                       Abner (which is mother? dates odd above)
        Laura Combs 67/19 m. Tom **Bingham**
            Ed Bingham 86/41 m. Zillia Trivette and Pearle Leonard
                       Mabel
                       Lucy m. Red Daniels
                       Faye m. ? Hayes
                       Mona m. Bill Norris jr
                                       William Gordon 41
                       Thomas m. Georgina McConnell 38
                       Edgar Bingham
                       Addie Bingham
                       Mary
   -Bingham-   Zillia

                              -105-

Myrtie (twin) m. Grady Hayes
      Thelma and Alma (twins) Hayes
      Ruby
Vertie (Twin) m ?
      Fred m. Willie Issacs
Jim Bingham m. Velma Wilson
Minnie b. 91 m.12 Vance Presnell b. 92
      Tommie Presnell 15 m. 36 Mary Nave
            Carolyn Belle 39
            Tommy Spencer 42

      Larrie 19
      Gray Presnell 22
      Jack Presnell 28 m. Mildred Harrison
            Jack Jr   1947
      Jim 32
      Ralph 35
Will Bingham m. Bessie Hayes
      Bill Howard m. 46 Ruth Osborne
-Bingham-   Coy m. Canova Morrell
Ralph m. Grace Sherwood
      Grey 27
      Sherwood 33
Mary m. Joe McNeil
      Bynum 35/35
Ruth m. ? Andrews
Albert m. Gladys Mast
Elliott
Dora Combs 69 m. William Barlow
Emma Combs 71 m. 88 John **Shell** 1860-1940
Lunda Lorena Shell 89 m. 09 Grant **Lowrence** b 87
      Howard Lowrence 16 m. 37 Marian Kincaid
            Gerald 38
      Raymond 10 m. 29 Mary Alice Skilman b12
            Charles 31
      Dallas 12 m 32 Blanch Bernice Brown
            Maxine 33
            Carol Jean 40
      Bynum Lowrence 18 m. 40 Eunice McKemp
Jean 20 m. 42 Clyde Greene

Addie Beulah Shell 90 m.09 Fred **Hagaman**
      Ralph Hagaman 10/13
      Norva 12 m. 38 Louise Johnson
      Madge 15 m 35 Osborne Harmon
      Annie 18

Ival and Ivan 21 died as infants

James Hagaman 22 m. ? Greene

Lucy 26

Sue 30 m. 50 Raymonf Harmon

Nancy Caroline 34

Westley Shell 92 m 19 Ida Valdezt

                  Jacquelin 24

Charles Shell   94 m. 1. Elizabeth Coffy 2.

                  David 30

                  Allen 34

                  Don 40

Ora Clara Shell 98 m. 19 Bynum Grogan

                  Dean 20

                  Jack Shell 22

                  Emma Joe Anne 33 m. 50 Oscar Harmon

Carl Shell 97 m. 20 Vera Foxwell 2. Virginia ?

                  Olis 21

                  Jack 22

                  Tom 24

                  Trula 28 m 50 ? Moss

Dora Shell 02 m. 22 Vardrey **Mast**

                  Harold Mast 23

                  Dorothy 25

                  Walter Harington Mast 24 m 50 Shirley Swift

                  Leo Mast 28

                  Benny 32

                  Johnny 37

Don Shell 07

Earl Shell 11 m. 1. Marian Potter 2. Amanda Nagle

                  Marian's boy 34/34

Addie Combs 1873-1886

Eliza Amanda Combs 1877/1877 one day

Barzilla and his 2nd wife Betsey - Their Children

Rachael MCBRIDE - m. George Hilliard 2nd. m. Nona Church 3rd Jasper Bailey

                  Dorcas dau of George

Ellen MCBRIDE m. 1. Bruce **Harmon**

    Lee m. ? Harmon

              Delia

              Pearle m.? Oakes (She is mother of Betty Mae Trivette who married Lawrence Hagaman)

Manley Harmon - died

Julia m. Dan **Woodring**
      Ival m. ? Asslinger
      Nelle Mae
      Ella Faye m ? Phillips
Mary m. Willie **Harmon**
      Roy
      Rebecca m. ? Wiseman
      George m. Rose Palmer
      Martha d. 36
      Ira
      Ed
      Della m. Fred Edmisten
      Inez
      Cloise
Mat Harmon m Nat May
John Harmon
Eunice Harmon
Claude Harmon m. Myrtle Green m. Glenn Bingham

Louisa McBRIDE   m. Jacob **Younce**
Mary   m. John Harmon (son of Calvin Harmon)
Nancy m. Will **Church**
      John Church m. Mat Cook
      Wiley Church m. Ellen Burton
      Jim Church m. Vada York
      Betsey Anne m Sam Harmon
      Becky m. Sam Evans

Nancy MCBRIDE m. Will **Cannon**
John Cannon m. Hannah Stansbury
Mary (twin) m. Jim Hodge
Martha (twin) m. Joe Evans
Nelia m. Arthur Evans
Belle m. Jim Hagne
Horace Cannon m. Emma Vos
Lewis Cannon m. ? Brady

Manley McBRIDE m. ?
Mary   m. ? Jones
      China   m. Charles Harmon
Willie
Rachel m. ? McCanliss
Bob m Eliza Regan

John McBRIDE   wife may have been Claude - no real information on him

Note: These records were on 20 pages of onion skin paper typed on carbon that have come to me from my mother who obtained them in the mid 1950's from someone else. It may have been Nan Lee Dougherty but I am not sure. The entries were sometimes confusing with frequent backtracking to pick up another line. I have tried to sort everyone out as best I could. There is a similar record of the Farthings and the Masts. The records were collected up to about 1952 but most end by 1940.

Many entries had full dates for births, deaths and marriages. I dropped most of those. Nancy 07 means she was born in 18 or 19 07 depending on the century. Deaths are the year and entered as 07/19 or 07 d.19 or 07/19. Marriages are usually entered as m. if date known m.12. Children are indented for each generation. Clearly there were a lot of family intermarriages as the record shows.

Appendix J
HIRAM **MCBRIDE** and MARY HERVEY **FARTHING** DESCENDANTS

Hiram was the second born child of Barzilla McBride and Rachael Wilson

Hiram **McBRIDE** - born Aug 9, 1818, died July 30, 1880 (62)
- married Mary Hervey Farthing Dec 1, 1844
she died May 26, 1869 (51 yrs 3 mo)

The Life of Hiram is written up in the main text.
- children of Hiram and Mary Hervey Farthin
A. Nancy McBRIDE -Mar.5 1846 - July 29,1931
married Lewis W. **FARTHING** -Nov. 24, 1870.
children-
i-Nora Etta May Farthing 12,1872 married Roah **Norris** Sept.20,1903
Roah born 1825 died 1907
children
a. Sue born Nov.16, 1903 married Ray Swift 1931
children
Jan ice Ray '34
b. Lewis Farthing Norris b.Mar.25 1905
m arried   Trocia Greene '30
-children-
Ben 1932
Ro bby Lynn34
Bo bby Gene34
Jim my 36d36
Du dley 38
c. Lynn Brown b.May 6, 1907

-ii- Grace Farthing -Oct 25 1873-Jy ? m. Ephraim **Norris** b.1878-   m. Jan 7,1903

         children-

              a -Ruth 1904 m.19 36   Dr.Addison Woolfolk

              b -Hazel 1906 married Levi Gates 31

              c -Paul 1907 married Mona Greer 31

                 children

                       Eddie 32

                       Johnny 36

              d -Ruby Norris b. 1911 m. 1.Paul Loeffler m .1938

              children

                       Grace 1940

                               2.Jn. Weidinger m. 42

-iii- -Emma Farthing Dec 23,1880 married-Oscar **PHILLIPS** m. March
                                 1 8,1908

     -PHILLIPS-   children-

              a. Sarah Sue 09 married N.E.Wilson m. 32

                       R.Hen derlight m. 42

              b -Oscar Lewis b&d 1910

                   c - Ch almer 1911

                   d - Clark McBride b 1913 d 15

                   e - Mary Emma 14

                   f - Paul 19   married 19 42 Eula Grant

B. -Polly McBRIDE -born Apr.9,1847- married Thomas **DOUGHERTY**   Jan 13, 1870.
He was killed by a cant hook.

-DAUGHERTY -   children

-i- Eugene O Daugherty married Mary Ann Walker 01

      children

         Ruth

         John B

         Bruce

         Ed

         Eugene

-ii- -Mary-May 1,1873 married Ap 2,99   Macon Shoun

      children

         Fred married   Irene Brooks

         Frank

         Eva

         Jack

         Ray married Rena Robinson

            children

            Eva Sue

-iii- -Fannie -b Aug 15, 1874   d.Aug 1950 m. Alvin Gambill 1902
children

           Tom

         Eugene

Elizabeth

Mildred

-iv- -Frank Dougherty-Nv15.75 d.-36 married Lillian King June 1919   child
F.C.

-v- -Susie -1877-1920

-vi - -Cora -1878-19 married John Rominger 14

-vii- -Judson 1880-1947 married May McLain 1914
children

        Eleanor 1915 married Tom Arrant 38

        Polly 1917 married Bob Gibson 40

        Judson 18 married Marie Lowery47

-viii- -Maggie 1882(twin)

-ix- -Minnie 1882 - 1948 married John Reese

-x- - Hunter Daugherty May 11,1885 married Nan Lee

-xi- - David 1887-1902

C. William Butler **MCBRIDE** b. apr 28 1849 died 1943 m.Betsey **Mast.** She was born March 13 1846 d. jy 3 1916

children

-i- Minnie oct 21 1871 m. Henderson **Shoun** jn 3 95, he died dec 27 46

    -SHOUN- Children

    Anne March 18 96 m. Walter Ccook 28 adopted a girl and a boy

    Nell dec 27 97 m. Charles Nelson jn 29

    Grady

    Betty Ann

    Lewis Shoun apr 02 m. louise Hobson 27

        Joan

        John

        Edna

        William Paul Shoun

        Constance 19 04 m Bernard Stalling 1940

        Bernard William Shoun 43 killed by car

        Andrew Shoun

        Joe Shoun 1908 m. Mary Lee Shull 1937

        Betsey jy 18 1912 m. Frank **Millsaps**

-ii- Lula McBRIDE nov. 23 1873 - nevre married died mar 12 52

-iii- James C. **McBRIDE** b Nov 16 1875 m. Mollie Farthing oc 12 1904

    -McBRIDE- children

      Frank 07 m. Thelma Frost 32

        James Eugene 39

      Katherine E McBride 09 m. Robert Kelly 37

        Mollie Anne 38

William D. McBride 11 m. Mae Dalton 38
Glenda Ray 39
William Larry 40
George McBride apr 18 13

D. Rachael dec 10 1850 m. Jordon **HENSON** Jn 27 1875 d. jy 22 1925 (he died Aug 23)
-i- Leonidas 1876 m. Bert Gouge 1905
-HENSON-   Jack o6 d. 14
Zek e
T om
Mild red m Charles Kimbrough / Clois Jordon
-ii- Harry Henson 78 m. Cecile Johnson 08 he died 43
L eota 09 m. Virgil McQueen
Fred jy 19 11 d apr 26 35
G ray jy 13
Bo nnie 15 m. H. Lawson
A nn 16
Ern est 17
Russell
Rachael 24
Dora and Dean 26   Dean died 27
-iii- T win Girls of Jordan and Rachael died
-iv - Milton Henson b 1880 m. Pearl Cross 07 he d. 26
A rlie m. Lou Thompson
J.D. m . a thompson
Su sie
Carter Hen son m. Martha Newman
-v - Pattie b. 82
-v i- Beckey b. 84 d. 86
-v ii- Minnie 87 (deaf)
-v iii- Jordon McArta Henson b. 1890

E . Barzilla **MCBRIDE** b sept 28 1852 m. Emma Tryon he d. jy 24, she d. 38
-i- Bu tler
-ii- Flo yd m. Lillie Mast oct 3 05 then m Willie Floyd d. 1952
Fran cis
Rach ael
Cu rtis m. Rhoda
-iii- Mary b. Nov 6 81 d. 1885
-iv - Frank
-v - Gracie
-v i- Iva m. Elmo Matherly
Jo hn
Fran k

Iv a Dean m. Homer Farthing
-v ii-   Pearl m. Grady Bradley
Jo sephine
Ken neth
Max ine
Marg ie
-v iii-   Lillian m. Buiser
-ix -   Jessie   m. Maude

F . John **McBRIDE** b. mar 20 1854 m. Carrie Mast apr 14 1872 he d. jan 31 19 38
(carrie b dec 6 54 d. apr 21 27)
- i- Mary McBRIDE 73 m. Will **PERRY** m. 93

-PERRY-   G race 94 d. 94
G rady 95 m. Earle Campbell m. 22
Fred   22
Hattie 2 4
Jew el 26 m Carl Parlier 45
A nnie May 28 m. F. Green
Carlen e 32
Mau d 97
Jo hn Perry 99 m. Allie Rowe m. 25
Sy lvia Jeanne 29
Kenneth 33
T helma 05
Do n C. 08   m. Blanche Williams m. 28
Marie 29 d. 29
Carson 31
Myra Lou 33 d. 33
Lula Belle 35 d. 35
Peggy Joyce 36
Carrie L ou 1912 d 1919
–ii- Clay **McBRIDE** b. jy 27 1875 m. Floy Farthing apr 19 1900 d.nov 1912

-MCBRIDE-   Reginald 1901 m. Louise Shipley m.1926
R.J. jr 27
Dorothy 32
Hal 0 3 m. Gertha Lee m. 27
Bo nnie Jean 31
Roby 32
Joy Lee 35
John Thomas 38
G race 06 m. Ben McCracken m 27
Wiley Ross 28
Betty Joe 30
Samuel Ben 33
T horne 09 m. Jay Peterson m. 37

Albert Thorne 39

Juanita Eliz 40

Jo sie 1912 m. Dexter Bell   m. 32

Frank 33

Howard 35

Carol Ann 41

-iii- Smith **McBRIDE** b. Apr 1 1880 m. Irene Cottrell dec 23 03 b. 84 d. 33

Byron May 05 M. Mildred and Olga

David 32

L ouise 07 m. Joe Mast

Kenneth 25

Curtiss 29

Barbara 32

Bo nnie 09 m. Mike Glancey

Dean 12 m. Mildred Gidson m. 36

Anne 38

a son 39

-iv- Mattie McBride b. sept 7 1885 m. Arthur **Johnson** aug 5 1906

Ned Johnson1909 d. 27

Texie Pearl b/d 1912

Ethel b/d 1914

Paul b/d 1918

John b/d 1919

Hal Johnson b 1921 m. Pauline Reese 1945

Ned 46

L on Clark Johnson b. 1923

-v- Lillie McBride b. Sep 10 1887d. 1947 m. Robert L **Henson** dec 27 1908

Mary Kate 1912m.Frank Campbell 37

Mary Francis 40

Henry Clay Henson1913 m. Aileen Hendrick

vi- Essie McBride b.jy 12 1889 m. Ed Henson jn 5 1910

Beulah 1911 m. Robert Horton 35

Carl 1938

Gertrude 39

??? Rachael 1921

Pearl 1913 m. Herman Green m.31
Carlock 31
Pat 33

G.　　Emily MCBRIDE b. sep 26 1855 m. John H. **Mast**　(she died Oct 27 1878)
ch ild Emma Florence

H.　　Martha MCBRIDE b sep 27 1857 m. Enoch **SWIFT**　oct 22 1874 (b. 1848 d. 1935)
-i- Wiley Swift 75　m. Bulus Bagby 02 (he d. 49)
Wiley Thomas
-SWIFT-　　　　　　　　　　　　　　　　　David m. Ruth Lentz
Francis
Bulus

-SWIFT-
-ii- David Swift b. se 3 '77 m. Bess Crosswhite (he d. 36)
-iii- Robert Swift b. se 5 ' 79 m. Bessie Greene 04 (he d. 39)
Gladys 05 m. Robert Barnhardt 40
Robert Swift 07 m. Mabel Teague 39
Mollie Dare 40
Olen 43
Susan 08 m. Earle Blackburn 29
Eugene 30
Bill 32
Betty 35
Peggy 36
David 39
Mary Francis 45
Albert Swift 12 m. Naomi Steelman 39
Pauline 13 d. 35
Dudley 15
Martha 17 m. Dean Adams 35
Carol Avens 44
Joyce Ann 45
Dora Dean 47
Russell 20 d. 28
Lydia Vance b 28 m. David Joyner
Pauline 43
Sally Pat 45 - died in fire
Charlotte Ann 47 d in fir
Max 28. d 28
-iv- Rose b. Jan 21 11'82 m. Selma Fuller 1910
-v- Clark Swift　b. Jn 9 '84 m. Maggie Phillips '24
Burt 26
Sarah 28 m. Paul Arrant 51

-vi- Mary b. jan 9 1887 m. Stanlet **Harris** 1919

　　　　　　　　　　　Stanley Austin 20 m. Glenn Farthing '43

-HARRIS-　　　　　　　　　　　　　Edwin Farthing 47

　　　　　　　　　　　　　　　　　Elizabeth 50

　　　　　　　　　　　　　　　　　Richard Aubin 51

　　　　　　　　Martha 23

-vii- Don Swift b. mar 29 1889 m. Mae Young

-viii- Hattie b. Jan 22 1892 m. Jackson Johnson

　　　　　　　　Louise m. Nerva Hagaman 38

　　　　　　　　Nancy Louise 39

　　　　　　　　　　Jane

　　　　　　　　　　Ruby m. James Hill

　　　　　　　　　　boy

　　　　　　　　　　Janice Martha 51

　　　　　　　　m. Charles Lewsis 34

-ix- Scott Swift b. apr 19 1894 m. Nettie Greer

　　　　　　　　　　Shirley May m. Leo Mast 1950

　　　　　　　　　　Patricia Ann 35

-x- Max Swift b jn 6 1900 d. 1928

I　Jane McBRIDE b. oct 23 1859 m. George **SWIFT** jn 22 1876 at McBrides Mills NC

　　　(sh e died aug 30 1921)

　　　　　　　note: of 12 kids 6 died before growing up

-i- Carl Swift '77 d. 03

-ii- Donald Swift '79   d .86

-iii-Bert Swift '81 d 98

-iv- Pickney Swift '84 d. 86

-v- Butler Swift '87 m. Ada Warren 1914

　　　　　　　　　　　Willis m. Cloe Palmer

　　　　　　　　　　　Paul (killed in france jy 19' 45)

　　　　　　　　　　　Francis

　　　　　　　　　　　Emogene

　　　　　　　　　　　Ray

　　　　　　　　　　　Jimmy

　　　　　　　　　　　Velma Kate

-vi- Millie '90 m. Jethro Wilson 33

-vii-Vic '91 m. Floyd **Warren** '18   she d. 23

　　　　　　　　　　　　Russell

-viii- Dean '93 m.Crete **Hagaman** '21 d. 35

　　　　　　　　　　Dean Jr 23 m. Patsy Teams

　　　　　　　　　　Carlton 28

-ix- Clarence Swift '96 m. Nannie Farthing '30

-x- Clay Swift '98 d. '99

-xi- Kate '00 m. Asa **Reese** 21

　　　　　　　　　　Asa L. 21 m. Jodie Farthing 46

                                                Dean June
                                                Marylin Joe 50
                                    Norman Reese 23
                                    Kathleen 24
                                    Richard Reese 25
                                    Gladys 28
                                    Betty Jane 29
                                    Clint Reese 31
                                    Glenn Asby 34
                                    Dorcas Dean 35
                                    Lance Lynn 38
                -xii- Jim Swift '03 d. 09

J.   Carrie (Sis) **McBride** b. oct 24 1862 m. An dy **TESTER** Mar 27 1887
        (she died jy 7 '41)   (he was born feb 4 1861 d. dec 11 1918)
-TESTER-   -i- Vergie 1888- 1951 m. Floyd **HARMON** 09
                                    Roger 10 m. Rowena Cannon
                                    Carrie 15
                                    Ella Faye 19 m. Willard Combs
                                    Beryl 22 m. a Presnell
                -ii- Coy Tester 89 m. Ethie Milsaps 13
                                    Louvina 16
                                    Blenna b/d 16
                                    Ralph 20
                                    Lewis 24
                -iii- Newton Tester 90 m. Una Greene 13 (he killed accident 51)
                                    Fred 14 m. Georgina Arnett '35
                                                Mack 36
                                                Wanda Kate 38
                                    Susie 15
                                    Ruth 20 m. a Warren
                                    Albert   m. Floy Harmon 40
                                    Charles 27
                                    Carrie Louisa 29 m. a Rowe
                                    Mary 32
                                    Wiley 35
                -iv- Sally 93 m. Lewis **Johnson** 15
                                    Earl 15 m. Lassie Gay Green
                                                Ethel Jean 36
                                    Roy 18
                                    Phyllis 25
                -v- Thomas Clark Tester 96 m. Carrie Cooke '17
                                    Basil 18 m. Kate Farthing 36
                                                Son 40

Bernice 18 m. Archie McGuire 38
Clarke Dale 39

-vi- Christopher Tester 1899 d. 1916
-vii- Ray Tester 1901 m. Ida Ward 24

Clyde 25
Rosa Lee 26
Paul 28
Nannie 31
Doris

K. Thomas Clarke **McBRide** b. May 27 18 64 m. Mary **Mast** Aug 11 1887.
He died May 2 1921 She Mar 8 47 - See their tree.

Appendix K

The **History of the 58th North Carolina Infantry.**

Sgt. Finley Patterson Mast served in this unit, so this is the story of his experiences in the Civil War. This history is included also because this is where most of the McBride and Mast relatives served in the war.

Background of the 58th North Carolina State Troops

It may seem inappropriate to begin the chronicle of the 58th North Carolina in 1861, since it was not formed until July 1862. However, some key incidents occurred in 1861 which influenced the regiment after it mustered into service. In 1861 North Carolina called on her sons to defend what she perceived to be her inalienable rights--states rights. Leaving the Union was not an easy decision for Tar Heels and the dye was not cast until Lincoln called for volunteers to suppress the rebellion in the deep South. Young mountain farm boys left the nest for the first time, left to put on a gray uniform. Many families supplied more than one son to a company or regiment. Some families gave all their sons to the cause. The 58th North Carolina was no different, and soon became a family itself, bound together by a common heritage, experience, philosophy, and blood.   Despite the commonalities, there were some significant differences in the recruitment region. Caldwell and McDowell counties, for example, were considered foothills and not mountains, and were perhaps more cosmopolitan than their comrades across the Blue Ridge. The 58th North Carolina Infantry was recruited on the eastern rim of the Appalachian Mountains in early 1862. The area was largely in the Mississippi River drainage basin, and the men were more akin to their brethren in Tennessee and Kentucky than other Carolinians in the Piedmont or Coastal Plain. The geography of their mountains made small farms, of 200 acres, the norm rather than the exception. Small farmers had few if any slaves and little or no need for them.

The mountaineers had little vested interest in the economic reasons for the War for Southern Independence. Most of the men who enlisted in the 58th North Carolina shared General Robert E. Lee's feelings that they did not want a civil war, but they also could not, in good faith, shed the blood of their fellow Tar Heels. Despite the litany of reasons these mountaineers had for remaining Unionist or neutral, they were not and in 1861 embraced secession.

In 1861, the Southern Army was made up of volunteers, men who wanted to be there. When the ordinance of secession passed in May1861, there was a flood of volunteers from the Tar Heel State into the new Southern Armies. The prevailing mood at the time was that these volunteers would be enough to secure independence. The idea that one Southerner could whip three to ten Yankees was common in early 1861 as well. The fact that the war was not over in 90 days dispelled this myth and other Southern boys knew what they had to do in the early 1862--join the army! Many North Carolinians were so anxious they joined the Confederate Army before North Carolina seceded. This enthusiasm was even found in Appalachian Carolina!

Another contingent of men who eventually made up the 58th North Carolina, were Union men who had no intention of ever joining a rebel army. In 1862 however, a draft law was passed and many felt it was inevitable that they would have to join and did so voluntarily rather than be stuck with the stigma conscripts would suffer. Some joined the 58th in hopes of getting close enough to Federal lines to desert and go north. The Confederate Congress also extended the terms of enlistment from 12 months to 3 years. It had also enacted the first draft in North America and required all men aged 18 to 35 to register and by default, almost all would be called.

Many of these men did wait and were conscripted in 1863 and sent to join the 58th North Carolina. Many of these late joiners had served in local militia and had some, if limited and ineffectual, military training and could be sent to join the unit without further instruction. It would appear that this unit had desertions at about the same rate as other Appalachian units. Many captured soldiers claimed to have been loyal and deserted to avail themselves of the amnesty proclamation. Some were stragglers and wanted to make their rendezvous with the Yankees as simple as possible. Some were believed by the federal military and were released north of the Ohio. Some were not believed and were sent to prisoner of war camps in the north. Some of the churches would deal with deserters after the war was over. Many of the churches divided over the issue of slavery prior to the outbreak of the war into Northern and Southern factions. The Primitive Baptist Church did not so divide, but in the period 1866 - 1868, excommunicated their members who deserted from the Confederate Army or who joined the Union League also called the "Red Stringers" which was synonymous with the Heroes of America. The result was the formation of Northern or "Mountain Union" Baptist Churches after the war, at Fox Creek Church in Grayson County, Virginia in 1867. Calvinists had a inclination to be bold in battle. They did not and do not think it possible to die before it is one's time to die and when that time arrived, it mattered not what the person was doing, as he will die. This theological viewpoint is evidenced in articles of faith adopted by sects in the south, and were derived from the 1683 London Confession of Faith.

Edward Pollard, author of The Lost Cause wrote: In armies thus recruited [by conscription], desertions were the events of every day. There were other causes of desertion. Owing to the gross mismanagement of the commissariat, and a proper effort to mobilize the subsistence of the Confederacy, the armies were almost constantly on short rations, sometimes without a scrap of meat, and frequently in a condition bordering on absolute starvation. The Confederate soldier, almost starving himself, heard constantly of destitution at home, and was distressed with the suffering of his family, and was constantly plied with temptation to go to their protection and relief. In the case of the 58th North Carolina's butternuts many felt compelled to go home to escape being "cannon fodder" for the Gallant Hood of Texas.

A burning desire to aid helpless families from the likes of George Kirk caused others to return to the Carolina mountains, without permission. Bushwhackers, known as outliers in the mountains, were rampant in Western North Carolina during and immediately following the war. Any able bodied horse was stolen from 1863 onward by Union partisans or Confederate quartermaster agents. These men came through the region and took produce at prices much below the market value. The Confederate tithe law also burdened farmers in the hills. Despite this, the women of the area increased production the best they could and in some cases, increased production over prewar levels. What food there was had to be buried to be saved from these bushwhackers and Confederate agents.

Regimental Organization March - July 1862

In late 1861 John B. Palmer conceived a notion to recruit a legion of cavalry, infantry and artillery from the North Carolina mountains near his Mitchell County home. This effort was partially successful and by the next summer Palmer had recruited 10 companies of infantry and three of cavalry but no known artillery unit. The legion concept, however, had fallen into disfavor with Confederate Officials and most of those already formed were broken down into smaller units. Palmer's was no exception. The three cavalry companies Palmer recruited became the core of the 5th North Carolina Cavalry Battalion which was later consolidated with the 7th North Carolina Cavalry Battalion to form the 65th North Carolina State Troops or6th North Carolina Cavalry. The 10 infantry companies were joined by an 11th company, which became Company H of the 58th, was recruited for another Legion beginning raised by Zebulon Vance of the 26th North Carolina. Vance was later elected governor of the Tar Heel State. Company H joined the 58th at Johnson City, Tennessee in August 1862. The 58th North Carolina was originally known as the 58th North Carolina Partisan Rangers and was redesignated 58th North Carolina State Troops after the unit assumed a more regular role in the war. The 58th was mustered into the service of the State of North Carolina on July 24, 1862, with a complement of 10 companies, and began active service. Company M, formed in September, 1862 joined and brought the total to an even dozen companies.

Company D

Captain D. C. Harmon's Company, was organized on June 27, 1862 in Watauga County, North Carolina. Harmon, like his previous four peers, resigned in 1862 and was succeeded by Benjamin Franklin Baird. Finley Mast and his brother were sergeants in this company. Later a cousin joined as a 1st Lt. Finley actually joined on June 15th before the company was formally organized.

Company I

Captain John A. Miller's Company, was organized on July 15, 1862 in Watauga County, North Carolina. Miller was followed by William R. Hodges and J. C. McGhee in the captaincy of Company I.

Company L

Captain W. Gentry's Company, was organized on July 20, 1862 in Ashe County, North Carolina. Gentry was succeeded by Calvin Eller and L. Hurley.

Company M

Captain J. L. Phillips' Company was organized on September 26, 1862 in Watauga and Ashe County, North Carolina. This company merged with Company G in 1863.

First Assignments August 1862 - August 1863

In late July and in early August 1862 the 58th North Carolina State Troops moved out of their mountain homes to their first post at Johnson City, (then Johnson's Depot) Tennessee. At Johnson City the command drilled briefly before being sent out to man various posts in Upper East Tennessee. J. W. Dugger recorded that the first camp near Johnson Depot was called Camp Stokes.

On August 23, 1862, J. F. Belton, Assistant Adjutant-General at Knoxville,

Tennessee, wrote to General Carter Littlepage Stevenson, that the 58th North Carolina was divided up, with one company at Carter's Depot, two companies at Zollicoffer and some at Johnson's Depot. On August 25th, Palmer was ordered: *"Your regiment having been ordered to report to Brig. Gen. C. L. Stevenson, you will see that it is not encumbered with any superfluous or unnecessary baggage, the soldier taking only his proper kit. But 5 wagons will be allowed to a regiment and not more than one tent to each company. All other property, including the trunks of the officers, must be left at the railroad or turned over to the proper department for storage."*

The men were supplied with three days' rations and 40 rounds of cartridges. Twenty rounds extra per man should be carried with the baggage. On August 26, 1862, Belton noted in a dispatch to Stevenson that the 58th had been ordered up as reinforcements. The 58th left Camp Stokes on the 27th and reached Camp Reynolds, near Cumberland Gap on the 30th. The regiment was assigned to General Stevenson's division of E. Kirby Smith's Army of East Tennessee. Smith was coordinating with Braxton Bragg for a full-scale invasion of Kentucky--the untested 58th North Carolina would soon get their chance. Stevenson's command, which was investing Cumberland Gap, held by Federal forces under the command of General George Washington Morgan of Pennsylvania. Morgan's position, made untenable by Confederate pressure all over Kentucky, and to the banks of the Ohio opposite Cincinnati, forced him to withdraw, leaving the Confederates in control of the vital communication link at Cumberland Gap.

The 58th North Carolina was assigned duties paroling captured prisoners and repairing damage the fleeing Yankees had done for a few days. J. W. Dugger recorded that the 58th moved up to Cumberland Gap on September 16 and remained there until October 25, 1862. Communications between H. S. Bradford, Assistant Adjutant-General and Brigadier General Stevenson on September 18, 1862, gave the order for the 58th North Carolina, which had been left at Cumberland Gap, Tennessee to clear the road and remove all obstructions. On September 19, 1862 the 58th was mentioned in the dispatch from Major General J. P. McCown to General Stevenson. McCown ordered Stevenson to pursue the Federals under General George Washington Morgan if he should retreat toward Lexington, Kentucky. Stevenson was ordered to leave one regiment of Palmer's Command in place in order to guard the salt-works at Saltville, Smyth County, Virginia.

Dugger noted that the 58th North Carolina remained in camp at Cumberland Gap until October 25. On that date the regiment marched 11 miles, 16 more on the 26th in the snow and finally camped in *"a nice grove."* On the 27th Palmer's men marched five miles and pitched their tents at Big Creek Gap.

An organizational table for the Army of East Tennessee troops under Kirby Smith, placed the 58th in the Second Brigade under command of Brigadier General Archibald Gracie, Jr. The brigade consisted of:

Second Brigade - Brigadier General Archibald Gracie, Jr.

43d Alabama - Colonel Y. M. Moody

55th Georgia - Colonel C. B. Harkie

58th North Carolina - Colonel John B. Palmer

and others

An organizational table for troops in the Department of East Tennessee, commanded by Lieutenant General E. Kirby Smith on November 20, 1862 the 58th North Carolina was in the Second Brigade of Third Division under the Command of General Henry Heth. Heth's Division, located on the line of the Virginia-Tennessee railroad, was constituted as follows:

First Brigade, commanded by Brigadier General W. G. M. Davis

1st Florida Cavalry - Colonel George Troup Maxwell

6th Florida - Colonel Jesse Johnson Finley

7th Florida - Colonel Madison Starke Perry

63rd Tennessee - Colonel Richard Gammon Fain

Marion (Florida) Artillery - Captain J. M. Martin

Second Brigade - Brigadier General Archibald Gracie, Jr.

43rd Alabama - Colonel Y. M. Moody

55th Georgia - Colonel C. B. Harkie

58th North Carolina - Colonel John B. Palmer

and others

A brief glimpse of life in camp was found in a letter from George McGuire to McCajah and Nancy Tugman. This letter was written in the camp of the 58th North Carolina at Big Creek Gap in Campbell County, Tennessee on December 18, 1862, a week before Christmas. The letter reads in part:

Dear brother and sister it is with pleasur that i seat myself this morning to write a few lines to you in token of my best respects to you i can say to you that i am in tollerable helth at this time hoping these few lines will find you all well and doping well i can in form you that i receid a very fond[?] leter from you yester day which gave me great satisfaction to hear from you and to hear that you was all well i have bin vey bad of with a cough and cold and stopt up in my head and lungs but i am a getting beter there's a head of sickness here in camp is not half of our compny that is able for duty. Moses Greer and Solomon Greer is both dead and six other in our company we dont no how long we will stay hear now how soon we will be atacked by the Yanks but if tha come we will give them the best we have got in our shop i am in a bad fix to write to day for i expected to get to go home about this time and have got noked out of it and it hert me a sit bad i receid a letter from home a few days a go and tha is was all well....

Part of the 58th was apparently detached just before Christmas 1862. J. W. Dugger noted that his company marched to Jacksborough on December 22 and remained there until January 16, when they returned to Big Creek Gap. A December 27, 1862 organizational table for troops in the Department of East Tennessee, commanded by Lieutenant General Edmund Kirby Smith, headquartered at Knoxville made the following change in the Brigade of which the 58th North Carolina was part. Palmer's Brigade, under command of Colonel J. B. Palmer, was stationed at Big Creek Gap.

A February 20, 1863 field return for the Department of East Tennessee gives Palmer's Command's Strength, located at Big Creek Gap, as 125 officers and 1526 enlisted men.

The 58th North Carolina finally left Big Creek Gap on March 29, with instructions to proceed to Clinton, in Anderson County, Tennessee. The regiment reached their new positions on the Clinch River on the 30th. An organizational table dated April 25, 1863, showed that Palmer's command was considerably reduced in size and was headquartered at Clinton, Anderson County, Tennessee.

55th Georgia - Major Daniel S. Printup

58th North Carolina - Major John C. Keener

64th North Carolina - Lieutenant Colonel James A. Keith Barbour Alabama Artillery - Captain R. F. Kolb

J. W. Dugger noted that the 58th left Clinton on May 6 and marched two miles. The next day the regiment marched 23 miles, and on the 8th they continued on to Wartburg, Tennessee where they stopped. On the 14th Palmer's men moved to Montgomery, Tennessee, 15 miles away. The next day the 58th's men cooked rations all night and then marched 20 miles. On the 16th, the men marched 20 more miles and reached Wolf River in Kentucky where they camped. The following morning at 4 a.m. the regiment moved toward Monticello, Kentucky which was reached on the 18th. After remaining at Monticello for a week, the 58th returned to Wolf River on May 25 and then on the 27th started out for Clinton, Tennessee once more, where the men made camp on May 30. On May 22, 1863 Federal Major General J. G. Foster reported from New Berne, North Carolina that in the demonstrations against Kingston, North Carolina that his forces had surrounded the 58th North Carolina on four sides and captured 200-300 of that regiment. This report was in error, as the 58th did not leave the mountains during this period. The 58th remained at Clinton for three weeks, when they fell back 10 miles. On the 21st, they fell back another 10 miles and lay in a line of battle all night. There was considerable marching and countermarching during late June and early July 1863. Federals were putting considerable pressure on middle Tennessee and emergencies were cropping in many places. Southern commanders rushed troops from place to place to meet the possible contingencies. The 58th North Carolina reached Louden, Tennessee on June 28 to meet an expected Federal push on Knoxville from the South. Confederates had moved the garrison at Knoxville to Tullahoma, and the 58th was moved South to replace the troops who moved out. The 58th remained at Louden for two weeks. Palmer's regiment marched for Bell's Bridge on July 11 and reached it on the 12th. The regiment remained there until August 4. On July 31, 1863 the organization of the Army of Tennessee, commanded by Major General Simon Bolivar Buckner, placed the 58th in Frazer's Brigade headquartered at Bell's Bridge.

On August 3, 1863, Bucker ordered Frazer's command to move to various locations from Bell's Bridge. Frazer's headquarters was to be located at Cumberland Gap.

...the 58th North Carolina was ordered to Big Creek Gap to relieve the infantry garrison there; the 65th Georgia, now at Knoxville, will march to Jacksborough as soon as relieved by the 6th Florida; The 55th Georgia to be relieved by the 58th North Carolina, to move to Cumberland Gap; The 64th North Carolina ordered from Strawberry Plains to Cumberland Gap via Bell's Bridge. This rearrangement of assignments was in some ways was a fortunate turn of events for the men of the 58th - Cumberland Gap fell on September 9, 1863 and the men captured there were sent to Camp Douglas where more died than they would likely take in battle deaths in battle. The 58th North Carolina's place was assumed by the 64th Virginia Mounted Infantry which lost 425 men captured at the Gap, 150 of whom died in Yankee prisons.

The 58th North Carolina left Bell's Bridge on August 4 and returned to Big Creek Gap, which was reached on the 6th. After two weeks at Big Creek Gap, the regiment began a retrograde movement on the 22nd and arrived in Jacksborough that evening. About 4 a.m. on the 23rd, Palmer moved his men to Campbell Station, which was reached about 10 p.m. and during the night rations were cooked for the anticipated movements over the next few days. On the morning of the 24th Dugger noted that "*took up their line of march for Lenoir's Station arriving the same day.*" Dugger continued: *Stayed at Lenoir's 4 days lay in line of battle 2 days. Retired from Lenoir's Station the 29th of Aug. at 4 o'clock in the after-noon and arrived at Louden that night at 11 o'clock. Started next morning at 5 o'clock and marched 12 miles and took up camp near Sweet Water, Tenn. About 8 o'clock, were ordered to fall in line in ten minutes. Marched 4 miles and took up camp in a field. Starting next morning at 4 o'clock marched 11 miles to Riceville, Tenn., and camped about 5 o'clock. Before day next morning started and marched past Charlestown 6 miles and camped at a large spring about 2 o'clock. Remained there and went on picket that night. Next day, Sept. the 3rd, started at 12 and marched until 1 that night and camped at Georgetown, Tennessee.*

Chickamauga and Chattanooga September - November 1863

The 58th and Buckner's forces reached Bragg's Army of Tennessee at Ringgold Gap, Georgia on September 9, 1863 as reinforcements. Buckner's men had burned the bridge across the Tennessee River at Loudon, and all other bridges as they retreated to Chattanooga from Knoxville. Colonel John Frazer was surrounded at Cumberland Gap, Major General Sam Jones at Abingdon was attempting to gather enough men to relieve the Cumberland Gap, but was unsuccessful. It was too late, the Gap under, Frazer unconditionally surrendered on the 9th. Confederates, busy blaming each other for the disaster, overlooked the key problem for Cumberland Gap and the Army of Tennessee. This problem was the fall of Vicksburg which freed up thousands of Union soldiers for other campaigns in Tennessee and other points deeper in the heart of Dixie. The 58th North Carolina, under Colonel John B. Palmer was hastily assigned to an impromptu brigade. The 58th's comrades were not completely settled but the 58th would serve the rest of the war with the 63rd Virginia. This organization suited some men in both units. They were friends, neighbors and relatives back home, despite the separating state line.

The field of battle extended from Chickamauga Creek to Missionary Ridge. Bragg had moved his men out of Lafayette to that line on the morning of September 18, to meet Rosecran's Federals. The events of the Battle were found in a September 25, 1863, report of Colonel John H. Kelly, of the 8th Arkansas Infantry.

Captain Isaac H. Bailey of the 58th North Carolina wrote of the events leading up to the Battle of Chickamauga at Bakersfield, North Carolina in 1901. At that time he recounted:

As we approached the creek from LaFayette, the enemy was discovered in a large corn field on the opposite side. Our regiment, the 58th North Carolina, together with the balance of the brigade, was put in line of battle to the left. A brisk skirmish was kept up until after dark, in which a portion of General Gracie's Brigade was engaged. We, the 58th North Carolina, bivouacked that night in front on the battlefield (corn field) and without fire.

Early light on Saturday, September 19, 1863 found the two vast armies staring at each other. Kelly's Brigade was formed, according to Harper, "*at the upper side of a what field, forty yards below the fence and woods that ran parallel with our division.*" Bailey's account continued: After remaining in line about 45 minutes the command was given: 'Unfurl your banners.' At this moment the sun broke forth, dispelling the fog, and as our banners floated out on the breeze the Federals, our enemy, General Boynton's command commenced playing "Yankee Doodle" and to move out eastward on an almost parallel line with outs. Almost immediately we were ordered to marked in a parallel direction, the enemy inclining to the right and to the left.

...[T]here was soon a terrible cannonading around us, but with little damage--none to the Fifty-eighth North Carolina. Very soon after this we captured a battery of artillery on a round eminence in a corn field, and greatly hoped to get to guard them, but by the time we had exchanged a few chews of tobacco, we were ordered away. For the balance of the day, with the rest of the brigade, we were held in reserve.

Kentucky Brigadier William Preston, in his after-action reported this situation on September 19:

...My troops remained in ranks without further reply, patiently enduring the fire. About 12 o'clock, in compliance with an order received from Major-General Buckner, I moved my command by the right flank, from about six or eight hundred yards, to a position somewhat west of north from Hunt's field. Trigg's brigade occupied the front, in a woodland near a small cabin. Gracie was formed near Trigg, and Kelly was posted in the rear, supporting Leyden's battalion of artillery. No further event of importance occurred during the day to Gracie's or Kelly's brigades.... Night coming on, Trigg bivouacked in the woodland and near the edge of the cornfield, while Gracie and Kelly occupied a position in front of a little hut, near which Major-General Buckner had established his headquarters.

On September 25, 1863 Major James M. French commander 63rd Virginia Infantry reported on the events of September 19-20, 1863 at Chickamaugua. French reported that on the 19th his troops were detached as guard for the ordnance train. On the evening of the 19th, they were ordered to rejoin Kelly's Brigade, but left two companies of the 63rd Virginia and the 65th Georgia to guard General Braxton Bragg's ordnance train. On the morning of the 20th, the 58th was moved with the remainder of the brigade in supporting distance of a battery.

William Preston's after-action report continued by noting that Gracie's and Kelly's brigades were "*vigorously engaged in constructing defenses to strengthen the left*" during the night. *This allowed Preston's artillery, Williams's and Leyden's battalions, the "cover of good field entrenchments."*

Captain Isaac H. Bailey, of the 58th's Company B continued his narrative of events:

At about 7 o'clock Sunday morning, the 20th, the two flanking companies, A and B, commanded by Captains Bailey and Toby, of the Fifty-eighth North Carolina Volunteers, together with five companies from the other regiments, were put under the command of Lieutenant Colonel Kirby, of the Fifty-eighth, and ordered in the direction of Alexander's bridge across the west prong of Chicamauga river as skirmishers to feel the strength of the enemy in that direction.

We proceeded about one and a fourth miles when we came to an open field lying along the Chicamauga river some three fourths of a mile in length and about the same in breadth. When we had gone nearly half way down through the field, we could see fortifications all up and down the river the full length of the field and about twentyfive yards from the river bank. Notwithstanding we knew that the enemy was behind the breastworks, we had to advance to feel his strength. So we slowly advanced until we came to the fortifications of fence rails leaning from our advance in the direction of the river to where the enemy had fallen back to and under tha bank of the river to draw us over, then to fire on us as we would have to retreat over the fortifications just passed. As soon as the line of skirmishers had passed over the fortifications, the enemy fired from their ranks, three or four men deep, a most galling and enfilading fire into our ranks. We had now ascertained by sad and painful experience what we had been sent out to do. We were then obliged to retreat through the rail fortification upon the woods and across the old fields of broom straw waving in the melancholy wind, and over a number of our most loved comrades left dead on the field.

One of them, Thos. G. Tipton, had just saved the writer's life. William Preston's report filled in information about mid-day on September 20, 1863:

On Sunday, about midday, the battle became quite fierce along the right towards Chattanooga, and there was a general advance of the left wing under Lieutenant General Longstreet. Stewart's division and Trigg's brigade were moved forward northwestwardly, in the direction of Brotherton's house, on the Chattanooga road. Under an order from Major-General Buckner, I advances with Gracie's and Kelly's brigades, with the exception of the 65th Georgia, Colonel Moore, which was left to protect Jeffries's battery, near Hunt's field, on the left. Gracie's and Kelly's brigades were formed in line of battle across the Chattanooga road in front of Brotherton's house, and Trigg a short distance in the rear. The enemy, in some fields on the north, maintained an active fire of shot and shell on my troops until about half- past three o'clock, when I received an order to mov towards Dyer's house and field to support Brigadier General Kershaw. Guided by Captain Terrill, I advanced with Gracie's and Kelly's brigades. Trigg's having been retained near Brotherton's by Major-General Buckner to resist an apprehended attack of cavalry on our left and rear. After moving through the woodland between the Chattanooga road and Dyer's farm house, I reached a large field extending northward to some wooded ravines and heights.

The 58th North Carolina, moved with the brigade about 3:00 p.m.in the direction of Chattanooga. The 58th was on the right, 5th Kentucky on the left and eight companies of the 63rd Virginia in the center. However, the brigade was soon moved to the left to relieve General Anderson's Brigade. The 58th moved from a thicket toward the enemy's lines under heavy fire, to within 15 paces of the Federals. The Federals called out as friends and the attack was broken off. This gave the Yankees time to recover, and take up positions on the ridge. The 58th North Carolina fell back, according to French, exposing his left flank. The 63rd was then subjected to "enfilading fire from the enemy." Several of the officers and men were killed and wounded, and the battle raged until sundown, when the Federals broke off the engagement according to James Milton French's official report.

About 3:30 p.m. Longstreet ordered Prestons' division to go through Kershaw's ranks and attack the southern slope, Horseshoe Ridge, of Snodgrass Hill. Kelly and the 58th was on the left, Archibald Gracie and his Alabama brigade were on the right. When these brigades reached the front lines, they were intermingled. They marched forward, "as on parade," without firing until on the terrace in front of Federal General Brannan's Division, less than 40 paces away in the open. The Federals were protected by fieldworks, fallen trees, and other debris, and yet they traded shot for shot for over an hour.

Captain Isaac Bailey later wrote that the 58th North Carolina on the right, the 63rd Virginia in the center and the 5th Kentucky on the left, in that order, moved up in line of battle. The left of their line rested on the Chattanooga road. The Federals they faced had already repelled at least seven Confederate assaults. Bailey continued:

The approach to these ridges was along spurs and were ridges intersected ridges and through intervening depressions or hollows, all more or less wooded, but more open and exposed opposite the right of the brigade. One of the assaults had been male by General Anderson's brigade. Before we could reach him in such a way as to successfully relive, he had been repulsed The line being again formed, the Fifty-eighth North Carolina, which was on the right, moved with steadiness through this comparatively open space till the extreme right arrived within ten or twelve feet of the enemy. The line of the brigade formed with the line of the enemy an angle of perhaps 83 to 24 degrees, the right of the Fifty-eighth being at the angle. After exchanging fire with the enemy for about one and three-fourths of an hour, we attempted to dislodge him by assault, and for this purpose the Fifty-eighth North Carolina was transferred from the right to the left of the line, and moved forward, swinging somewhat to the right. When we arrived at the base of the hill, the enemy was hear to cry: "We surrender! We surrender!" Colonel John H. Kelly... immediately stepped to the front, two horses having been shot from under him within the past few minutes, and called upon the officer who seemed to be in command and demanded that if he proposed to surrender he should lay down his arms.

When told to lay down their guns, the Yankees began firing on the Rebs. Kelly's Brigade was within 40 yards. In a postwar letter to the Confederate Veteran, a Federal soldier, who was there reported that the Federals thought the Southerners were surrendering. The brigade fell back in the confusion, but was soon reinforced by Trigg's Brigade, and the combined force captured 249 Federals, which were sent to the rear. Preston gave credit to Trigg's and Kelly's brigades for capturing the 22nd Michigan, the 89th Ohio and part of the 21st Ohio during the battle. Colonel Hiram Hawkins of the 5th Kentucky was credited with capturing "two colonels, one lieutenant colonel, a number of company officers" and 249 prisoners. This crediting Trigg with captures made by the valiant actions of Kelly's and Gracies' Brigades seems to have caused a great deal of resentment in the 58th North Carolina and 63rd Virginia toward their future comrades of the 54th Virginia, as well as the 5th Kentucky.

William Preston's report continued:

...I then directed Colonel Kelly to form his brigade on the left of Gracie, and to change direction to the right as he advanced. The owner of the farm, John Dyer, one of my gunners, gave me a most accurate and valuable description of the local topography, and I directed Kelly to cover and protect Gracie's right. Whilst bringing Kelly into position, Gracie's brigade disappeared in the wood, advancing against the battery hill. I ordered Captain Blackburn, my volunteer Aid-de-Camp, to follow and ascertain from General Gracie by what authority he had moved.... Gracie replied that he had been ordered to advance by ...Kershaw, who was in the ravine just beyond the field. The movement was slightly premature, as Kelly was not formed, but I at once ordered his brigade to oblique to the right again, so as to press toward the slope of the hill in the rear, while Gracie was attacking in front... Gracie's brigade advanced between four and five o'clock, and Kelly moved about

ten minutes afterwards to assail the second hill on the ridge, 300 or 400 hundred yards west of the battery hill. I ordered him to change direction obliquely to the right, which was promptly done, in a few minutes, the brigade passed beyond the troops halted on the left of Kershaw's brigade, in the ravine, and engaged the enemy on the ridge, [300-400] yards beyond. Then a desperate combat ensued, the hostile forces being not more than thirty or forty yards apart. Kelly gained the hill after a bloody struggle, and the enemy vainly sought to dislodge him from it. Just as I first formed and moved Kelly into action, I met Major-General Hindman and staff, on the summit of the hill, near Dyer's field. The General, though suffering from a contusion in the neck, from a fragment of shell, remained in the saddle.... I instructed him [Capt. Harvey Jones] to inform Gracie that the hill must be held at all hazards, and that I would send Colonel Trigg to his support in a few minutes. Soon after Colonel Kelly sent me word, by Lieutenant McDaniel, that he could not hold the hill without succor, and I gave him a similar response. This was about the period of the heaviest fire, and I rode forward to where Colonel Kelly was engaged on the hill, and Lieutenant McDaniel brought him to me. I reiterated the order, and the assurance of Trigg's speedy arrival, passed on to the right, where I met General Gracie. He reported his ammunition was almost exhausted, and was withdrawing his men to replenish his cartridge-boxes. In the meantime General Buckner had sent me Colonel Trigg's brigade, which, advancing in double quick time, arrived at a critical moment, while the battle was raging fiercely. One of Trigg's regiments went to the support of General Gracie, while the remainder of the brigade was ordered to form on the left of Kelly, and to attack the enemy on the ridge. This fresh brigade, moving over the troops halted in the valley below, assaulted with great ardor the enemy on the left of Kelly, and quickly carried the ridge. The fresh and strengthened line of fire from this fine com- mand reanimated our men, and disheartened the enemy, who relinquished their first position, and fell back to a second ridge, occupied by a strong force behind fieldworks. A momentary lull ensued.... I sent, at this time for Colonel Kelly, who reported in person, and informed me that the enemy in his front seemed in confusion. I directed him to use his discretion and press the advantage by advancing as far as practicable, with Trigg wheeling to the right toward the declivity of the battery hill, stretching towards Chatta nooga. It was now moonlight, and Kelly, returning to his command, after a few minutes absence from it, the fire reopened, and continuing for a short time, ceased. It was the last fire of the day, and closed the battle.

Isaac Bailey of the 58th continued:

After a desperately contested fight from 3:30 p.m. to nearly nightfall, we succeeded in gaining the hill from which the enemy made three or four unsuccessful attempts to dislodge us by assault. However, owing to the conformation of the ground, the 58th North Carolina was exposed to a galling fire from the front and on both flanks, the left flanking company being within ten or twelve feet of the enemy. In this action the regiment lost about half of its numbers by official report of Colonel Kelly, commanding the brigade. Company A, Captain Toby, started on the charge with 34 muskets and reached the top of the hill with only 12, losing 22. In conjunction with Colonel R. C. Trigg, 54th Virginia, commanding another brigade, we captured two regiments of the enemy, which surrendered to Colonel Trigg during the temporary absence of Colonel Kelly, commanding our brigade. As the column commenced moving with the prisoners a volley was fired into our ranks causing a good deal of confusion, it then being dark....

The gallantry shown at Chickamauga would earn Kelly a general's commission. "*Nothing in this battle, marked with gallantry so frequently that it became commonplace, surpassed the courage of these two brigades[Kelly's and Gracie's] as they watched their ranks thin minute by minute and*

still doggedly refused to yield an inch of ground. Glenn Tucker related, that Turchin thought "only new troops could accomplish such a wonderful feat."

Thomas, a Federal division commander, was not beaten but was surrounded and could not attack and could only hope to retreat in darkness. The assault at Horseshoe Ridge of Snodgrass Hill was comparable to Pickett's and Pettigrew's Charges on Cemetery Ridge at Gettysburg. Captain Isaac Bailey recounted some of the casualties of the 58th thusly:

Early in the action Lieutenant Colonel Edmund Kirby, while gallantly cheering his men, fell pierced by four bullets. Major Dula was wounded early in the engagement. Colonel Palmer, the only field officer with the regiment, was here wounded, but sill continued in command, with his senior Captain, Isaac H. Bailey, to aid him as Major and Lieutenant Colonel, after which Captain Bailey fell almost mortally wounded, left leg broken, shot through the right side and one ear almost severed from his head. Thirteen commissioned officers, including the Adjutant, had been killed and wounded, two-thirds of the right flanking company, Captain Toby's, having been killed and wounded, and about seven tenths of the left flanking company, Captain Bailey's.-

The Confederate victory at the Battle of Chickamauga was complete by about 7 p.m. on September 20, 1863. Kelly's Brigade's strength entering the battle was 876. Its reported casualties were: killed 62; wounded 238, missing and presumed captured 29, total 329 for a 37.55% loss according to the official report. The 58th lost 46 killed, 114 wounded and one missing, for 161 casualties, over 50% of the regiment's pre-battle strength, and sustained 49% of the total casualties for the brigade. The 63rd Virginia lost at least 19 killed, 28 wounded and one missing, while the 5th Kentucky suffered 14 killed, 75 wounded, one captured and one missing according to Colonel Hawkins' report. Despite the official report, totals on muster rolls of the regiments involved indicate the brigade lost at least 79 killed, 217 wounded, and three captured or missing for a total of 319, ten fewer than initial reports indicate, but higher levels of killed in actions. The 58th North Carolina camped on the battlefield the nights of September 20-22, perhaps surrounded by their dead. Fatigue details were assigned to dig graves, others were on picket, while others had the odious duty of carrying the dead to their graves. William Preston was not oblivious to the aftermath of the battle inhis October 31, 1863 battle report. On September 21, Preston order the burial of the dead. The hill Gracie's men had assaulted was afire from the musketry which had sparked the dry brush along that ridge. Many bodies were burned beyond recognition. As a result of the battle of Chickamagua, those units engaged were asked, by the Confederate authorities, to select those who had been most gallant in the battle.

Brigadier General Preston remarked in his official report about the Battle of Chickamauga:

The troops of my division had never been engaged in any important battle, having been stationed during the war chiefly in Southwestern Virginia and East Tennessee, to defend their mountain passes from invasion. Held in reserve while the conflict raged around them for a day and a half, they manifested a noble ardor to share in its dangers and it glories. Though long in service and not aspiring to the title of veterans, I felt strong confidence in their patriotism, courage and discipline. The hour for the trial of all these great qualities arrived; every hope was justified, and I feel assured that both officers and men, won honorable and enduring renown upon the memorable field of Chickamauga.

Colonel John B. Palmer went back to Western North Carolina to recover from his wounds, and while there, received orders to assume command of the Department of Western North Carolina. Palmer's headquarters was at Asheville and he remained in Western North Carolina until the end of the war. Palmer was relieved by General James Green Martin in mid August, 1864. Despite this relief, Palmer did not return to the 58th. President Davis called on the Army of Tennessee quartered on the summit above Chattanooga on October 9, 1863 and inspected the soldiers. Davis rode along the entire line, in range of Union cannon at Chattanooga, below. Glenn Tucker, author of Chickamauga: Bloody Battle in the West, wrote in his chapter on Horseshoe Ridge that the 58th North Carolina, recruited from Northwest North Carolina and led by Colonel Palmer was reviewed by the generals. North Carolina Governor Vance had supplied Longstreet's corps with new gray uniforms, while the 58th was in rags and barefoot. The 58th had passed out of state and were orphaned and not given new uniforms. Kelly's Brigade was ordered not to cheer as Governor Vance and the dignitaries passed in review, so they took off their ragged caps and waved them to the generals, who were touched by the gesture.

James Clark, of the 63rd Virginia, wrote his wife Martha on February 15, 1864 from Dalton, Georgia: "*We have had more reviews in the past month than I ever saw. I can't see what good they do, have us every trotting round for them to look at. Every Gen. that has a wife & she come to see him must have us paraded round for her to look at.*" After Chickamauga Colonel Kelly was transferred to a command a cavalry division in Wheeler's cavalry corps. The 58th and 60th North Carolina, 54th and 63rd Virginia regiments were permanently made a brigade under Brigadier General Alexander Welch Reynolds, "Old Gauley" of Clark County, Virginia, in Buckner's division, Hardee's corps on November 12, 1863.

The 58th spent most of October and November 1863 on the heights above Chattanooga as part of Reynold's Brigage. Speculation about the command's duties include construction of breastworks and supporting artillery units bombarding Chattanooga below. Reynolds' Brigade was recalled from Buckner's division shortly after it departed Missionary Ridge for Knoxville and was somewhat in limbo when the Battle of Missionary Ridge began. Reynolds' Brigade was deployed in a thin line on Missionary Ridge, with no reserve according to Captain George W. F. Harper. Major General U. S. Grant, commanding the Federal Army of the Cumberland, ordered his men to attack. It was an unlikely assault, the Confederates dug in on the heights made it seem like Pickett's charge with roles reversed. Reynolds' Brigade, assigned to Stevenson's division had been on the Southern left on the 21st, was sent to reinforce General Patrick Cleburne's division. The brigade held that place for three days, and repulsed attacks from blue coats under General Phil Sheridan. James Lee McDonough in his excellent work, Chattanooga - A Death Grip on the Confederacy noted that early on November 23, Bragg ordered Cleburne to reinforce Longstreet at Knoxville. By noon most of Johnson's division, except Reynolds' Brigade, was moving to Loudon on the Western and Atlantic rail road.

Some Confederates were deployed in rifle pits at the foot of Missionary Ridge, the rest on the crest of the ridge. Reynolds' boys in the rifle pits were, according to Captain Harper, "annoyed by the premature explosion of the shells from our batteries on the ridge in the rear, firing upon the enemy in front. A veteran of Company H, with a grim sense of humor, suggested to his Captain that the command occupy the other side of the breastwork--a brisk musketry fire then coming from the enemy. The suggestion was not adopted. Heavy lines of Federal infantrymen ap- proached the Confederate entrenchments and confusion reigned in the Southern ranks. Reynolds' brigade, posted between Deas' and Bate's Brigades were ordered to the top of the mountain as the Federals began their approach. Reynolds' men were intended to fill a gap at the crest of the ridge between Bate's and Anderson's brigades. The reason for withdrawal, however, was unknown to the men through whom they passed, adding confusion to the situation. Some of

Reynolds soldiers passed through Colonel Jesse J. Finley's Florida Brigade and recent comrades of the 54th, while scaling the heights, which caused confusion just as the battle began. Reynolds' mixed brigade, did not fix themselves in the 150-yard wide breach in the Confederate line on the top of Missionary Ridge. Captain James Garrity's Alabama Artillery Battery filled the gap alone, and they had no support. Reynolds' regiments were deployed across the Crutchfield road behind Bate's Division, over a quarter mile from the breach in the line they were supposed to fill. The Confederate line was breached in Anderson's Brigade, not in theunplugged position Reynolds should have been in. Had Reynolds' been closer to Anderson than Bates perhaps their reputation would have been less bloodied. General Bate sent Major James Thomas Weaver of the 60th North Carolina to try to reinforce Anderson's Brigade and to counter attack. Reynolds' boys ran more than a quarter mile and reached Bate's right flank, but they were too late, Federals were pouring through. Bate reported "Union troops turned our guns upon us and opened a fire of musketry from our right and rear. This...caused my right to give back." Blue coated soldiers took Bate's position and were "rapidly enveloping [his] division." George Washington Harper wrote, "*General John C. Breckinridge, in command at this point, when the troops were withdrawn about midnight enquired for the regiment then filing into the road, and being told, raised his hat and complimented the 'Tar Heels' very highly on their part in the fight.*"

About midnight, November 25-26, Reynolds' withdrew toward Dalton, Georgia. Reynolds' men were accused by Braxton Bragg for the Confederate rout at Missionary Ridge. Their mistake, however, was in not informing their comrades of their orders. Another problem seems to havebeen the inability to communicate orders to the men responsible for their implementation. James Clark, Company F, 63rd Virginia wrote: "*The yankees did not follow us but a short distance. We drove them back & tooka good many prisoners.*" In Clark's estimation Reynolds' Brigade quickly regained their composure, and reorganized into an effective force again. The Confederate line was breached in Anderson's Brigade defense zone, not in the unplugged position Reynolds should have been in. Had Reynolds' position been closer to Anderson than Bate perhaps their reputation would have been less bloodied. General Bate sent Major Weaver with Reynolds' Brigade to try to reinforce Anderson's Brigade--to counter attack. When Reynolds' men realized the error they ran 500 yards north to Bate's right flank. They were too late, Sheridan's Federals poured through. Instead of facing tired Federal lines, they found Yanks on an adrenaline high, renewing the attack. Reynolds' Brigade, led by Major James Thomas Weaver of the 60th North Carolina, fell apart, with the troops running to the rear in bewilderment. Bate wrote, "*Union troops turned our guns upon usand opened a fire of musketry from our right and rear. This... caused my right to give back.*" Federals seized the summit on Bate's left and rapidly enveloped the division.

Reynolds' report written on December 15, 1863 at Dalton, Georgia, noted that he had moved under orders from Anderson. He described the brigade's action: *At 7 o'clock on the morning of the 25th, I joined my Brigade posted in the rifle pits at the foot of Missionary Ridge & covering a space of some fourteen-hundred yards on the left of Gen Patton Anderson's Division. At 10. o'clock A'M the enemy attacked my line. Permitting them to approach to within 200 yards of the rifle pits, I ordered fire to be opened on them, and after an action of about one hour, they were driven back with considerable loss & did not again attempt to force my position. In this short action, the officers & men of my Command, without exception, conducted them-selves wit coolness & gallantry. At 2 o'clock P.M. I received orders to fall back from the rifle pits to the crest of Missionary Ridge, which I did by alternate Companies, deployed as skirmishers, and formed my line of battle on the ground designated. I will here state, that some of the Companies of the 60th N.C. Regt. which were on the extreme left of the line, in moveing up the ridge, were obliged, on account of peculiar topography of the ground, to oblique somewhat too far to the right and on reaching the top of the Ridge, found themselves separated from their command, & owing to the difficulty of joining their own Regt. they remained in line with Gen. Bate's Brigade. A short time after I had taken my position on the crest of the Ridge, I observed the Enemy advancing to the attack in three lines of battle. There being two pieces of artillery posted on the left of my line, I directed them to open fire on the enemy, which was done with excellent effect. The enemy having reached our abandoned rifle pits, I was directed by Gen Anderson Comd'g the Division, who was then present with my Brigade, to cause the guns to be depressed, & open on them with canister. This was instantly done, & so terrible was the effect of this fire on the dense lines of the Enemy, that it caused them to falter for an instant, but closing up their ranks, they again advanced to the charge. In a short time the enemy came within range of musketry, & my Brigade opened on them in fine Style and as they advanced rapidly up the face of the ridge my fire & that of the troops on my right, was so severe that for a time the enemy were checked . Unfortunately at this juncture, when every heart beat high with hope, & victory was almost within our grasp, the troops posted in the rifle pits on the right of my Brigade broke & fled in... disorder. The enemy seeing the advantage that must result from this disgraceful & inexplicable panic on the part of hitherto invincible troops, at once crossed the hill on my right on opened a heavy fire on my lines, completely enfilading my position; This of course rendered necessary an immediate change of position. I therefore changed front to rear on the left Battalion. My troops performing this delicate & dangerous manoeuver under the fire of the enemy in admirable style & without the least confusion or irregularity. As soon as my new line was formed I opened fire by Company, and continued to engage the enemy until I found that the troops on my left had also given way, and the enemy occupied the Ridge on my left & now rear. Having now no supports whatever, I considered it more prudent to withdraw my small, but gallant Brigade than to remain, with the almost certainty of capture. I therefore retired (it was now dusk) by the right flank down the ridge, sheltering my troops as much as possible from the fire of the enemy who by this time had opened our own captured guns upon me from two different & commanding points on the ridge. Learning that Genl. Bates & the troops on my left were proceeding towards the Pontoon bridge at Birds Mill, I move in the direction of our extreme right, where I yet heard firing. I did this on principle, that in the absence of orders, it was my duty to go to the support of those yet engaged. On reaching the road leading to Shallow Ford Chickamauga River, I received orders to conduct my com mand to Shallow Ford Bridge & report to Genl Mannigault, who would place my Command in position. I reached this point about 10 o'clock & after remaining some two hours, took up the line of march for Chickamauga. It is with no little pleasure & pride that I am enabled to say that both in the riflepits at the foot of the Ridge & during the engagement on the ridge, all the officers & me of my Brigade acted with the gallantry & coolness of vet erans. Throughout all the movements none left the ranks, but obeyed every order promptly & without the slightest confusion or disorder. I am indebted to my Regt. Comd'rs Col Hardy 58 & 60 N.C. Regts. Lt. Col. Wade Comd'g 54 Va Regt. & Maj French Comd'g 63rd Va Regt, for a hearty cooperation & much assistance in all my movements during the day. Maj. French was struck by a fragment of a shell, but though painfully wounded, refused to leave the field until the action was over. Maj. Weaver of the 60. N.C. Regt. & who was in command of my extreme left, also deserve honorable mention for conspicuous gallantry in conducting the retreat of his command from the Riflepits to the top of the Ridge. He was the last man to leave the trenches & displayed an intrepidity & in different to danger seldom surpassed. Capt. A. T. Stewart 58th N.C. & Lieut. Jacob Anderson Comd'g Co. "F" 54th Va Regt. acted with great gallantry, encouraging & Setting examples of heroism to their men. Richard B. Ally, Color bearer, Srgt. Wm. McKinnon & Private A. M. Chumbly Co. "F." all of 54 Va Regt, & Sergt Dr. W. H. Estes 58 N.C. were conspicuous for bravery. Co. "F" 54th Va. Regt. particularly distinguished itself as sharp shooters, performing most effective service.*

Casualties for the 58th North Carolina were heavy in the loss at Missionary Ridge. Many men were taken prisoner, some deliberately. The 58th appears on return of casualties of General Stevenson's Division, for the period November 24-25, 1863, but no number was given by Reynolds. An organizational table for Buckner's Division, Army of Tennessee, made in just before Missionary Ridge, for the Chattanooga-Ringgold campaign, shows that Reynolds' Brigade was composed of the 58th North Carolina nominally under Colonel John B. Palmer, the 60th North Carolina under Major James T. Weaver, the 54th Virginia under Lieutenant Colonel John J. Wade and the 63rd Virginia was led by Major James Milton French. December 1863 - September 1864.

The Atlanta Campaign

General Joseph Eggleston Johnston took the helm of the despondent Army of Tennessee on December 27, 1863. The despised Braxton Bragg was gone and the Army of Tennessee quickly adopted Johnston as their own "Uncle Joe." Johnston understood the Army of Tennessee needed time to recover, to resupply, to train for the unavoidable battles to come.

The Mobile Register reported the Army of Tennessee had no "barefooted soldiers" for the first time in its existence. Johnston was also busy gathering supplied to sustain his soldiers in the spring campaign. He was, in fact, gathering all the Confederate soldiers that could be spared outside Virginia. The winter quarters for the Army of Tennessee were near Dalton,about 100 miles north of Atlanta. Reynolds' Virginians called their side of the brigade area "Camp Extra Billy Smith" for the recently elected governor of the Virginia, the Tar Heels called their side Camp Zeb Vance after their state's popular wartime governor. It was a time to heal the wounds and live down the embarrassment of Missionary Ridge. Reynolds' men remained relatively sedate until February 1864.

Disease was the worst enemy of the 58th North Carolina this winter--several died of disease in the first quarter of 1864. Disease had been a major factor in the regiment's readiness when it was stationed in East Tennessee and was again effecting the 58th. It had a depressing effect on morale. Age would play an important factor in the battles to come in the hot Southern summer. After all, these were mountain men, used to a colder climate than the Georgia boys who were about them. Dalton, about 100 miles north of Atlanta, was on the rail line and in direct line from Chattanooga. Johnston remained in Dalton despite its military disadvantages, because he did not want to give up the people to Federal occupation. There were conflicting reports on the morale of the troops at Dalton in the winter of 1863-4. Some newspaper men commented that the Army of Tennessee was completely demoralized and another countered the charge with the idea that they were "*hungry for revenge.*"

Many of these reports were no doubt propaganda issued by editors and were intended to prevent panic in the civilian populace. On February 25, 1864, dateline Dalton, Georgia, Brigadier General Reynolds reported on a skirmish with Federal forces at Rocky Face Ridge or Stoney Side, about eight miles from Dalton. Reynolds reported that his engagements had been entirely successful, and reported casualties as follows: The 58th and 60th North Carolina regiments took 24 wounded three mortally, the 54th Virginia had twelve wounded and the 63rd Virginia sustained only five wounded. The muster report of Company G, reports that the Federals were making advances on Tunnel Hill, near the rail line in mid-February 1864. Stevenson's Division was ordered for their camp site, just west of Dalton into action. The command marched on the night of February 23, and arrived near the "demonstration" on the 24th. The brigade was not put into the line of battle until the 25th, and according to members of the regiment, "whooped the Yankees". James Clark of the 63rd Virginia, wrote on February 28, 1864, *"Our Brigade has been in front all the time. We lost about 40 killed & wounded out of the Brigade."* General Alexander Reynolds, in a letter to his sister from Dalton, Georgia on February 29, 1864, wrote:

The Battle of 'Stone Side' was my own fight, I was in supreme command. I selected the field and my troops alone gained the victory. My command consisted of my Brigade, and 3 Regt. of Gen Clayton's Alabama troops, in all 2500 men and opposed by Granger's Army Corps, Yanks, about 7000 men. The fight began about 9 o'c. a.m. our skirmishers having engaged them about 6 o'c. a.m. The enemy advanced in 3 lines of battle with great confidence expected to overwhelm me at 10 o'c. the battle raged furiously all along my line. The thunder of cannon & clatter of musketry was...deafening, yet our boys stood fast and pounded in their volleys with terrible effect.... I ordered an advance. Shouts went up which rent the air and the Yankees broke. They soon reformed and again came to the charge. We met them again and drove them, being reinforced they made their third and heaviest attack. The lines swayed to and fro for some time. I rode forward and ordered a charge and this line entirely routed them. I never felt so glorious in my life. It was a complete victory and thank God. I won it, even my fair horse, "Gauley" seemed to feel and enjoy it. I am proud of my brave boys.... We are all (my brigade) are very anxious to get to Western Va. My veterans would show you all in that country how to whip Yankees. I think that I could clean out the country.... I hope we will succeed if I could get there....

Most of Reynolds' soldiers were pleased with their brigadier. Discontent still pervaded the 54th Virginia, but for the time being this dissatisfaction was dormant. The Virginians of the brigade also yearned to return to the Old Dominion, but such was not to be. Most of the Tar Heels seem to have been content to be in Georgia. It was all a matter or perception, all of Reynolds' mountaineers were closer to home in Georgia than they would have been in the Army of Northern Virginia. During the fight at Rocky Face Ridge, Reynolds was in overall command of his own brigade, Edmund Winston Pettus' Brigade, Hotchkiss' Artillery battalion and Company B, Hawkins' battalion of sharpshooters. Pettus would later command the Virginia remnant of Reynolds' Brigade in the last days of the war in North Carolina. George Washington Harper was relatively quite in his memoir about Rocky Face Ridge, only noting, *"A number of casualties occurred in the Fifty-eighth. Among the killed was James Inglis, Sergeant-Major, a Scotchman by birth, whose death was deeply regretted by his comrades."*

Lieutenant Poindexter "Pine" Blevins of Ashe County, North Carolina wrote his family from "*Camp of the 58th and 60th V.I. Regts, Near Dalton, Ga.*" on March 27, 1864. Most of his letter was devoted to religious discussions, but did give his opinion of the military situation. Blevins wrote:

...our great army is appearently still at this time, owing to the bad condition of the Roads has prevented any ground movement of these western armys, but the weather is very pleasant at this time, and no doubt but a few days will soon. Begin or renew the Bloody strife. My opinion is that the Yankees is laying in large suplies at Chattanooga to support their vast army in their attempt to drive Gen Johnston's army back and if successfull to feed them as they advance toward Atlanta. I trust and pray that disappointment and defeat, my over shadow Gen Grants paths, plans and undertakings, and demoralls his army in their attmept to trample and subjugate the people of the confederate states. Barbarity and cruelty continues to follow their whole line of march as the helpless women and children is witness against them, that is caught inside of the Enemys lines in his advance, his last attact on Dalton did not leave him guiltless of unhumine cruelty, and such I fear will follow his whole line of March if peradventure he should be successfull in his plans and undertaking. May the Blest Lord in his infinite Merceis cause us as a nation to humble our selves in the very dust of humility so that such may not be our fate - May His cause prosper and true Christian faith grow stronger and stronger and true and genuine religion may cover the whole land of America as the waters cover the chanels of the great deep. If this was the case them you could have the pleasure of meeting with long absent friends, to wit, Brother, and Husbands, poor unthankfull Beings as I am, I truly desire if it is the Lords will to live to see such a day come, that I can have the great pleasure of meeting with good Christians at the Baptist Chapel, on such Beutiful Sabbath as to day is insted of being called out in the field for inspection of arms and accoutrements the deathly weapons of war. which has allways been mortifying to me to have such duties to perform on the Holy Sabbath day but it is a rule and a custom of war and we have to obey all orders of our Gen'z....

One of Reynolds' Virginia soldiers commented about the winter of 1863-4: "*Our fare here was of the poorest kind; viz: stale bread and fat bacon and sometimes not much of that.*" Another wrote his parents in Grayson County, Virginia on April 1, 1864. In this letter he noted that his daily ration was « pound of bacon or a pound of beef and 1« pounds ofcorn meal. He also noted that they had "*draud one days rations of stuff tha called it flour but tha was mistakin it was chaf or wheat ground and was not bolted. It was nuff to take the worms out of a gaspin chickens throat.*"

Those present were reported to be in good spirits, had good training, good clothing. The only category not categorized as "good" was arms. It was noted on the muster rolls that many muskets were damaged. It would appear that most of the regiment was supplied with .69 caliber muskets this late in the war. Muskets were supplemented with captured Federal rifles, shotguns, and with some weapons manufactured in Greensboro, North Carolina. Armaments were irreplaceable and this regiment debited a soldiers pay for careless loss of ordnance. The 63rd Virginia's Captain Clark noted on May 1, 1864, that none "of our boys was sick." It was noted on postwar rosters for subelements of the brigade that they were in skirmishes and "partial engagements almost daily in the early part of May 1864." This was true of the entire Georgia Campaign, the fighting did not cease at any time for more than a week.

During the first days of May, 1864, the last days the regiment would spent in Dalton, Georgia, an event occurred which made a lasting impression on the men of the Army of Tennessee and the 58th. On this sunny spring day, 14 men were executed for desertion, eight of these men were from the 58th North Carolina. One of these men, Jacob Austin of Union County, North Carolina was a conscript assigned to Company E. He was forced into the 58th on Christmas Eve 1863 and deserted 28 days later. He was captured, court-martialed and sentenced to death. Many soldiers did not feel these sentences were fair, as many others were pardoned for similar offenses, but some officers felt that a show of this kind of necessary to stem the tide of unauthorized absences. Other soldiers were sentenced to extra duty, some humiliation, or loss of pay. These executions had the desired effect, at least in the 58th North Carolina--desertion virtually ended in the regiment. Of course, by May 1864, most of those who remained were hard core supporters of the Southern cause or those with an over developed sense of duty. In fairness to those who had been pardoned or received light sentences, the eight men of the 58th who were executed were reported to be strong Union men and had engaged in partisan warfare against the Confed- erate Government when they were not in ranks. Those pardoned or who received light sentences were considered men who would return to duty, but just needed some time at home. Perception was everything at the court-martials held in Reynolds' Brigade.

On May 7, 1864 the Army of Tennessee again focused on the business at hand - war! Sherman again advanced on the Army of Tennessee at Dalton, Georgia, and the Army of Tennessee engaged Federal Forces at Resaca, with Reynolds' Brigade in the thick of the battle suffering many killed, wounded and completely disabled for the duration of the war, many disabled for the duration of their lives. Major George Washington Finley Harper wrote in the history of the 58th North Carolina that the Brigade suffered terrible losses in the battles around Atlanta, but cannot give complete details as he was wounded in early May. He goes further and says that Reynolds' Brigade was consolidated with Brown's Tennessee Brigade under General Joseph P. Palmer of Murfreesboro, Tennessee.

On May 9, 1864 the 58th participated in the battle of Rocky Face Ridge. Rocky Face Ridge, a 500 foot rock cliff, was defended by General Stevenson's Division which included Reynolds' Brigade and the 58th. Federal Brigadier General Charles G. Harker's Brigade assaulted the summit, and reached the top, in single file progression. Harker's men got to the gap between Stevenson and Cheatham. Stevenson reported that the fight was obstinate and bloody, but the Federals could not capture the crest of the Ridge. Union losses in the engagement were 837, with Confederate losses estimated at 600. It has been reported that Sherman decided that the Ridge could not be taken without severe loss of life. He returned to his plan of flanking maneuvers and forced the Southern Boys off the mountain by tactics. In 1913 Calvin Livesay wrote "*Early in the spring of '64 we began to move toward Atlanta fighting more or less all the way. We had quite a battle at Resaca. Breast works were thrown up and we had a lively time. Here Johnston was driven back....and General Reynolds wounded. We were now put in Brown's Brigade of Tennesseans. We never saw General Reynolds any more.*" [Livesay was mistaken, Reynolds was wounded at New Hope Church]. Resaca was a depot town on the Western and Atlantic Railway. As prelude to the engagement of May 13-14, Federal General Thomas advanced on Johnston's center at Dalton. He was joined by General Schoffield from Cleveland, Tennessee, and attempted to flank Johnston and take his vital supply and communications center at Resaca. This maneuver forced the Southern boys from Dalton back to Resaca on May 14. Confederates under Johnston had been busy over the winter preparing a network of entrenchments from Dalton to Atlanta. Johnston was painfully aware that Sherman would have to make a serious mistake for a Confederate military victory to occur in Georgia. He saw his and The Army of Tennessee's mission was to hold the Federals in check until the Northern election in November.

Reynolds' Brigade in Stevenson's Division was in the fore of the assault led by Federal Brigadier General A. S. Williams' and his XX Corps, and secured positions that were their objectives. Stevenson, to the left of Lieutenant General A. P. Stewart, informed Stewart that he would attack precisely at 4 p.m. At 6:00 p.m., Johnston counter attacked on the Right with Hoods' troops, supported by one of Hardee's Divisions, of which Stevenson's Division and Reynolds' Brigade were one, and General William H. T. Walker's division. Hood advanced about 2 miles and was in position to do damage to the Federal flank, when General Williams was sent, just in time, to repel Hood. There was some confusion in passing orders, Hood issuing some, and having Johnston countermand them. It appears that the confusion in communications through the thick brush may have led to the Southern defeat at Resaca. This was Johnston's only true defeat in the Atlanta Campaign. Stevenson's divisions bore the brunt of the Federal assault columns. Federal soldiers advanced to within 30 paces, but Stevenson's line held. Sherman flanked to Lay's ferry, about 3 miles below Resaca, and crossed the Oostanaula River on two pontoon bridges. Confederate losses at Rocky Face Ridge and Resaca were about 2,800 of their 67,000 man force. Federal losses have been reported to have been 2,997 of their 104,000 men. Johnston's Army fell back to pre-determined positions at Cassville, Georgia, setting up the next engagement. Bromfield Ridley, chronicler of the Army of Tennessee wrote:

...There was one place, though, where Sherman, had he been the able general many supposed, would have taken some of Johnston's glory from him. The only time he ever got Johnston apparently in a 'nine hole' was at Resaca on May 15, 1864."

Johnston had taken up positions on high ground at Cassville on May 18. His Corps commanders, Hood and Polk, thought it folly. He gave up the ground, "*a step which I have regretted ever since.*" His men fell back through Allatoona Pass on May 19. The 58th North Carolina participated in the battle, as is evidenced by casualties reported in the muster rolls. Since the regiment was assigned to Hardee's Corps, it may safely assumed that they were on the Southern left, near Wheeler's Cavalry. Sherman had ordered his army to attempt another flanking movement. As with so many battles in the "Western Theatre", there is no contemporary information as to the regiment's specific participation. The Army of Tennessee crossed the Etowah River during the night of May 19-20. On May 25, 1864, the pursuing Sherman had crossed the Etowah River and was travelling cross country toward Marietta, Georgia via Dallas, Georgia, with 100,000 soldiers and 20 days worth of supplies. The Southerners were entrenched, in a heavy thicket, with General Hood's main line centered at New Hope Church a few miles northeast of Dallas. Polk's Corps was closer to Dallas. The Federals advanced toward the Confederate lines, that were so well concealed that they may not have known were there. Federals were allowed to reach within 25 to 30 paces before they were cut down with a thunderstorm of fire from the concealed Confederates. Johnston had ordered Stewarts Division to form a line of battle about 5 p.m. This line was one man deep, and held their position against a three man deep federal advance. If the line had broken, then Stevenson's Division would have been completely lost. Stevenson was to the rear of Stewart on another road, facing another Federal assault. Federal General Hooker reported 1665 killed or wounded, and was unable to recover many of them between the lines and in the brush. Stevenson's Division was saved again, and the Army of Tennessee was happy. During these engagements Reynolds' Brigade losttheir beloved leader at New Hope. General Reynolds was severely wounded. After New Hope that one Federal officer supposedly remarked that the "Rebels carried their breastworks with them." Carter Stevenson wrote of the Battle of New Hope Church: *Upon my arrival at New Hope church, I put my command in position on the right of General Stewart, and very soon thereafter the enemy assaulted him in force.... While in position near New Hope church, I regret to state that I lost the services of Brigadier-General Reynolds, who there received a painful, but I hope not a dangerous wound.*

On May 27, Federal General Howard led 14,000 Union troops against Hood, initiating the battle of Pickett's Mill. Hood's line held firm. Ridley recorded in 1898, that this battled was "another heartrending scene of death and destruction." Broomfield Ridley wrote of the affair, that the men saw the Atlanta Campaign as a chess game between Sherman and Johnston, with Johnston making the key moves and Sherman responding in bewilderment. Johnston was a master of the game, he had half the pieces of Sherman, was able to avoid a Federal checkmate for months. In a May 26, 1864 dispatch from E. M. McCook to Brigadier General W. L. Elliott, Chief of Cavalry, Department of the Cumberland [Federals], McCook notes that he took 13 prisoners, from the 58th North Carolina, 36th Georgia and 54th Virginia, Hood's corps, Reynolds and Cummings brigades. McCook said in his battle report *"I don't think they want to fight this side [west side] of the Chattahoochee."* Despite McCook's observation, skirmishing was constant for two days. On the May 27th Southern General Cleburne's division attacked Federal General McPherson at Dallas, Georgia. The 58th North Carolina was not involved in this heavy skirmish--it was recovering from the effects of New Hope Church. In the early days of June 1864, Sherman was busy with his drive to the Chattahoochee River. Johnston was busy trying to stop him with much skirmishing, again almost every day according to post war recollections. There was constant skirmishing, from Mid-May until Atlanta fell. A heavy toll was taken in the Army of Tennessee. The 63rd Virginia's James Clark's June 16 letter to Martha noted:

The enemy has been trying to flank us but we have foiled him in all his efforts. We have some fighting everyday. Yesterday had some strong shelling, not much damage done. The enemy don't seem disposed to fight but gain territory by strategy. Old Joe seems to have stopped him at least for a while as we are only a few miles nearer Marietta now than weeks ago... two of the regiment has been branded as deserters and received that punishment.... A few days before we left Dalton I saw 14 deserters shot. They were from the N.C. regiment that belongs to out Brigade. It was the worst sight I ever saw, too horible to think about. Yet some of them was not killed the first time & some of them not touched. Their cries was horrible in the extreme. Men were ordered up one at a time to put their guns close to their hearts or heads & fired. One poor fellow told them if they were going to kill him for God sake to do it & not shoot his flesh to pieces. They all seemed to be very much effected about their future; except one who believed there was no God & died firm in his belief.... I am afraid what Virginians is here will not hold the fair name of which Virginians has in the eastern army. One company of the 54 regt. went to the yankees a few nights ago, officers & all. They were from Floyd County... all but 3. They would not go.... The lice grows pretty large down here in the hot country.... Grass grows fine, good many ticks, lizzards, scorpions & green snakes.

On June 18 Johnston pulled back into a new line from the crest of Kennesaw Mountain to Olley's Creek. Hood's corps was to the right in the direction of Marietta, Lieutenant General Leonidas Polk's corps, (he was killed June 14), now commanded by General William W. Loring, was along the crest of Kennesaw Mountain and Hardee's Corps was blocking the road from the west to Marietta. The whole area settled into a siege. On June 22, 1864, Stevenson's division was ordered to charge the Federal positions near Mt. Zion Church. Captain Clark wrote on June 28 from Camp Hear Baptist, "*We drove them back to their fortifications found them strongly fortified & could not drive them any further.*"

Reynolds' brigade reached a point about 100 yards from the Federal breast works andcould go no further, nor go back. One soldier wrote, "*We were protected by a ravine & lay there until it got dark & came away. If the yankees had come on us we would have been compelled to surrender but they were too cowardly to come.*"

One of Reynolds' soldiers grumbled in a letter home, "*I think our Gen. ought to be sure what they are doing before they attempt to charge. We lost a good many men & gained nothing.*" Stevenson reported said it was the "*hottest place he ever saw.*" Stevenson served in many of themajor battles of the western theater. The Battle of Mt. Zion Church, also called Kolb's Farm in Federal reports, began on the morning of June 22.

Stevenson's men were routed. Johnston was angry with Hood for a poorly planned, disastrous attack which cost Reynolds' Brigade dearly. Federal losses were under 250, while Confederate casualties approached 1100. Sherman was determined to break the stalemate and destroy the Confederates. He attacked on June 27, 1864, and the Battle of Kennesaw Mountain began. The 58th, still in Hood's Corps, found itself this time in the Confederate Center, faced off against Thomas' Federals. Federal losses were about 3,000, while the Confederates only lost about 1,000 men killed and wounded. Reynolds' Brigade recovering from Mt. Zion Church, played only a very limited active roll in the battle of Kennesaw Mountain. The 58th North Carolina Wounds were slight, if any, as none of regiment have any notation of wounds received at Kennesaw Mountain.

One of Reynolds' Virginians noted on July 15, 1864 they had not been out of the sound of artillery fire since May 7. He also felt the food had improved, writing, "*We have been the best fed army I ever saw. It is not of the nicest king but plentie corn bread & bacon but we are lacking vegetables such as potatoes, cabbage,* tomatoes, etc." In this same letter to his father, Clark noted, "*The enemy seems to be resting on the other side which I suppose he is in great need. Johnson has contested every inch of ground from here to Dalton. The enemy has payed dearly for all territory he has gained.*"

In the early Summer of 1864, the beloved "Uncle Joe" Johnston was supplanted by Lieutenant General John Bell Hood. The news spread through the Army of Tennessee on the night of July 17 like wildfire. Johnston had been the object of partisan scheming in Richmond by President Davis, Hood, and Braxton Bragg.

Desertions which plagued much of the Army of Tennessee were not a major concern in the 58th, due in large part to the executions carried out on malefactors.

On July 20, 1864, Hood's Army of Tennessee disastrously attacked Sherman's Army. Casualties were high in the Confederate ranks. By July 22, the Army of Tennessee had been fully reorganized, General Hood then commanding. On the 22nd Hood ordered a second reckless attack on the Federals and was again repulsed. The Confederates fell back into Atlanta. The 58th was among the defenders, in the center of the defensive works. Several of the 58th's soldiers were reported in their service records as having been wounded, killed or captured "near Atlanta" in June, July and August 1864.

Specific regimental duties were not recorded, as with so many of the activities of the 58th. Some of the soldiers have items recorded in their records which give the modern reader some clues. Some were shot by snipers while on picket duty. Others were the unwilling recipients of Federal grape shot. A few just disappeared. The siege of Atlanta lasted until the end of August. Sherman's Army made a flanking march to the south of Atlanta toward Macon and threatened to cut Hood's Army off from the rest of the South. Memories of Vicksburg were clear to many in the Army of Tennessee. To meet the new challenge and avoid total disaster he abandoned Atlanta. The Federals occupied and burned the city on September 2, 1864. The fall of Atlanta was probably the single most disastrous event of the war for the Confederacy. It killed the peace movement in the North and gave Lincoln's reelection campaign the boost it needed.

During September 2-3, 1864 the Battle of Jonesboro, last of the Atlanta campaign, occurred and the 58th North Carolina was involved in the fight. Jonesboro, on the Macon Railway, was the last defense of Macon. The battle caused the Confederate to fall back to Lovejoy's Station.

Federal General Absalom Baird reported a third of his soldiers, engaged at Jonesboro were killed or wounded, "*thus attesting to the severity of the fight.*" The Reynolds Brigade were among his opponents and there is no reason to believe that the Southerners had it any easier. The Southern dead and wounded are unknown for the battle of Jonesboro, but appear to have been fewer than Federals have reported, but the number taken prisoner more than made up for the bloody casualties, except in the mind of those who might live to tell the terrible tale. After the evacuation of Atlanta Hood devised a scheme, with the blessing of President Davis, to recover the city. The President met with Hood and addressed his Army at Macon. The men of the 58th North Carolina were present for Davis' speech. Davis and Hood devised new tactics.

From Lovejoy's, the Army of Tennessee moved to the town of Palmetto on the Atlanta and Montgomery Railroad. The troops moved towards Chattahoochee River on September 27, crossing on October 1, 1864. On October 5, Hood ordered his 40,000 men to undertake an assault on Allatoona Pass.

Hood's assault on Federal opponents was only partially successful. The Army of Tennessee and the Army of the Cumberland had exchanged roles, but Hood had no realistic hope of matching Sherman's success. On October 12, 1864 Hood's troops attacked and captured Dalton, which had been their 1863-4 winter quarters. Major Harper's account of the 58th North Carolina is unclear about the time Reynolds' Brigade broke camp at Dalton the second time. The regiment was involved in futile Confederate actions to cut Sherman's supply and communication lines, though no specific records for their activities exist.

Reynolds' Brigade crossed the Tennessee River at Florence, Alabama on November 2, 1864, and was held there inactive until November 20, 1864 awaiting supplies. From Florence, Alabama on November 18, 1864 an organizational table for Major General Carter Stevenson's Division, Brown's and Reynolds' Brigades, consolidated was issued and the brigade was organized:

58th North Carolina, Captain Samuel M. Silver

60th North Carolina, Lieutenant Colonel James T. Weaver

3rd & 18th Tennessee, Lieutenant Colonel William R. Butler

and others

The Army of Tennessee invaded Tennessee and was involved in heavy skirmishing in front of Columbia, Tennessee on November 24-27, 1864. Records do not survive to indicate the participation of the 58th North Carolina.

On November 28, 1864, the 58th North Carolina and Palmer's Brigade led the advance of Stephen Dill Lee's Corps on the Mount Pleasant Pike, pushing a dozen regiments and six batteries of retiring Federals, entering the town of Columbia, Tennessee, on the Duck River, which had been under Federal occupation for two years. At this point the brigade was able to rescue some stores from a burning Federal blockhouse. The 58th North Carolina was left at Columbia to guard 1,700 Federal Prisoners sent to the unit, and to garrison the town. This detail enabled the regiment to miss Hood's twin disasters at Franklin and Nashville, Tennessee. At this time the regiment was reported to have an effective strength of 246 men, total present of 311, with an aggregate present total of 338. On December 14, 1864, the 58th North Carolina was ordered to Corinth, Mississippi with the prisoners. Here they were relieved of the guard, and on December 26, 1864, was ordered to Okalona, Mississippi to drive off a cavalry raid which had cut the rail line there. The remainder of the Brigade were not lucky, and traveled on with Hood to his great defeat. The 58th North Carolina rejoined Palmer's now very small brigade on the return of Hood's Army to Tupelo, Mississippi in January 1865.

Palmer's Brigade missed the disastrous battle at Franklin, Tennessee on November 30, 1864. To their good fortune, Hood had them detached for other duty, guarding the ordnance train. Hood's carelessness resulted in about 7,000 rebel dead. Lieutenant Colonel James M. Ray of the 60th North Carolina wrote that after the encounter at Columbia, Tennessee, the Confederates delayed instead of pursuing the retreating Federals, giving them time to regroup and entrench at Franklin.

Reynolds's Brigade officially made the transition to become Palmer's brigade during this time. Joseph Benjamin Palmer, 1825-1890, having a name very similar to the organizer of the 58th North Carolina has caused some confusion in records relating to the regiment. Palmer, a prewar Unionist, attorney, and politician entered the Confederate Army upon Tennessee's secession. He led a consolidated brigade in the Franklin-Nashville Campaign, but was detached during both big fights. His command, attached to Edward Walthall's Division did take part in covering the retreat. In the final reorganization of the Army of Tennessee he was placed in command of a brigade composed of the remnants of 38 Tennessee regiments and two battalions. His brief association with the men of Reynolds' Brigade went well, but he lost them in the April 9, 1865 reorganization.

The retreat began at Nashville. The retreat ended in surrender at Greensboro 5 months later. Palmer's brigade fell back to Murfreesboro, Tennessee where the popular Lieutenant Colonel James T. Weaver of the 60th North Carolina was killed by a sniper in General Forest's command and was listed as an accident.

Contemporary records show Hood's 33 day Tennessee campaign began with 26,000 "*of all arms*". When the Army of Tennessee crossed back across the Tennessee River had "less than 18,000." The army crossed the river at Brainbridge, Tennessee "was moved via Tuscumbia and Iuka toTupelo, Mississippi, where they could rest and re-organize." The 58th North Carolina rejoined Palmer's command at that point. The strength of the Army on January 20, 1865 was 16,913, nearly 2,000 fewer than had crossed the Tennessee less than a month before. The Franklin-Nashville Campaign cost Hood 50 cannon, leaving him with only 59. The Federal's lost 16 block-houses, 4 locomotives and 100 rail cars, 10 miles of rail track and several hundred horses and mules, as well as several thousand Northern boys killed or wounded.

A January 19, 1865 abstract from the return of Major General Stevenson's division, Lee's corps showed that Palmer's Brigade had the strength, presented in the following table. Brigadier General Edmund W. Pettus was temporarily commanding the division. The 58th North Carolina alone made up a quarter of the nine regiment strong brigade effective strength.

Hood was resigned his command on January 25, 1865 at Tupelo, Mississippi. His transient replacement was Lieutenant General Richard Taylor, son of President Zachary Taylor.

February - April 1865 Capitulation in Carolina

Palmer's Brigade including the 58th, rode the rails to Branchville, South Carolina. On February 4, 1865 they challenged Sherman again and took an active part in several actions at several crossings of the North and South Edisto, repulsing the Federals "in all cases." The 58th was involved in the skirmish at Orangeburg, South Carolina, where some were captured and others wounded. No records survive to indicate the number killed. The Wytheville Dispatch after the war ran a story about Jackson Grubb and Joseph Headrick of Company H, 63rd Virginia and their encounter in South Carolina, near Orangeburg, with Federal Soldiers. From the Grubb and Headrick version of events, an Union soldier was found dead in the swamps. Retribution, part of Sherman's total war philosophy was taken seriously by his bummers. Grubb and Headrick of Company H, who had been captured near Orangeburg, were included in a party of prisoners forced to draw lots, to see who would die in revenge for the dead Yankee. A South Carolinian lost and was executed. G. D. Gouge took a few minutes out of the hectic army schedule at Branchville, South Carolina on Feburary 8 to drop a few lines to his sister in Yancey County:

We are still near Branchville, S.C., where Colonel Silver left us and are expecting a fight every day. The Yankees are so near that we can hear their drums every morning and some of them came up in sight yesterday but went back without firing guns. I can say to you that we have been seeing hard times this fall and winter, but we are very well pleased with getting so near home. We think if we can't come home, we can hear from you oftener. I have been in hopes that they would make peace sometime this spring, but we have just heard this morning that would not receive our commissioners at Washington unless they would come back to the union and free the negro in our country, and if this be so, I see no chance for the war to stop soon.

Palmer's Brigade reached Columbia, South Carolina by February 14, burning bridges behind them. Calvin Livesay told of seeing "*a sea of blue on the south bank.*" General Johnston was disappointed to find no reinforcements at Charleston, and was distressed to give up another state capital.

Palmer's Brigade had the "*honor*" of acting as a rear guard to hold the south bank of the Congaree River until February 16. Palmer's command then withdrew and burned the bridge behind it. Johnston was operating a delaying action so that Columbia could be evacuated. The Army of Tennessee began its march north on February 17. Palmer's Brigade reached Charlotte, North Carolina on February 23 after wading across the shallow, frigid, Catawba River. After a few days in Charlotte the 58th moved to Salisbury and stopped there a few days. The Army of Tennessee was shifted on March 2, 1865 by train to Smithfield Station, now Selma, North Carolina, where General Joseph E. Johnston had been reinstated in command. Johnston was trying to consolidate his shrinking army.

The men of the 58th North Carolina and of Palmer's Brigade were by now nearly naked--each soldier only a single blanket--or less. Rations were very scarce. The Army of Tennessee passed the severe winter of 1864-65 in active field service. Despite severe exposure of the men and officers, there were no complaints. The men knew complaints would do no good and if they did complain, they did it with their feet and desert- ed. Palmer's Brigade did not take part in the hard fought battle of Averasboro, North Carolina on March 16, 1865. Other events were awaiting them, and the battle-worn soldiers of the regiment were no doubt glad they were not called into action.

On March 19, 1865, Lee's Corps was given to Major General Daniel Harvey Hill. Hill's March 31, 1865 report shows Stevenson's division, with Palmer's Brigade, had an effective strength of 1,181, and was the strongest division in the corps. The division had about the same strength of a full regiment in 1861. The effect strength of the three divisions composing the corps' effective strength was 2,687. Hill wrote of the events of March 19: "At 3:15 p.m. the whole corps advanced in two lines, Deas' brigade and Palmer's, Stovall's and Jackson's constituting the front line; Manigault's Pettus' and Baker's the rear line, 300 yards retired." Palmer's troops passed through the first Federal line in under 15 minutes. The Yankees retired to breastworks 300 yards in the rear of their first line. Palmer's Brigade led the efforts that pushed them from there as well. Hill received a map made by the engineers of the Federal position, and found them to be parallel to the Goldsborough and Fayetteville Road, and a second set of trenches perpendicular to the first fronting on the swamp. At this point Hill was ordered to halt and reform. At this point in the battle General Palmer's Brigade assaulted the field works perpendicular to the road.

Other events required the withdrawal of the small reserves, which the Federals discovered. The Yankees counterattacked, flanking Palmer, Baker and Carter. Hill realized this, but not before 200-300 of his Tennessee troops under Colonel Anderson Searcy of the 45th Tennessee were cut off. They made their way completely through Sherman's bummers and rejoined Hill's command 9 days later. Hill stated, in his battle report, that there would have been a disaster but that General Walthall arrived "to fill the gap and check the Yankee advance." General Palmer's troops disengaged to join General Pettus' Brigade by Hill's order. They rested until about sundown. At dusk the Federals advanced on Pettus, but he "drove them back without difficulty."General Hill reported that his captured men were due to incorrect intelligence and an incorrect decision on his part, based on incorrect information. Further, Hill reported that the Yankees fought the worst thathe had ever seen them at the Battle of Bentonville, and that his men seemed to have "*renewed vigour.*" His corps claimed to have captured 339 prisoners and a Napoleon gun. Hill thought the number of prisoners were exaggerated but extended commendations to Brigadier General Palmer for his soldierly bearing. Stevenson's division lost nine officers and 22 soldiers killed, 19 officers and 176 men wounded in the battle. Stevenson's Bentonville report does not substantially differ from Hill's on the performance of Palmer's Brigade. Stevenson highly praised Palmer and his men.

He reported that Palmer's Brigade lost 5 officers and 8 men killed, 13 officers and 108 men wounded on March 19th, none on the 20th, and 1 officer killed on March 21. Stevenson claimed 57 prisoners had been taken by his division. Stevenson wrote of Palmer's brigade's performance at Bentonville, "*Never was more dash and gallantry displayed than was exhibited by Palmer's Brigade in their successful assaults upon the breastworks of the enemy.*"

It appears that Finley Mast was captured about this time and sent to Ohio as a prisoner of war.

General Palmer's report dated March 29, 1865, claims a loss of 13 killed, 113 wounded and 55 prisoners at Bentonville. Palmer commended Lieutenant Colonel A. F. Boggess of the 26th Tennessee who, "*fell in the gallant discharge of his duties, a noble specimen of the man, officer, and soldier.*" Palmer also commented on Colonel R. M. Saffell, 26th Tennessee, writing, "*being a super-numerary officer, volunteered with Colonel Ashby's calvary, to resist the enemy attempting to turn our left flank on the 21st, and was killed while gallantly leading a charge and repulsing them*".

General Palmer's report also noted that Captain George W. F. Harper commanding the 58th North Carolina, Captain Eli Spangler commanding the 54th Virginia and Lieutenant Colonel Connally H. Lynch, commanding the 63rd Virginia and 60th North Carolina, "*each handled their commands with ability and bore themselves handsomely through the day, as did Colonel Searcy and the officers under him, commanding the Tennessee consolidation.*" At Bentonville, Palmer's command consisted of the 58th and 60th North Carolina, the 54th and 63rd Virginia and a detachment of several consolidated Tennessee regiments under Colonel Anderson Searcy. The 58th North Carolina numbered less than 300 effective troops, but was in both better and stronger condition than Palmer's other regiments. Joseph B. Palmer, now promoted to brigadier general, in command of the brigade, was chosen to lead the assault. Palmer's attack, initially successful, but bogged down, was relieved by Pettus' Brigade, which took the lead. The Federals regrouped in a reinforced position, and Palmer's Brigade again joined the front lines with the 58th North Carolina on the left of the battle line, the 63rd Virginia toward the center. The fight got thicker as evening progressed, and the lines thinner and the Brigade found itself nearly encircled, but held position until 8 p.m. when firing ceased. About midnight of March 19, the brigade withdrew, and reformed for battle in the morning of the 20th. On March 22, 1865 the Army of Tennessee withdrew by rail to Smithfield, North Carolina. While there, the Army of Tennessee was reorganized. Brigades, Regiments and Companies, by this time all very small, were consolidated. The 63rd was reorganized with the 54th into the 54th Battalion Virginia Infantry (The Consolidation order was dated April 9,1865). The 54th Virginia battalion was reported as serving in Pettus' Brigade, Stevenson's Division, Lee's Corps Army of Tennessee. The 58th and 60th North Carolina Regiments were consolidated into the 58th & 60th North Carolina Infantry Regiment Consolidated and reassigned to Brantley's Brigade, D. H. Hill's Division, 2nd Corps, Army of Tennessee, ending their association with old comrades of Reynolds Brigade formed 18 months before. These units were involved in some minor skirmishing until April 25th when an armistice was announced. Johnston surrendered the Army of Tennessee on April 27, 1865. The army was paroled at Greensboro, North Carolina, May 1-2, 1865.

There is no reason to believe that men of other companies did not do the same, that is, just go home in mid-April 1865. Most, therefore, missed the final payment for their services. General Johnston ordered that the Confederate treasury be divided amongst his men. It amounted to one and one seventh Mexican silver dollar per man. Every man received one silver dollar and every seventh man received an extra one. The one silver dollar was certainly worth more than the $154.00 worth of Confederate currency that each private was due for the last 14 months of the war.

From postwar recollections of members of the 58th North Carolina and 63rd Virginia, these western troops were taken by rail to Statesville, where they began the march, not walk, home, which was at least 100 miles away for most of these men. They began arriving at their homes in mid-May, 1865. Most families hadn't seem them in at least 2 years. Many surprised relatives who had presumed them dead.

The above are extracts are from an online document by the late Jeffrey Craig Weaver

Appendix L

Other Facts

Record of Postmasters:

Mast P.O.

Newton L. Mast 6/4/1887 Discontinued 5/17/1902, mail to Amantha Reestablished 5/23/1904 Newton L. Mast 6/4/1887 James B. Mast 3/19/1929 Discontinued 10/10/1931, mail to Amantha

McBride's Mill P.O.

Hiram McBride 5/11/1869

Sugar Grove P.O.

Joseph Matheson 9/6/1853, Joseph H. Mast 3/11/1857, John Mast 5/26/1858, Martin L. Banner 9/13/1866, John Zorun 11/19/1867, Eliza J. Mast 4/7/1868, John A. Mast 10/31/1873, Finley Mast 11/9/1887, Addie Mast 8/11/1892, Mattie Mast 7/8/1893, Abram T. Banner 9/28/1898, Mattie Mast 7/15/1899, Floy Mast 9/25/1913, Iva A. Matherly 7/6/1918, Joseph C. Mast 3/8/1919, Vadry B. Mast 6/23/1920, Cannon G. Ward 9/25/1964.

Some Marriage records from Ashe Co.

Sophina McBride married Ezra More 6/7/1857

James McBride married Mary Anne Shoupe 9/14/1844   Eli Mast, Bondsman

Eleanor McBride married Landrine Eggers 9/4/1824

Hannah McBride married Thomas Dougherty 1845

Mast, Jacob (1738-1808)

Jacob Mast was born in Switzerland. He migrated to America an orphan boy in company with his four sisters and younger brother John. All were in the care of their uncle Johannes Mast and landed in Philadelphia, Pennsylvania on 3 November 1750. Their first abode in the new world was in the vicinity of Hamburg, Berks County, PA, where the Amish had founded their first organized congregation in America by 1749. In that year Bishop Jacob Hertzler arrived from Switzerland and became their first leader. During 1754-1764, "the years of bloodshed" in Berks County, when the Indians returned to reclaim the land, the Masts were driven from their home in 1760, and found refuge at the headwaters of the Conestoga, where Jacob Mast in 1764 took out a warrant for land comprising 170 acres for 325 pounds, situated in Caernarvon Township, Berks County, PA.

Jacob Mast was married at the age of 25 to Magdalene Holly, who had accompanied him on his voyage to America. To this union were born 12 children, all of whom married and had offspring. In 1786 he succeeded Jacob Hertzler as bishop, the second Amish bishop in America and the first ordained here. He was one of the charter members of the present Conestoga Mennonite (MC) Church near Morgantown, which became the first permanent Amish Mennonite church in

America. His manuscripts indicate a fair education for the times. The record of his public sale of personal property shows that he owned a goodly number of books.

As bishop, Mast presided over the following congregations in Berks County: Northkill, Maiden Creek, Tulpehocken, and Conestoga; in Chester County, one congregation Goshen, where a meetinghouse had been built near Malvern; the earliest in Lancaster County was in the vicinity of Compassville, and White Horse; these were also under his oversight. He died in 1808 and was buried on his farm.

Mast, John P. (1826-1888)

John P. Mast (1826-11 June 1888) was born near Elverson, PA, and was a lifelong resident of Caernarvon Township, Berks County, PA. He was a great-grandson of Bishop Jacob Mast and was himself an able and faithful leader in the same district where his great grandfather had served for 22 years. As a preacher he was practical and eloquent. He drew his lessons from everyday life and had a wide acquaintance in Amish Mennonite circles in both the United States and Canada. He was married to Anna Zook, but had no children. He was ordained to the ministry in his thirties by a unanimous vote from his congregation. He died 11 June 1888. His name was for many years a household word throughout his community.

- extracts from the Global Anabaptist Mennonite Encyclopedia Online

Appendix M

The following are extracts from **"History of Watauga County NC with Sketches of Prominent Families"** by John Preston Arthur 1915.

Mast Family - Joseph Mast, the first of the name to come to Valle Crucis, Watauga County, was born in Randolph County, North Carolina, March 25, 1764, and on the 30th of May, 1783, married Eve Bowers, who had been born between the Saluda and Broad rivers, South Carolina, December 30, 1758. Joseph was a son of John, who was a brother of the Jacob Mast who became bishop of the Amish Mennonite Church in Conestoga, Pa., in 1788. They had left their native Switzerland together and sailed from Rotterdam in the ship "Brotherhood," which reached Philadelphia November 3, 1750. John Mast was born in 1740, and shortly after becoming twenty years of age left his brother, Jacob, who had married and was living near the site of what is now Elverson, Pa. John wandered on foot through many lonely forests, but finally settled in Randolph County, where joseph was born. There he married a lady whose given name was Barbara. From Joseph and Eve Mast have descended many of the most substantial and worthy citizens of Western North Carolina, while the Mast family generally are people of influence and standing in Pennsylvania, Ohio, Nebraska, Iowa, Montana, Orange, Florida, Illlinois, Missouri, California, Kansas, and, in fact, nearly every State in the Union. C. Z. Mast, of Elverson, Pa., in 1911 published a volume of nearly a thousand pages, ll of which are devoted to an excellent record of all the Masts in America.

John A. Mast was born on Brush Creek September 22, 1829. He married Martha Moore, of John's River, December 5, 1850. He died February 6, 1892. His paternal grandfather, John Mast, and maternal grandfather, Cutliff Harman, were among the pioneers of this section and were Germans, settling on Cove Creek. His wife, Martha Mast, was born April 13, 1833. She died February 15, 1905.

Joseph Harrison Mast - His father was John Mast and his mother, Susan Harman, who are buried at the Taylor burying-ground at Valle Crucis. John Mast's father was Joseph, and he lived where Finley Mast now lives, while Cutliff Harman lived where David Harman now lives. Joseph H. Mast was born April 9, 1829, and married Clarissa P. Moore October 12, 1848. Her father was Daniel Moore, of the Globe, Caldwell County. Their children were: Sophronia, wife of Newton Banner, born July 15, 1850; Andrew J., born February 25, 1852; Leona, born December 2, 1853; Martha V., born April 20, 1856; John H., born October 19, 1858; Allie J., born May 8, 1861; Sarah C. born August 19, 1863; Daniel H., born June 26, 1866; Joseph C., born May 8, 1869. He settled at his present home at Sugar Grove in 1848, and built the dam and grist mill of the present Mast mill before the Civil War, bolting the ground wheat by an old reel still in existence, though J. C. and J. H. Mast, his sons, changed that old mill into the first roller mill in Watauga County in 1897, E. F. Bingham building the second half a mile above. His children married as follows: Andrew Jackson married Joana King, Leona A. married Robert Mast; Martha V. Married Thomas Sullivan; John H. married, first, Eleline, daughter of Hiram McBride, and second, Nancy, daughter of Hiram Wilson; Alice J. married Finley Mast; Sarah C. married John Smith; Daniel H. married Ruia Lowrance; Joseph C. married, first, Nora Phillips, and, second, Ada Madron, of Bristol, Va. Joseph H. Mast, Sr., died September 8, 1915.

The brothers and a sister of J. H. Mast, Sr., were: Noah, who married Elizabeth Roland; Leson, who married Sally Dugger; Eli, who married Callie Dugger; Jack, who married Martha Moore, of the Globe, and Finley P., who married Rhoda Smith.

This history of Asa Reece is important because of references to Hiram McBride and names which appear in the family...

Asa Reese, Pioneer - Valentine Reese came from Germany to America about 1750 and married Christina Harman, settling at the old Bowers Place now called Trade, Tenn. Their son John was born in 1770 and married Sarah Eggers, John died at age seventy and his wife at age ninety-six. They reared ten children.

Hiram McBride was born in 1798 and married Rhoda Smith. They settled in Watauga. They had six children, and after Rhoda's death Hiram married Martha McCall and sired six more. A divorce followed, and two years later Hiram married his third wife, Jane Widby, by whom he had one child, a daughter. Hiram died July

9, 1872, aged seventy-four years. Asa, son of Hiram and Rhoda, was born May 9, 1820, and married Catharine Wagner February 27, 1845, settling two miles from what is now Mountain City, Tenn. His wife joined the Baptist Church in February, 1872, and he in December, 1876. They had ten children, one of whom, a girl, dying in childhood. Asa died November 27, 1898, and was buried near his home and daughter, Rhoda. Asa's children were Jehiel, Asa, Joh, Nelson, Cinderella, Mahetebel. After the death of his first wife Hiram Reese moved his family to what was known as the old Jim Reese house, below Phillip Greer's on Cove Creek, in 1830. In 1832, during a cold spell, a family named Hutchinson, with their team, were added to the family of fourteen already at the small house, where they remained till warm weather, without money and without price. During this time Asa and his brother had to sleep on the open porch, with a snow coverlet frequently to keep them warm. In copartnership with Samuel Reese, of Buncombe, Hiram Reese lost much money wagoning to South Carolina, and the sheriff sold him out for debt about 1834-35, and the family was broken up. In the fall of 1838 Asa, with Alfred Adams (father of T. P. Adams) and Sarah Mast, took a trip to Sequachy Valley, Tenn., near Collins River, Warren County, Asa's father having consented that the boy should keep all he earned after reaching nineteen years of age. In the fall of 1840 Asa, with Hiram McBride, Riley Wilson, two of Asa's uncles, a girl named Roland, and two daughters of Jacob Reese, went to the Platt Purchase, Mr., 300 miles west of the Mississippi River, where he stopped with his uncle, James Webb, crossing the Platt River at New Market. But McBride got home-sick and returned. Asa returned to this state in the spring of 1844 in company with John Ellington and Reuben Sutherland going to his uncle, Bennett Smith's, and his cousins, George and Polly Hayes. In the summer of 1844 he worked for awhile with the Fairchild ladies on Howard's Creek, where he flirted with a girl named Winkler whom these ladies had hired to weave for them, much to their disgust. But Asa concluded that "old maids are the most jealous, superstitious, whinning old things that belong to the human family." He decided not to enlist for the Mexican War after visiting his father in Russell County, Virginia, and finding him in poverty he declared he loved him as much and reverenced him more than if he had given him a couple of thousands of dollars, adding that children who are aided by their parents often forget them, and sometimes their God, as well. While Asa was a small boy he and his brother attended Sunday School in a small old log house which stood at the mouth of a hollow, just below where the widow, Ann Farthing, used to live on Beaver Dams. This must have been about 1828, and was undoubtedly the first Sunday School of which there is any record known to this writer. Thus, to the many other good deeds, the Farthings have the glory of having instituted Sunday Schools, now universal, then unknown. The house in which Asa was born stood on a branch of Sharpe's Creek and was built of logs, with puncheon floor. The chimney was built of stone inside and of wood outside to the top of the mantelpiece, above which it was of sticks and clay. It was covered with old-fashioned clap-boards. His father had a smoke house for his meat, though many hung their meat in the gables of their homes, thus giving all kinds of meat a chance to become smoked yellow, including hog, beef, bear, venison, coon, etc.

This family may have been connected in several ways.

Wilson Family - Charles Wilson came to North Carolina from Pennsylvania about the time of the Revolutionary War. His wife is said to have been a sister of Gen. Nathaniel Greene, of Rhode Island. Charles was in General Greene's army and was killed at Guilford. Hiram Wilson married a Miss Smith and they settled on Cove Creek about 1815. Their children were John, who married Mary Mast; Lucretia, who married Isaac Wilson, a distant kinsman; Sarah, who married Dudley Farthing; Isaac, who married Miss Caroline Greer; Ellen, who married Reuben Farthing; Albert P, who was born April 14, 1826, and married Elizabeth Councill, a daughter of Jesse; Clarissa, who married George Younce; Hiram, who married Alex. Baird, and Wm. Carroll, who married a Miss Adams, a daughter of Alfred Adams. Hiram, Isaac and Carroll were killed in the Civil War, and Albert P. was wounded twice, John having died just prior to the Civil War.

Baird Family - Ezekiel Baird was the father of Bedent and William Baird, and came to North Carolina from New Jersey. William went West, where he died. Bedent married Mary, a daughter of Cutliff Harman, and lived one mile down the Watauga River from Valle Crucis on its left bank where Walter Baird now lives, although Bedent's old house has been replaced by the present large frame dwelling. Bedent's sons were Alexander, who married Nancy Vanderpool, and lived on the waters of Brushy Fork; Franklin, who married Catharine Moody, daughter of Edward, who lived at what is now Foscoe. Franklin lived one mile down the Watauga, where James Church now lives, and just above Walter's; Palmer, who married, first, Elizabeth McBride, and lived on Beech Mountain, three miles from Bedent's; Blodgett, who moved to Tennessee and married a lady near Nashville. He was absent forty years before he was heared of at Valle Crucis. The next was Euclid, named for the geometrician, and he married Louisa Council, daughter of Jordan Council the first, and lived where ex-Sheriff W. B. Baird now lives. Franklin's children were: Jackson, who married Tempe Shull; William, who married Sarah McNab; Susan, who married James Lowrance; David F., who married Elizabeth Wagner; Thomas Carroll, who went to Texas, where he died unmarried about 1861. Alexander's children were: Bedney, who went West and married Susan Jane Merchant; Abram, who married Elizabeth Hartley; Warren, who married Rebecca Hartley; Ezekiel, who married Sarah Wilson; Jonathan, who died in the Civil War; Phoebe, who never married; Elizabeth, who married Hiram Wilson.

Palmer's children were: John, who married Miss Shupe; Andrew, who died in the Civil War, unmarried; Ann, who married Wm. Grimsley; Caroline, who married _____; Eliza, who never married. Blodgett's children are not known to his

Watauga relatives. Euclid's children were: Benjamin, who married Celia gragg; John, who married Emeline Shell; Hiram, who died in the Civil War; Thomas, who went West and died unmarried; Sarah, who married John Hackney; Charlotte, who married Eli Brown; Mary, who married Hiram Gragg. Rittenhouse's children were: William B., who married Eliza Gragg.

David F.'s children are: Victoria, who married T. H. Taylor; Allie, who married J. M. Shull; Nora, who married D. C. Mast; Susan who married Jack B. Horton; Emma, who married W. W. Mast; Lula, who married J. C. Moore; Thomas C., who married Emma Mast

Brown Family - James Brown Came from Holland to Wilkes County and settled near Holman's Ford of the Yadkin -- the Dutch equivalent of Brown sounding very much as the English word is pronounced. He had ten sons, of whom is still remembered Joseph, who settled just below Three Forks Church, He married a Miss Hagler, of the "Big Waters of Pee Dee," in South Carolina. Their Children were; Thomas, Elizabeth, Jesse, Sallie, Nancy and James, Thomas Married Susan Greene, a daughter of John "Flatty;" Joseph married Nancy Farthing, daughter of Rev. Wm. Farthing; Elizabeth died unmarried; Jessee married a Miss Webb, of Judge James L. Webb's family; Sallie married Reuben P. Farthing; Nancy married Daniel Bradley

Jordan Councill's Grandchildren - Jesse's children were: Sallie, who married Jesse Ray and lived on Old Fields Creek; Nancy, who married Thomas Green and lived at the mouth of Meat Camp; Elizabeth, who married Albert P. Wilson and lived on Cove Creek after the Civil War, when he sold the place to Hiram McBride, of Tennessee, and came to Boone where his wife died. He now lives near Three Forks Baptist Church.

The Eggers Family - Landrine Eggers came from London to the eastern part of this State first and then to Ashe County. He was born in 1747 and died March 17, 1883. He was married, first, to a lady whose name has been forgotten and second, to Joanna Green whose family lived near Three Forks Church and were members of that body. Children of first marriage have been forgotten, but those of the second are: Hugh, the date of whose birth and the name of whose wife are not now known, and one daughter, Lydia, who was born December 14, 1791, and married James Swift, who died January 8, 1858, leaving the following children: Franklin, born August 11, 1816; Elias, born February 5, 1818; Morgan, born October 23, 1819; James, born December 3, 1821; Martha, born January 1, 1824; Margaret, born August 26, 1826; Elizabeth, born June 20, 1828; Wilburn, born October 7, 1831; Mary, born March 16, 1833; Rebecca, born April 15, 1835. Hugh's children were: Landrine, born September 10, 1805; Malinda, born February 11, 1802; Washington, born August 21, 1808; Nancy, born April 15, 1836; Jehiel S., born October 20, 1834; Martha C., born September 27, 1837, and the following, the dates of whose births are unknown: Cleveland, Abner and Joel. Landrine the second married Ellen McBride, daughter os Wm., of Rowan County, born August 5, 1800; died December 5, 1872. The children of Landrine the second were: Brazilla, born June 10, 1825, married Sarah Isaacs; Ransom, born January 5, 1827, married Rachel Isaacs; Hugh and Sarah, twins, born December 26, 1828, of whom Hugh married Alva Kilby, and Sarah, John Isaacs; Landrine the third, born November 18, 1830; Anna born July 21, 1832, married Franklin Reese; Richard, born February 1, 1834, married Elizabeth Reese; John, born December 2, 1835, married Martha Stout; Ellen, born January 16, 1839, married Maston Davis

Note: We know from the application for pension papers, filed by Landrine Eggers in the Ashe County Court on 10 November 1832 that this is incorrect. The papers state "He was born in New Jersey near the valley of Freehold and when he was age nine years old his father removed to the Highlands of New York in the neighborhood of Goshen." "He was born in 1747 and died March 17, 1833." Note: These dates are not correct. From the pension papers: "Now sitting Landrine Eggers of the county of Ashe in the state of North Carolina, resident being age seventy five years, the eleventh day of last March.." The statement was sworn to on the 10th day of November 1832, making his date of birth 11 March 1757. Also sworn to, on the same day, by Jesse Coffey and Bedent Baird: "We Jesse Coffey, a clergyman residing in the county of Ashe, and Bedent Baird of the same hereby certify that we are well acquainted with the applicant, Landrine Eggers who has subscribed and sworn to the above declaration, that we believe him to be aged seventy five years.."

Farthing Family - Dudley Farthing was born in Virginia, April 6, 1749. He was the son of William Farthing and his wife, Mary. Dudley Farthing died in Wake County February 22, 1826. His wife was Annie, daughter of WM. Watkins and Phoebe, his wife. She was born July 4, 1747, in Virginia and died February 13, 1812, in Wake County. Their children were: Phoebe, born November 15, 1778, and she married John Link, February 3, 1803; Mary, born July 3, 1780, and died March 22, 1826; William, born August 25, 1782, married Polly W. Hallyburton, February 9, 1804; John, born September 26, 1784, married Lucy Goss, first, who died April 9, 1827, and then Polly Amos; he died February 29, 1868; Reuben, born September 1, 1787, married _____; died August 14, 1834; Eliza, born February 22, 1790, and died August 3, 1790. The children of the Rev. William W. Farthing were: Dudley, born November 29, 1804, married Nancy Mast in 1831; he died July 8, 1895, and she September 22 1882; Patsy, born December 4, 1805, married Thomas Shearer, an uncle of Robert Shearer; they moved to Kansas between 1850 and 1855; Nancy was born February 21, 1807, married Joseph Brown and went to Missouri; Reuben P;, born June 28, 1808, married Sallie Brown, and died December 20, 1889; John Atkins, born July 21, 1809, married, first, Melissa Curtis, and, second, Keziah Farthing; William Brown, born December 20, 1810, and married Annie Kindle; Edward F., born April 30, 1812, and died May 3, 1812; Thomas, born May 9, 1813, married Ermine Hallyburton; Annie Watkins, born September 5, 1814, married Wm. Young Farthing, father of W. S. Farthing; Harriet, born March 22, 1816, married James Brown, and died May 16, 1897; Mary Hervey, born February 21, 1818, married Hiram McBride, died May 26,1869; Abner Clopton, born October 6, 1819, and married Mary Narcissus Farthing; Paul, born April 17, 1821, married Rachel Farthing; he died in a Federal prison at Camp Chase in 1865; Stephen, born January 3, 1823, married Margaret Adams, and died January 25, 1882. Dudley Farthing's wife was Nancy, daughter of John Mast and Susan Harman, and she was born May 18, 1809. Their children were: William Judson, born February 6, 1832, and went to Texas in 1859, where he died unmarried September 10, 1865; Susan, born July 12, 1833, and is yet alive; James Martin, born July 25, 1835 and was killed December 13, 1862, in the battle of Fredericksburg, Va.; Mary White, born January 9, 1837, married Newton Moore in 1860 and died May 11, 1914, in Virginia; Thomas Jefferson, born August 13, 1838 never married, died of pneumonia at Lynchburg May 21, 1862; John Young, born May 17, 1840, married Polly Farthing; Henry Harrison, born October 7, 1841, Married Sarah Catharine Baker November 29, 1872; Martha B., born August 24, 1843, died in infancy; Joseph, born August 9, 1844, died in infancy; Lewis Williams, born November 6, 1845, married Nancy McBride, daughter of Hiram; Sarah Carolina born January 31, 1849, married Warren Greene, first, and then Anderson Cable; Wiley Hill, born March 23, 1850, married Rachel Louisa Farthing, sister of W. S. Farthing, and lives near Blountville, Tenn.; Nancy Emeline, born January 6, 1852, and never married. John Farthing was a brother of Rev. William Watkins Farthing and a son of Dudley the first. He was born in Durham, then in Orange County, July 29, 1812, and in the fall of 1826 came with his brother, W. W., to Beaver Dams, but he lost his wife there and also his brother, W. W. John's first wife was Miss Lucy Goss, and he returned to Durham and married Polly Amos and came back to Watauga in 1831 and settled where Zionville now is, where he owned most of the land; The children byy his first wife were: William Young, who married Ann W. Farthing; Dudley, who married Sarah Wilson; Sherman, who was killed by a tree near Zionville just before 1840, thus preventing his expected marriage; Nancy, who married Wm. Ferrall; Rachel W., who married Paul Farthing, a son of Wm. F. Farthing, a son of Wm. W. Farthing; Keziah, who married John A. Farthing, who lived where W. S. Farthing now lives; Lucy White, who never married; Anne, who married Caswell King in Wake County, was an infant when her mother died in Watauga, and was taken back by her father, John Farthing, and reared by Keziah Cozart in Wake County. In her old age she came agin to Watauga, where she died.

The children by the second marriage were: Reuben, who married Ellen Wilson, first, and then a Miss Harman; Elijah, who married Amanda Oliver; John, who died when nineteen years of age; Sallie, who married John Adams.

John Farthing's father was Dudley Farthing, who died in Wake, his wife having been Annie Watkins, whom he married February 2, 1778. The first Dudley Farthing had, beside William Watkins and John, Reuben, who married a Miss Hargus, his descendants still live in and near Durham.

The Farthings came originally from Wales to Pittsylvania County, Virginia, from there they went to Person County, North Carolina, where Annie Watkins was reared. The Rev. William Watkins Farthing was a minister and traveled some for the old Missionary Society of North Carolina, which antedated the Baptist State Convention, and he was traveling and preaching when he first got acquainted with Watauga County. His sons, Reuben, John A;, Abner C. and Stephen J., were ministers, the two youngest having been ordained under authority of Bethel and the two elder under that of the Cove Creek churches. Rev. J. Harrison Farthing, son of Abner C., is a minister, as are also Calvin S., son of Thomas; Robert Milton, a son of Calvin S., and he preaches in Tennessee, and Rev. L. Whitfield also preaches.

Dudley Farthing was a son of Rev. W. W. Farthing; married Nancy Mast, a daughter of John Mast, who lived where Finley Mast now lives. He had been a member of the Ashe County court prior to the establishment of Watauga County, having been appointed in 1832 to fill out the term of Abram Vanderpool, and from that time till the constitution was changed in 1868 he was chairman of the Watauga Court of Pleas and Quarter Sessions. He presided with great dignity and administered his office with sound judgement and ability. No superior court judge who ever came to Watauga County presided over his court with more justness, impartiality or legal learning than Dudley Farthing. He was elected county commissioner after 1868 and became chairman of the board. According to the recollection of his son, Col. Henry H. Farthing, there was reason to suspect that $1,000.00 of the county funds was missing, and Judge Farthing declared that at the next meeting that matter would be investigated. The court house was burned before that meeting and with all the records except Deed Book F. He was born November 4, 1804, and died July 8, 1895. He was just twenty-two years old when he moved with his father to Watauga county. It is said that when corn was scarce he would not sell it for money, saying that a man with money could get it anywhere, but a man who had no money could get it only where he was known and his needs obvious. He lost little if anything by thus crediting his neighbors in distress. Dudley Farthing lived where Mrs. Susan Farthing lives now, in a frame house built about 1850, three-quarters of a mile southwest from Bethel Church. He and his wife are buried there, Stephen Farthing inherited the W. W. Farthing home place and objected to additional interments in graveyard above the old home place. There is a graveyard which W. S. Farthing and others used for burial of their relatives east from the old Farthing graveyard.

Harman Family - In 1791 Cutliff Harman came from Randolph County and bought 522 acres of land on Cove Creek from James Gwyn, to whom it had been granted August 6, 1791, according to Malden C. Harman in Watauga Democrat of

April, 1891. Cutliff married Susan Fouts, and was about ninety years of age when he died in 1838, his wife having died several years before, and he having married Elizabeth Parker, a widow. He had ten children by his first marriage; none by his second. Among his children were: Mary, who married Bedant Baird; Andrew who married Sabra Hix; Eli, who married the widow Rhoda Dyer (born Dugger); Mathias, who moved to Indiana; Catherine, who married Benjamin Ward and went west; Rebecca, who married Frank Adams and moved to Indiana; Rachel, who married Holden Davis; Sarah, who married John Mast; Nancy, who married Thomas Curtis; Rev. D.C. Harman was a son of Eli Harman and was born April 17, 1826 and died December 23, 1904.

McBride Family - John McBride came from the north of Ireland and settled in New Jersey, from there he moved to Rowan County with the New Jersey settlers. He married Mary Baird in Rowan and their children were: Brazilla, who married Rachel Wilson in Rowan; Timothy, who went to Missouri, where he remained, and William, who married a Miss Swicegood in Rowan and died there. One of the daughters married Levi Heath; Ellen married Landrine Eggers, while another daughter married David Goss, who moved to Missouri. Brazilla was in the War of 1812 and named his first son for Andrew Jackson.

Brazilla's children were: Andrew Jackson, who married Polly Green; Hiram, who married Mary Farthing; Silas, who married Emily Green; Brazilla Carroll, who married Catharine Brinkley of West Tennessee; Sarah, who married Harrison Johnson; Ann, who married Squire Green; Mary Amanda, who married John Combs; Emily, who married Jonathan Green.

Brazilla's second wife was Elizabeth Eggers, and their children were: Manly, who married Martha Norris; John, who married Miss Greer; Rachel, who married George Hilliard; Ellen, who married Bruce Harman; Louisa, who married Jacob Younce; Martha, who died unmarried at the age of sixteen; Nancy, who married William Church; Elizabeth, who married Richard McGuire.

The following was taken from the gravestones in the Cove Creek graveyard:

Rev. Brazilla McBride was born September 27, 1790, and died December 10, 1858; Hiram McBride was born August 9, 1818, died May 26, 1869; Rachel, wife of Brazilla McBride, born February 15, 1797, died August 18, 1839.

From the A. J. McBride graveyard the following was taken: Rev. Andrew J. McBride was born November 27, 1822, and died November 12, 1891; Silas McBride was born November 18, 1827, and when he died he was aged seventy-two yeare, six months and twenty days; Elijah Green was born November 4, 1800, died July 15, 1882. His wife was born October 10, 1803, and died January 8, 1879.

The Jersey Settlement, - A group of baptists from New Jersey went to Rowan County and then to the mountains and had Barzilla McBride as an early pastor but he is not listed as an early member. We can assume he and his father arrived after 1800. This congregation was ultra strict in the early days and acted as a court on morals.

Three Forks Baptist Church - This was the first church established west of the Blue Ridge, excepting only the one established at the Old Fields, which, according to Mr. Williams, was established "a few years after" --1779. It was organized November 6, 1790, according to the records now in the keeping of the clerk, Mr. John C. Brown of New River. These records show that "the Baptist Church of Jesus Christ in Wilkes County, New River, Three Forks Settlement," was organized by James Tomkins, Richard Greene and wife, Daniel Eggers and wife, William Miller, Elinor Greene and B. B. Eggers. This soon became the mother church, from which went out "arms" to the glove, to Ebeneezer and to South Fork and other places. Attendants came to Three Forks from all this section, many coming even from Tennessee. Among the first pastors of this mother church are: Richard Gentry, of Old Fields; John G. Bynum, who died in Georgia; Mr. Barlow, of Yadkin; Nathaniel Vannoy, George McNeil, of Wilkes; Joseph Harrison, of Three Forks; Jacob Greene, D. C. Harmon, Smith Ferguson, Brazilla McBride and Jacob Greene, of Cove Creek; Jackie Farthing, Reuben Farthing and A. C. Farthing, William Wilcox and Larkin Hodges. They earned their bread in the sweat of their faces and worked in the Master's vineyard without money and without price. They have all gone to their reward in heaven.

Today this church is known as Zionsville Baptist church. It dates from 1836 and was organized by Barzilla McBride on land donated by John Farthing. The first pastor was M.C. McBride.

Membership from 1790 to 1800.

As this was probably the only church around it gives a record of residents.

J a m e s Thompkins,	Avis Eggers,	James Chambers,
Richard Green,	E l i z a b e t h Tompkins,	Anna Champber,
Daniel Eggers,	Ben. Cutbirth,	John Faugerson,
Ellender Green,	Anna Wilcoxon,	Ebineezer Fairchild,
William Miller,	Lidia Council,	James Jackson,
Mary Miller,	Benj. Baylis,	Catharine Hull,
Phoebe Eggers,	Eliza. Cutbirth,	Joseph Sewel,
Sarah Coleman,	Sarah Baylis,	Ezekiel England,
		Rugh Tompkins,

Christeana Reese,
Valentine Reese,
Samuel Ayers,
Elijah Chambers,
Moses Hull,
Joseph Ayers,
W i l l i a m
Tompkins,
Benj. Green,
Sam'l Wilcoxon,
Sr.,
Garsham Tompkins,
John Reese,
Hodges Counsel,
Mary Fairchild,
Sarah Green,
Sarah Reese,
Charity Ayers,
James Proffitt,
James Calloway,
Jeremiah Green,
Sarah Hull,
Joannah Eggers,
James Faugerson,
Elizabeth Hull,
Martha Champers,
Landrine Eggers,
Nathan Horton,
Mathew Counsel,
Nancy Chambers,
Rachel Champers,
Jesse Counsel,
Comfort Wade,
Edward Stocksdale,
Edeith Stocksdale,
Joseph Tompkins,
Susannah Brown,
Sam'l Wilcoxon,
Jr.,
Thomas Wade,
Samuel Baker,
John Ayers,
Sam'l Castle,

Martha Castle,
Abraham Eaton,
Jno. Parr,
Mary Parr,
Jonathan Allen,
Jas. McCaleb,
Mary McCaleb,
Anne Doneky,
Catharine Allen,
Wm. Davis,
Rebakah Fairchild,
Richard Orzgathorp,
Jn. Vanderpool,
Ellen Vanderpool,
Catherine Hull,
Sam'l Vanderpool,
Sam'l Pitman,
W i n a n t
Vanderpool, Jr.,
Anna Vanderpool,
Winant Vanderpool,
Naomi Vanderpool,
Keziah Pitman,
Abraham Vanderpool,
Sarah Davis,
Abraham Linvil,
Susannah Vanderpool,
Peter Regan,
Rebekah Regan,
Catharine Linvil,
Margaret Linvil,
Maryann Isaacs,
Mathias Harmon,
Mary Harmon,
Jno. Holesclaw,
Jane Vanderpool,
Jacob Reese,
Catherine Brown,
Hannah Phillips,
Jeremiah Buck,
Sarah Shearer,
Jno. Shearer,
Vanentine Reese,

Jr.,
Mary Eggers,
Jonathan Buck,
John Brown,
Hannah Reese,
Elisha Chambers,
David Coleman,
James Jackson, Jr.,
Elizabeth Horton,
Henry Champers,
Rachel Brown,
Anna Reese,
Mary Reese,
Eliza Reese,
Isaac Reese,
Landrine Eggers'
negroman by
name, George,
Anthony Reese,
Asa Chambers,
Comfort Stocksdale,
Samuel Northern,
Susanna Fairchild,
Mary Owens,
William Owens,
Daniel Eggers, Jr.,
Henry Earnest,
Gracy Shearer,
Susannah Brown,
Debby Lewis,
Benja. Brown,
Mahala Eggers,
Elizabeth Morphew,
Margarete Chambers,
Robert Shearer,
Jane Triplet,
Richard Lewis,
John Ford,
Benja. Tompkins,
Lyons Wilcoxon,
Benja. Greer,
Barnet Owens,
Susanah Owens.

Of these there were received by experience: Three in 1790, three in 1791, twenty-nine in 1792, seven in 1793, none in 1794, two in 1795, none in 1796, one in 1797, one in 1798, sixty in 1799. Received by letter in 1790, one, in 1792, eight in 1793, one, in 1795, four in 1796, seven, in 1797, two, in 1798, six, in 1799, nine.

The following were dismissed by letter: Jeremiah Gree, in 1793 Samuel Ayers, Benj. Bayless, Sarah Bayless, Joseph Sewel, Garsham Tompkins, Ruth Tompkins, Joseph Tompkins, Wm. Tompkins in 1794 Jesse Counsel, Lydia Counsel, Mathew counsel in 1795 Elijah Chambers, Samuel Wilcoxon, Anna Wilcoxon, Sam'l Wilcoxon, Jr. in 1797 Jonathan Allen, Catharine allen, James McCaleb, Mary McCaleb, Thomas Wade, Comfort Wade, Mary Reese in 1798. Elizabeth Tompkins died in 1796.

The following were excommunicated: Sarah Hull, Exekiel England, Susannah Brown, Jesse Counsel in 1794 James Callaway, Samuel Ayers in 1795 William Miller, James Jackson, Landrine Eggers, Hodges counsel in 1796 Mary Miller, in 1797 Samuel Wilcoxon, Jr., Moses hull in 1798 Jno. Ayers, Daniel Eggers, Phoebe Eggers, Mahala Eggers, Martha Chambers in 1799 William Owens, in 1801. It must not be concluded, however, that these had been guilty of very serious offences, for most, if not all, of them were restored to full membership by recantation.

Farthing Family - The coming of the Farthing family to Beaver Dams gave a fresh impetus to the cause of the Baptist Church in this section. They arrived in the fall of 1826, having come from Orange, close to the Wake County line. Two brothers, William W. and John, arrived here first. William soon died, and John, having lost his wife, returned to Wake, where, having married again, he reappeared in Beaver Dams settlement in 1831 and settled where Zionville now flourishes. They organized Bethel Church on Beaver Dams, July 4, 1851, getting their constitution from the Cove Creek Church, and having a membership of ten. Three other churches were constituted from Bethel, viz: Beaver Dams, in September, 1874; Forest Grove, about 1889, and Timbered Ridge in 1906.

A Family of Preachers - The first Dudley Farthing, father of Rev. William W.

Farthing, who came to Bever Dams in October, 1826, was a public speaker of note in his home county, but he always said that as he could blow only a ram's horn and not a silver trumpet, he would not be a preacher. However his son, William, was a preacher of force and fame, and, although his health was such after his removal to this county he did not preach often. He left four sons, upon whose shoulders his mantel fell and with whom it bided. They were Reuben P., John A., Stephen and Abner C. Farthing, who for years were the captain jewels in the Baptist carcanet. And their descendants still wear the armor they laid aside, and are still battling in the vanguard of the army of the Lord as preachers and leaders. While still others, feeling that in the pulpit they would be as helpless as David would have been in the armor of Saul, in their own way and in God's good time are striking mighty blows in the sacred cause of righteousness. No family in Watauga County have done more for the general uplift than that of the Farthings.

Comment about Migration

Alexander Thomas, Andrew J. McBride, Marion Wilson, Jesse Bradley, and Wm. Isaacs, of the Cove Creek section, went to California in 1849, and McBride left a diary, but it has been misplaced within the last few years. It is said that his brother. Carroll, went with him, and that on their return Carroll stopped in Tipton County, Tennessee. While in the West they killed a deer, but Indians took it from them and forced them to run for their lives and to hide in a ravine.

It is also said that they made money in California but spent it all buying a waterproof cloth with which to make a pipe to draw off the water in a creek above the point at which they had discovered gold hoping to gather much from the bottom of the bed, not realizing that it was being washed down from above till too late.

Sheriffs of Watauga Co - Michael Cook, 1849 to 1852; John Horton, 1852 to 1856; D. C. McCanless, 1856 to 1859 (January); Sidney Deal, till 1860; A. J. McBride, from 1860 to 1866;(1) Jack Horton, from 1866 to 1876; A. J. McBride from 1874 to 1882; D. F. Baird, 1882 to 1894; W. H. Calloway, 1894 to 1900; W. B. Baird, 1900 to 1904; Some claim that A. J. McBride was sheriff during the Civil War and others that Jack Horton held the office from 1862 to 1876. Owing to the loss of the records 1873, it is impossible to ascertain the exact facts .

Camp Mast, CSA civil war, at Sugar Grove - Captain Price had a company of the Home Guards at Jefferson, while Major Harvey Bingham had two companies at a camp on Cove Creek, four miles above Valle Crucis, which had been named in honor of the Mast family. It was just below the old Mast Mill, now called Pete Mast's Mill. Geo. McGuire was captain of one company and Jordan Cook of the other. The land on which it stood is now occupied by the residence and grounds of Boone Deal. Only one-half of the force was in camp at any one time, the other half being at their homes every alternate week. The camp consisted of wooden shacks and tents. There were also some fortifications around it. Many wounded Confederate soldiers formed part of the garrison of Home Guards stationed there. The men were rather poorly armed, and Major Avery's battalion was on its way to supply them with better weapons in February, 1865 when it was surrendered, as will more fully appear later on.

The Battle on the Beech - In the fall of 1864 nine men went to James

Farthing's home, a mile and a half below what is now Ward's Store on lower Watauga River, robbed him, shot him and left him for dead. They then went a mile further up to Reuben P. Farthing 's, claiming to be Confederates. Thomas Farthing was up stairs in Reuben's house, wounded. But he had a pistol, and hearing what was passing below, put his head out of the widow and ordered the nine men to leave. They did so, but took several horses from one of Thomas Farthing's brothers as he was going with them to the pasture. Word was sent to Major Bingham, who immediately came with eighteen men. Rations for three days were then cooked by the Farthings for these men, and they followed the horses to Cranberry and recaptured them, returning to the old Joel Eggers place near Balm, where they stayed that night. Captain James Hartley was notified of their presence there, and supposing that they would return to Valle Crucis by the Bower's Gap, secreted himself and thirteen of his men there and awaited Bingham's approach. But Bingham had decided to return to Reuben Farthing's below Ward's Store for the purpose of returning the recaptured horses. There is a wagon road there now, but then there was only a trail. One of Hartley's runners informed him of Bingham's purpose, and Hartley, taking a near way up the ridge, arrived in time to confront them at the place now owned by Lee Gwaltney, seven miles from Ward's Store and one mile from what is now Balm. This spot is about half way between the Hanging Rock and the South Pinnacle of the Beech, but then known as the Abe Baird land. In the fight which ensued Richard Kilby was killed and Elliott Bingham, a brother of the Major's, so badly wounded that he died afterwards. These men belonged to major Bingham's battalion. None of Hartley's men was hurt. The Confederates retreated, although they greatly outnumbered the attacking force. A. J. McBride, of Bingham's command, although a preacher, cursed and swore when ordered to retreat.

Surrender of Camp Mast - It is difficult to get the exact date of the fall of this mountain stronghold, for weak as it was, it was all there was at that time, but T. P. Adams, of Dog Skin Creek, says it was the 5th of February, 1865. As he was one of the captured garrison, he probably knows. Assuming that this is the correct date, on the 4th of February of that year Captain James Champion, of Indiana, a recruiting officer for the Federals, gathered at Banner Elk about one hundred Union men, most of whom were armed after one fashion or another, But many of them had no weapons at all. He marched them that day to Valle Crucis, where they halted, killed one of Henry Taylor's beevs, cooked it and had supper. This dispatched, Captain Champion made them a speech, in which he told them of his plans. But, he added, that if there was any man in the party who expected to loot or rob or burn or destroy any property not strictly contraband, he must fall out, as all he expected to do or allow to be done was to burn the camp, capture the garrison and disable the arms found there. Out of 123 men in his command, twenty fell out, indicating that they had joined in the hope of plunder only. With James Isaacs for guide, the residue started, following the public road to the old Ben Councill place at what has been called Vilas since Cleveland's first post-master general was in office. They crossed Brushy Fork Creek at this point and took the ridge between that tream and Cove Creek, and came down upon Camp Mast just before a chill dawn. It seemed, however, as they passed over the frozen ground, that the clang of their horses' shoes had aroused every dog in Christendom, and just before reaching the camp a flock of sheep became frightened and fled helter-skelter down the ridge toward the camp, with bells jingling and sheep bleating, thus making a veritable pandemonium. But the camp was still asleep, and Champion's men were placed at regular intervals around it, each second man being required to build a fire. When the plaid dawn gave way to the roseate sunrise and reveille sounded, the sleepy garrison looked out upon the frozen hills but to discover that they were indeed encompassed round about, if not by an army with banners, at least by an apparent wall of smoke and fire. Champion had divided his force into three companies, one under I. V. Reese, the second under Aaron Voncannon, while he remained in charge of the third. General Franklin, General being his baptismal name and not a mere empty title of military rank, was sent forward with a flag of truce, returning soon afterwards with Captain George McGuire, who was native and to the manner born, but afterwards supected by some to have conspired with Champion for the surrender of the Camp, as the latter had selected a time when Major Harvey Bingham had gone to Ashe to confer with Captain Price as to some desired co-operation between the two forces. McGuire reported hat he had taken a vote and found that about sixty of his men favored surrende, while eleven voted to fight. He was sent back for the names of those on each side of the question, and soon returned with them. The minority was overruled and garrison surrendered, all being over by nine o'clock that winter morning. They were taken down Cove Creek, crossing Watauga River at the old Ben Baird place, and followed the old Bedent Baird Road over Beech Mountain to George Dugger's, and thence to where Sam Banner lived, where Keith Blalock's son joined them, taking charge of the prisoners. When these reached Ham Ray's at Shell Creek in Tennessee most of those who had voted to surrender were paroled and discharged, while all of those who had voted to fight, except T. P. Adams, were sent on to Camp Chace. McGuire went on, but not to Camp Chace. He rode with the officers and never returned to this State.

Paul and Reuben Farthing - When the question of surrendering was put to the garrison at Camp Mast, Paul Farthing declared that the surrender of the Camp meant the surrender of his life. Miss Sophronia Mast, a daughter of the venerable Joseph Mast, of Sugar Grove, and Miss Melinda Williams, now the wife of Mr. Wesley Holtsclaw, were returning at dawn from having sat up all night with a sick neighbor, when they discovered that they were within the lines of Champion's men encircling the camp. They were detained there, and while waiting to be allowed to proceed to their homes advised Paul Farthing and his nephew to escape by following the stream under the bushes growing on the bank of the creek flowing hard by, but they said it had grown too light and that they would be discovered and killed. Paul Farthing, however, gave Sophronia his pistol,, knife and pocket-book, and Dr. J. G. Rivers, who was also of the surrendered garrison, entrusted some things to Miss Williams, and these articles were afterwards faithfully delivered by these two young girls, Miss Mast afterwards becoming the wife of Captain Newton Banner. The two Farthings, Paul and his nephew, Reuben, did die at Camp Chase, just as they had predicted would be the case if it surrendered.

Stoneman's Raid - General Stoneman reached Boone in the forenoon of March 28, 1865. The day was fair. Some men in the house which stood where J. D. Councill's residence now stands, among whom was W. Waightstill Gragg, fired on the head of the column as it came down the road from Hodges Gap. This was enough: Warren Green was killed; so were Jacob M. Councill and Ephraim Norris. The following were wounded: Calvin Green, son of Alexander Green; Sheriff A. J. McBride, Thomas Holder, son of Elisha; John Brown, son of Joseph Brown, of Gap Creek, and W. Waightstill Gragg, of the First North Carolina Cavalry, who was then at home on a furlough. The house from which the shooting had been done, now J. D. Councill's, was converted into a hospital and the Federal surgeon did his best for the wounded. Calvin Green was taken to the old Jordan Councill house. He had been badly wounded, but recovered. McBride had been shot in the breast, but the ball followed a rib and lodged near his spine, from which the federal surgeon removed it, while McBride lay on his stomach on the floor, without anaesthetics of any kind. Holder's wound was in the hip and groin. He lived on Howard's Creek, but is now dead. Brown had his ankle broken. Gragg's wound was not very severe. He lived a short distance above the house now occupied by Benjamin Brannock. After the firing from the Councill house, Stoneman's men charged, and all who were in that house or near it ran through the fields toward the foot of Howard's Knob. Hence, all were wounded in the rear, except Mc Bride, who was hit in the breast. The house in which Jacob M. Councill was killed is called the Mark Hodge house.

Bedent Baird and Jersey Settlement - That many of the first settlers of this county came from New Jersey seems to be confirmed by the fact that D. Gilbert Tennent, of Asheville, has a book which is called the "History of the Old Tennent Church," compiled by Rev. Frank Symes, its pastor, and printed by George W. Burroughs, at Cranberry, N. J. In it is published a diagram of the pews of the church, one of which in 1750 was held by Zebulon and the other by David Baird. The church was then called the Freehold Church, but is now known as the Tennent Church. It still stands in Monmouth County, New Jersey. Just what relationship these Bairds hold to the Bedent Baird of Watauga aand the Bedent and Zebulon

Baird of Buncombe in 1790 seems to be a riddle beyond solution at the present day. But that Zeb Vance's mother, who was a Baird, was related to the Bairds of Watauga is about as certain as any unprovable fact can well be, for family names, family traits and physical family resemblances are so marked as to be unmistakable.

A Mysterious Enquiry - Early in January, 1858, Bedent Baird received a newspaper, on the margin of which was written a few lines, in which the claim was made that Bedent E. Baird was akin to the writer, who, however, failed to sign his name.(1) But he had given his post office, that of Lapland, in Buncombe County, but now called Marshall, the county seat of Madison. Bedent E. Baird, then, in 1858, in his eighty-eighth year, answered this unknown writer, sending his letter to Lapland, but he received no answer. From this letter we learn that John Baird and a brother came from Scotland in the Calendonia and settled in the Jerseys, meaning in New Jersey. This John Baird had married a woman named Mary Bedent, and they named their first child Bedent Baird, the very first of the name "that was ever on the face of the earth." Their seventh son was named Ezekiel and he married Susanna Blodgett, whose father was killed in the ambuscade near Fort Duquesne at the time Braddock also met his death. Ezekiel Baird moved to North Carolina, where Bedent E. Baird was born about 1770. Ezekiel Baird's brother, Bedent, was married three times "and reared three numerous families at or near the German Flats, Canada." Ezekiel Baird's other five brothers also married and reared families "who helped to break the forests and settle five or six of the southwestern States."

Demise of William Mast

An African Romance - On the 16th day of October, 1849, Mr. and Mrs. William Mast, then living where the Shipleys now live, near Valle Crucis, were poisoned by drinking wild parsnips in their coffee. It was said by some that a slave woman named Mill or Milley had been whipped for having stolen twenty dollars from Andrew Mast, and poisoned William Mast out of revenge. Others say the crime was committed by Mill and her slave lover, Silas Baker, in the hope that if Mill's master and mistress were dead, she would have to be sold, and that Jacob Mast, who was about to marry Miss Elizabeth Baker and move to Texas, would buy her and thus prevent these dusky lovers from future separation. Although there was no direct evidence against either, Mill was sold to John Whittington and taken to Tennessee, while Silas was taken to Texas with his mistress and her husband, Jacob Mast.

Cove Creek about 1915 - From Sugar Grove to the Tennessee line Cove Creek is so thickly settled as to be almost a continuous village. Several creeks come down from Rich Mountain and Fork Ridge, and on such streams many people live and thrive. For Cove Creek is recognized as the Egypt of Watauga County. It contains some of the most fertile land in the State. Its people are progressive and co-operate in all public enterprises. beginning at Zionville, near the Tennessee line, there is a succession of villages, including Mable, Amantha, Sherwood, Mast and Sugar Grove. Two large flouring mills are on the creek, while there is the first cheese factory ever established in the county in flourishing condition at Sugar Grove. Churches, schools and masonic lodges dot the hillsides. Hospitality reigns in every household. The people are prosperous and happy and helpful. From a point near the mouth of Sharp's Creek, looking toward Rich Mountain, is a view that is as beautiful as any in the mountains. A forest of young lin trees has been set out on one of the wornout hillsides and will soon be in fine condition; also grafted chestnut trees--that is, native chestnut trees on which have been grafted French and Italian shoots. A sang garden or orchard is flourishing nearby, while the town of Sugar Grove and vicinity is lighted up with electric lights. Bath tubs supplied with clear spring water are found in many of the dwellings, and an air of prosperity and progress pervades the entire community of Cove Creek. Automobiles and the latest improved farm machinery show the temper and spirit of the people. In short, there is not forward step which can be taken at this stage of its growth that Cove Creek has not taken. Silverstone, in the shadow of the Rich Mountain, is one of the lovliest of all the villages of this vicinity, though it is some distance from Cove Creek. It is, however, part and parcel of that locality.

Valle Crucis - According to a tradition well supported by the statements of many reputable citizens of the present day, Samuel Hix and his son-in-law, James D. Holtsclaw came in 1779 from Cheraw, S.C., through the Deep Gap, to what is now known as Valle Crucis, and erected a palisade of split logs, with their sharpened ends driven into the ground, so as to enclose about an acre and a half surrounding the Maple Spring between the present residence of Finley Mast and that of his brother, Squire W. B. Mast. This was because they feared Indians, not knowing of the agreement between the Watauga settlers and the Cherokees as to the land between the Virginia line and the ridge south of the Watauga River. After a time Hix became uneasy and retired to the wilderness near what is now Banner Elk, where he made a camp and supported himself by hunting and making maple syrup and sugar, thus avoiding service as an American or a Tory. At some time in his career he is said to have had a cabin in a cove in rear of the present residence of Squire W. B. Mast, then to have lived in the bottom above James M. Shull's present farm, afterwards moving down the Watauga River near Ward's Store, where he died long after the Revolutionary War. It is said that he never took the oath of allegiance ot the American cause and that whenever he came home for supplies his mischievous sons would frighten him by firing off a pistol made by hollowing out a buck-horn and loading the cavity with powder, the same being "touched off with a live coal." Just here it may be remarked--a fact not generally known--that a dead coal, which yet has elements of immortality in it to such an extent that, unless it is ground to powder, it remains charcoal indefinitely. Such coals, in beds of ashes, are still plowed up near the Lybrook farm, now the Grandfather Orphanage, one mile from Banner's Elk, still called by old people from the Hix Improvement, that being the place where Samuel Hix "laid out during the Revolutionary War." Whether he had a grant or other title to the Valle Crucis land seems immaterial now, as he had possession of it when Bedent Baird arrived toward the close of the eighteenth century, for Baird, with a pocketful of money, had to go a mile down river to get a home in this wilderness of rich land. Then Hix is said to have sold his holdings to Benjamin Ward for a rifle, dog and a sheepskin, Ward selling it later on to Reuben Mast, while Hix moved down to the mouth of Cove Creek. Ward soon got possession of this also, and sold it to a man named Summers, who was living in a cabin on the left bank of Watauga River during a great freshet which lifted the cabin from its foundation and carried it and its inmates, the entire Summers family, to death and oblivion in that night of horrors. A faithful dog belonging to the family swam after the cabin and when it finally lodged against a rock, the dog would allow no one to enter til he had been killed. The Hix Hole, just below David F. Baird's farm, is still so called because of the drowning there of James Hix and a Tester about 1835, when a bull was ridden into the river in order to recover the two bodies. Reuben Mast lived where D. F. Baird now lives, while Joel Mast lived where J. Hardee Talor resides. David Mast lived where Finley Mast's large mansion now stands. Henry Taylor, whose father was Butler Taylor, came from Davidson County to Sugar Grove about 1849, married Emeline, daughter of John Mast, of that place, then moved to Valle Crucis in time to get some of the money paid out for the construction of the Caldwell and Watauga turnpike. This road must have been begun prior to October, 1849, for Col. Joseph C. Shull remembers that William Mast had the contract to build the bridge across Watauga River one mile below Shull's Mills, and was at work on it the morning on which he drank the poison the slave girl, Mill, is supposed to have put in his coffee for breakfast, for he came to Col. Joseph C. Shull's father's home for medicine and returned to work on the bridge, but soon had to go home, dying that night at about the same time his wife died. It was to the valley above this that Bishop Ives came in 1843, where he erected the school and brotherhood described elsewhere. This valley was what the editor of the "Life of W. W. Skiles," Susan Fenimore Cooper, a descendant of Fenimore Cooper, author of the "Leather Stocking Tales," says the Indians would call a "one smoke valley" (p. 17), from the fact that but one family dwelt there in 1842. That family was that of Andrew Townsend, the miller, whose descendants still live nearby.

Sugar Grove - Cutliff Harmon came from Randolph County to this place in 1791 and bought 522 acres of land from James Gwyn, it having been granted to him May 18, 1791. Cutliff married Susan Fouts first and a widow by the name of

Elizabeth Parker after the death of his first wife. It is Sugar Grove that is the most progressive of the Cove Creek towns, having electric lights, a roller mill, the first in the county, and a cheese dairy, established 5th June, 1915. It has also one of the finest school houses in the county. It was here also that Camp Mast was located during the Civil War. The land in this section is considered as about the best in the county. Col. Joseph Harrison Mast, who died September 8, 1915, had his residence here. He was in his prime one of the best and most substantial citizens of the county and still holds the respect and affection of all who knew him. The first roller mill in the county was established here. These people know what co-operation means and act accordingly. The cheese factory is the first that was established in the South, and promises to be successful.

Beaver Dams - was the field in which the Farthing graveyard now is and where a log cabin stood. It was there that the first log-raising and log-rolling, or clearing, took place on Beaver Dams. Curtis's sons went west, but in 1910 a great grandson, Webb Mast, by name, came back and had a picture taken of the old Ben Webb house site. The Webb cabin stood above the place where Alfred Trivett now lives, Webb having moved to middle Tennessee after he sold to Rev. W. W. Farthing in 1826. One of Ben Webb's daughters married Reuben Mast and died in that old cabin. Reuben Mast then married one of Thomas Curtis's daughters and moved to Texas. It was in this first cabin that Bishop Asbury stayed on one of his trips through Beaver Dams and when it was covered by only a few boards.

References:

C.Z. Mast "A Brief History of Bishop Jacob Mast and Other Mast Pioneers" published 1911 on line at https://archive.org/details/briefhistoryofbi00mast

Walter Clark "Histories of the Several Regiments and Battalions from North Carolina in the Great War 61 65"

published 1901 5 vol. Vol 3 pg 447-54

George Washington Finley Harper "Sketch of the 58th Regiment (Infantry) North Carolina troops" 1901 Lenoir. 23 pages

J.B. Miller "The Watauga Boys in the Great Civil War" n/d

John B. Palmer "The 58th North Carolina at the Battle of Chicamauga" in "Our Living and Our Dead" vol 3, pages 454-5

Joseph H. Cru "Units of the Confederate States Army " 1987

John Preston "Bible and Tombstone History of Watauga co." pg 329, 681

I. Harding Hughes, Jr. " Valle Crucis, a History of an Uncommon Place" 1995.

Various Internet sites especially .genealogy.com and www.ancestry.com,

The family tree charts for Mast and McBride are available at Ancestry.com : Go to Trees: Search for "Robb Collins Family Tree". Leslie Susan Robb is the Home Person/editor. These charts cover most of the ancestors discussed here.

~~~~~~~~~~~~~

MAST FAMILY TREE

This tree and the following are created to show the direct ancestry line for ancestors of the children of Thomas Clarke McBride and his wife Elizabeth Mast. Many of the families are large so extensive charts are left out.

1	2	3	4	5th generation
Jacob Mast and Anna Mischler in Switzerland				Wife
|				
Jacob Mast				
John Mast &-	John (Son)			& Barbara (? Harmon)
4 sisters	Jacob			
	David			
	Nancy			
	Joseph &-----	Adam (son)		& Eve **Bowers**
	Elizabeth	**John** & – Nancy(dau)		& Susannah **Harmon**
	Hanah	David	David	
	Mary	Jacob	Noah	
	Mollie	Joel	Eli	
	Catherine	Reuben	Leason	
	Susannah	Noah	Elizabeth	
	Stephen	Elizabeth	Mary	
		Charlotte		
		Malinda		
		Caroline		
		Emmaline		
		Joseph Harrison		
		John A		
		Finley Patterson & –	Charlie (son)	& Rhoda **Smith**
			Mary Elizabeth	
			Jack Joheil	
			Lillie	
			Emma	

Col 1 - Jacob to Pennsylvania John to North Carolina

Col 2 - All went to Ohio except Joseph who went to Watauga NC. Women married into Curtis, Eller, Hoover, Wagoner, Sheets, Houts families. Men married Ware, Bowers,

Col 3 - David, Jacob, Reuben to Nacogdoches Texas, rest remained. Elizabeth married Councill and men married Cable, Harmon, Shull, Curtis, Fulcher, Webb,

Col 4 - Married in order Farthing, Roland, Dugger, Dugger, Shull, Wilson, Horton, Gragg, Mast, Taylor, Moore, Smith.

Col 5 - Married in order Baird, McBride, Laine, McBride, Beard

Comments:

McBRIDE FAMILY TREE

1	2	3	4	Generations

unknown in Ireland   Barzill Baird & Mary Susannah Bulman
                                                                     1729   Monmouth NJ   1753|

John McBride 1766 -1840 &   m. Nov 15 1786 Rowan   **& Anne Baird** (Beard)
    | Westchester NY 1766-1839

  Barzilla 1790-1858 & ----- Sarah (dau)   **& Rachael Wilson**

Andrew 98   **Hiram &** ---------------   Nancy (dau)   **& Mary Hervey Farthing**
Billy (wm)92   Andrew Jackson Polly
Nellie   Anne   William Butler
Sally   Silas   Rachael
Betsy(Eliz)91 Eliza   Barzilla
Timothy 95   Carol   John
Eleanor 00   Emily   Emily
               Amanda   Martha
Barzilla &   Rachel (dau)   Jane   & Betsy Eggers
               Ellen   Carrie
               Louisa   **Thomas Clarke &**– Rosalie (dau)   **& Mary Eliz. Mast**

          Martha   Annie Boone
          Nancy   William Grey
          Betsy   Lucy Imogene
          Manley   Wiley Preston Brown
          John   Carrie May
                                          Emily
                                          Thomas Finley
                                          Nellie Ashburn
                                          James Kenneth
                                          Rhoda Mast

Col 1 - Married in order: Wilson, Dancey, ?, Eggers, Wiseman, Goss

Col 2 - descendants moved to Arkansas and Missouri. Married in order: Johnson, Farthing, Greene, Greene, Pringle, Green, Combs, Hilliard/Church/Baily, Harmon/Henderson, Younce, Church, Cannon, Norris, Greer

Col 3 - Married in order: Farthing, Daugherty, Mast, Henson, Tryon, Mast, Mast, Swift, Swift, Tester, Mast

Col 4 - Married in order: Glass, Curtis, Mann, Hix, Collins, Dunn, died, Lilly, Collins, Seay, Eacott

THOMAS C. McBRIDE & MARY E. MAST FAMILY

Thomas Clark McBride (May 27 1864 - May 2, 1921

Mary Elizabeth Mast (Dec 19 1868 - Mar 8 1947

1	2	3	4	5	6	7	8	Generations

Rosalie McB(Jy 26,1888 -Ja 12, 1957)   married John Joseph Glass Dec, 1918

   David (adopted son) & Alice Black

         Stewart & Beverly Finlayson m. in 1969

         Michael b. 71, John Mitchell b. 74

         Constance & Howard Haislip

               Jeffery b. 68 d. 86

               Travis Clark b. 70 & Kristen McGuinn

                  Jeff b. 1995

         Bethany Diane b. 77 m. Will Hamner

               MariKaye

               Will

         Clayton & Jane Ripley m. 1973 & Brenda Blystone

               Michelle Elaine 77

               Garlin

               Bradley Hinkle (Brenda's son by 1st marriage)

Annie Boone McB(Apr 4 1892 - Fe 27 1958) m. Fred Curtis Sept 16, 1916

   Thomas Clark & Jean ?   & Fran ?

       Two sons

William Grey McB (Jy 18, 1890 - Mar 14, 1937) m. Mamie Mann Oct 6, 1912

  Emily Fay (Topsy) (1914 - 1989) & Earl Collins m. Jn 19, 1937

        Minnie Faye (b & d. 41)

 Sondra Earlene b. 43 & Jack Ritch Collins m 1966

        John Collins 68

  Connie Sue b. 48 & Ted Mullens m 1968

        Teddy Matthews Mullens b. 70

        Jeffrey Earl b. 74

  Mildred (1916 - 1987) & (Jack) Warren Lanier **Wyatt** m 1941

Warren Lanier (Lanny) Wyatt b. 48 & Ina Crawford m. 72

Zackory Thomas b. 84
Mackenzie Crawford b. 87

David Victor **Wyatt** b. 53 & Sandra Kaye Miller m. 1973
Daniel Andrews Wyatt b. 78
Joshua Michael Wyatt b. 80

Thomas Howard (Jack) **McBride** (1918 - 1983) & Mary Vaught m 1959
Debra Lee b. 61 & Thomas Duane **Jones** m. 1980
Thomas Duane Jones b. 81
Kella Nicole Jones b. 86
Adam Corey Jones b. 90

Kenneth Wayne **McBride** (1926 - 1974) & JoAnn Cook m. 1955
Kenneth Wayne McBride b. 56 & Mary Campbell m. 1979
Kevyn McBride b. 79 & Lisa m. 2014
Charlotte b. 15
Olivia b. 16
Jordan Aslee McBride b. 81
Kenton Michael McBride b. 83 & Holly m. 2013
Canden b. 14

Sharon Ann McBride (1958 - 1961)

Karen Faye b. 62 & Kelly Martin m 80, & Mark **Rodriguez** m. 89
Aaron Martin b. 81 & Mariana m. 2003
Edgar b. 2017
Adam Martin b. 83 & Fallon m. 2009
Liam b. 2011
Delaney b. 2013
Andrew Rodriguez b. 89
Marcus Aston Rodriguez b. 91
Alex Rodriguez b. 95

Michael Bruce McBride b. 66

Lucy Imogene McB (jy 17 1894 Feb 1 1969) & Dan T Hix   m. 1923   N/C

Wiley Preston Brown McB (Jan 9 1899 -Se 18, 1962) & Doris Collins m. 1932
  Mary (1933- 2013) & Myron **Okulski** (1931 - 1998) m. 53
            Mary Margaret Okulski b. 62 & Steven J. Trude m. 81
                        Brian Michael Trude b. 83
                        Jonathon Raymond Trude b. 84 & Casy Quinlen m.12
                              Hanley Elaine b. 15
                              Avalon Jay b.17

            Myra Elizabeth Okulski b. 56 & William Barry (77-91) m. ?
                        Jason Michael Barry b. 78
                        Joshua David Barry b. 81

            Martin McBride Okulski b. 59 & Francis Shad m. 89
                        John Schad Okulski b. 93
                        David Martin Okulski b. 94

            Michael Okulski b. 53 & Ann Shaw m. 84 & Ann Harrison m.
                                                      9 2
  Ann McBride (1935 - 2006) & James Harry **Vanderburg**   m. ?
            Jane Vanderburg & Roy **Cannup** jr
                        David Shane Canupp b. 77
                        Christopher Canupp b. 81

            James Vandenburg & Betty Sotero
                        Peter Vanderburg b. 74
                        Mary Jane Vanderburg b.75
                        James Vanderburg b. 77
                        Eric Vanderburg b. 81

            Wiley Burdette Vanderburg & Joanne Leigh
                        Thomas Vanderburg b. 81
                        Wiley Vanderburg b. 83
                        Steven Vanderburg b. 85

Carrie Mae McBride b. 1936 & Mike **Bishop**
Sherri Bishop
Mark   Bishop m. ?
Ward   Bishop m. ?

Carrie May McBride (May 29 1900 - 1994) & Tom G. **Dunn** m. 1921
Kathryn Dunn & ? & ? & Robert Defevre
Robert Dunn (- d. 84) & Darlene Flynn
Tom Dunn
Kari Ann Dunn
Patricia McBride Dunn
Susan Marie
Kathryn Elizabeth Dunn & Stephen Hoffman

Emily McBride (Apr 5, 1902 - Aug 8, 1913)

Thomas Finley McBride (Feb 14, 1904 - Nov 4, 1944) & Louise Lilley m. 1934
Virginia McBride & Joel **Altman**
Elizabeth Altman m. Philip Walsh
Caroline Altman
Dorothy **McBride** & ? Stetson

Nellie Ashburn McBride (Feb 10, 1906 - 1998) & Royce Leland **Collins** m. 23
(Betty) Dorothy Elizabeth Collins (1924 - 2014) & Jack **Snelling** (1916-06)
Joan Snelling b. 47 & Glenn **Repple**
Emily
Kaitlin
Debbie Snelling & Dr. Michael **Dunn**
Bryan
Kimberly

Joyce Madeline Collins (1926-2005) & Dick Robb & Bruce Issac & Dick
Ro bb
Richard Robb & Barbara O'Mally
Damon Robb
Leverette (Rhette) Royce Robb
Daniel (Danny) McBride Robb
Leslie Robb b. 58 & Larry **Hiens** & Mark Sheppard & Thadeus Dancer

Jared Heins b. 76

Kelly Heins b.78 & Benjamin Clark

Lily Grace Clark b. 07

Hazel Clark b. 11

Dustin Heins

Chad Sheppard b. 76

Genesis Iris Dancer b. 81

Raphael Dancer b. 81

Harriet McBride Collins (1928-1985) & Johnny C. **Fountain** (1930-1990)

Pam Fountain & Rick **Rankin** & Tom Carrier

Ashley Rankin

John Royce Fountain b. 60 & Nanette Green

Courtney Marie Fountain

James Kenneth McBride (Nov 7, 1907 - Jan 10, 1947)& Anita Seay m. 1934

Rhoda Mast McBride (Apr 22, 1910 - Oct 22, 79) & John Francis **Eacott** m. 35

John McBride Eacott b. Jy 19 1937 & Donna Margaret Phillips m. 1971

Erin Lee Eacott b. apr 19 1974 & Jason Mark Unger m. 2007

Aven Wynne Unger b. Jn 7 2009

Tessa Nell Eacott b. Se 13 2012

Jonathan Phillips Eacott b. Apr 29 1977 & Amy Lee Straus m. 2008

Mackenzie Suzanne Eacott b. jy 8 2014

Nathan Straus Eacott b. jy 8 2014

Jill McBride Eacott b. 1946 & Maurice Oscar **DeBruyne** m. 68

Brett DeBruyne b.73

Ryan Eacott Debruyne b. 75 & (Beth) Elizabeth Organ m. 2003

Holly DeBruyne b. 2011

Kate DeBruyne b. 2017

Tanner Jay DeBruyne b. 78 & Melissa m. 2007

Kendra b.2008

Julia b. 2010

Janifer Lee Eacott b.1948 & Gary Legault m.70 & Richard **Carlson** m. 79

Amy Lee Carlson b. 79 & (Gus) Kenneth Allen m. 2010

Carson Kenneth Allen b. 2012

Maylee Grace Allen b. 2015

TREES descending to either Thomas C. McBride or Mary Elizabeth Mast

GREEN - REEDER

John Greene   J ohn Reeder

1635 _____1645 |

    | |

  William Greene 1660-1722 _____ Joanna Reeder 1690   John Hunt ---- Margaret
Moore

         | |

      J eremiah Greene 1750 -1800 _____ Johanna Hunt 1718-1790

               |

John Wilson 1750-1800 _____ Sarah Green   John McBride 1760- 1796 __Ann Beard 1760

       | |

       Ra chel Wilson _____Barzilla McBride 1790 - 1858

                      |

             Hi ram McBride 1818 - 1880 ---- Mary Hervey Farthing 1818-1869

                                   |

                        Thomas Clark McBride 1864 -1921

~~~~~~

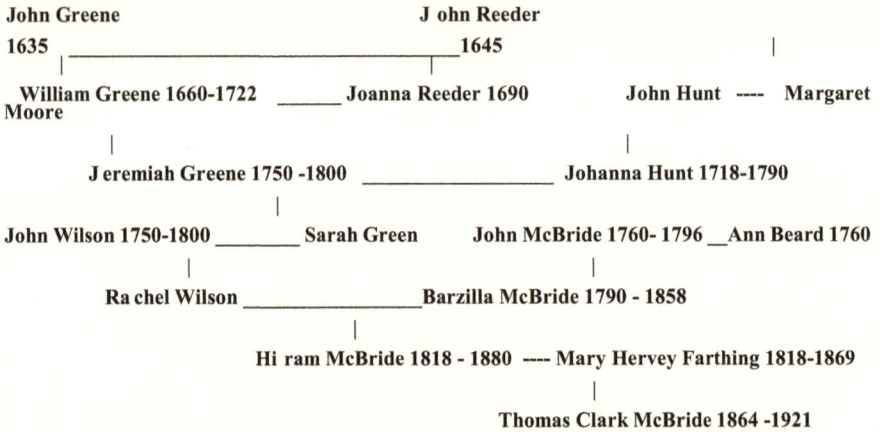

FARTHING - WATKINS

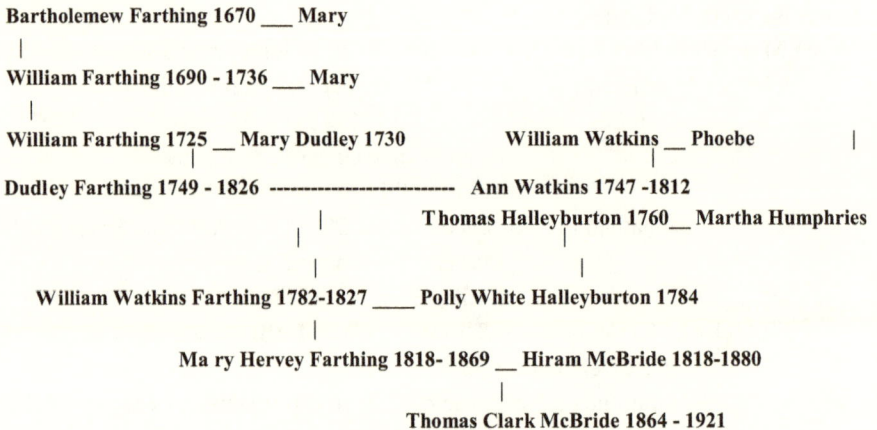

Bartholemew Farthing 1670 ___ Mary

 |

William Farthing 1690 - 1736 ___ Mary

 |

William Farthing 1725 __ Mary Dudley 1730   William Watkins __ Phoebe |

                      | |

Dudley Farthing 1749 - 1826 ---------------------------- Ann Watkins 1747 -1812

                            | Thomas Halleyburton 1760__ Martha Humphries

                            | |

   W illiam Watkins Farthing 1782-1827 ____ Polly White Halleyburton 1784

                              |

         Ma ry Hervey Farthing 1818- 1869 __ Hiram McBride 1818-1880

                                 |

                   Thomas Clark McBride 1864 - 1921

~~~~~~

MAST - HARMON

John Mast	George Bowers– Margaret	George Hermann –	Mary Margaret Wiley
1740	1740 _____?	1710 -1787	_____1720-1789

Joseph Mast 1764 _____ Eve Bowers 1758-1830   Cutliff Harmon __Susanna Fouts
                                                 1 748 - 1838

John Mast 1786-1868 _____ Susan Harmon 1791-1868

Finley Patterson Mast 1832-1924 _____Rhoda Smith 1839 -1919

    Mary Elizabeth Mast 1868 - 1947

PFAUTZ - HARMON

Michael Pfautz 1648 __ Catrina

Hans Michael Pfautz 1682-1741 __ Ursula Muehlenshauser 1682-1772
                       J ohn Jacob Kuntz   John Werner _Ann Ries   Hans_Marie

Jacob Pfautz 1700-1762 _ Anna Magdelen Kuntz Adam Varner 1798-75___Catherine Sigler 1698

John Michael Pfautz 1724-1803 _____Katrina Varner 1727-1800

                                     Susannah Fouts 1755-1817 _____ Cutliff Harmon 1748 - 1838

                                     Susan Harmon 1791 - 1868 ___ John Mast 1786 - 1868

                                                Finley P. Mast

                                     Mary Elizabeth Mast 1868-1947

note: Ann Ries descended from Conrad Schoeffer 1623-66; Hans Sigler 1677-1721, Marie Sigler 1677-1734; Catherine Sigler 1698-1774; John Werner 1680-1734

SMITH - FAIRCHILD

Robert Smith ___ Polly   Gamaliel Earls __Martha

George Smith 1747-1838 ___ Elizabeth Earls 1749-1842   Asa Fairchild __

Abner Smith 1781-1850 _____Mehetable Fairchild 1771-1855

                                 Jeheil Smith 1806 - 1885 _____ Elizabeth Dugger 1807-1902

                                 Rhoda Smith 1839 -1910 __ F.P Mast 1832 -1924

                                     Mary Elizabeth Mast 1868-1947

DUGGER - SMITH

William Dugger bef 1656

|

John Dugger

|

Daniel Dugger 1724- 1756___ Mary Scarborough

|

  Benjamin Dugger 1724- 1815 ___ Elizabeth ?   **Henry Earnest 1770**

                  | |

    David Dugger 1777 -1850 ___ Margaret Earnest 1787 -1835

                                |

            Elizabeth Dugger 1807-1902 _____ Jeheil Smith 1806 -1885

                                      |

                    Rhoda Smith 1839- 1919 — F.P. Mast 1832-1924

                                            |

                      Mary Elizabeth Mast 1868 - 1947

~~~~~~

Comments:

Finley P. Mast and his
wife Rhoda Smith

Finley Patterson Mast

About 1905
L to R back row
Aunt Mary Smith
Finley Mast
Myrtle Glenn, & Gladys
Jennie Mast & Dean
Ma Bingham
Rhoda Smith Mast
Front row - Jack Mast
Lucy Lawrence, Dog
Daulty Glenn
Ophelia Bingham
Alice Mast

Thomas Clark McBride

Mary Elizabeth Mast McBride

Left to Right, children of F.P. Mast
Charlie Mast
John (Jack) Johiel Mast
Emma Mast Baird
Mary Mast McBride
Mattie Mast Laine

William Grey McBride

1955
Wiley Preston Brown McBride
Nelle Ashburn Collins
Rhoda Mast Eacott
Rosalie McBride Glass

Thomas Finley McBride

James Kenneth McBride

Lucy Imogene McBride Hix

about 1954
Royce Collins
Fred Curtis
John (Jack) Eacott jr.
Jack Eacott
Rhoda Eacott
Nelle Collins
Annie Boone Curtis

Carrie May Dunn
Rhoda Eacott

Nelle Collins

Reunion 2002
Grandchildren of Thomas and Mary McBride.

John Eacott (Rhoda)
Carrie Bishop (Wiley)
Jill DeBruyne (Rhoda)
Dorothy McBride (Thomas)
Janifer Carlson (Rhoda)
Dorothy Betty Snelling (Nelle)
Ann Vanderburg (Wiley)
Mary Okulski (Wiley)

Possibly a photo of Emily McBride

Home of Hiram McBride 1852, where Thomas Clark McBride was raised.

www.ingramcontent.com/pod-product-compliance
Lightning Source LLC
Chambersburg PA
CBHW021230090426
42740CB00006B/472